DEMENTIA REHABILITATION

DEMENTIA REHABILITATION

Evidence-based Interventions and Clinical Recommendations

Edited by

LEE-FAY LOW
University of Sydney
Sydney, NSW, Australia

KATE LAVER
Flinders University
Adelaide, SA, Australia

ELSEVIER

ACADEMIC PRESS

An imprint of Elsevier

Academic Press is an imprint of Elsevier
125 London Wall, London EC2Y 5AS, United Kingdom
525 B Street, Suite 1650, San Diego, CA 92101, United States
50 Hampshire Street, 5th Floor, Cambridge, MA 02139, United States
The Boulevard, Langford Lane, Kidlington, Oxford OX5 1GB, United Kingdom

Notices
Knowledge and best practice in this field are constantly changing. As new research and experience
broaden our understanding, changes in research methods, professional practices, or medical
treatment may become necessary.

Practitioners and researchers must always rely on their own experience and knowledge in
evaluating and using any information, methods, compounds, or experiments described herein. In
using such information or methods they should be mindful of their own safety and the safety of
others, including parties for whom they have a professional responsibility.

To the fullest extent of the law, neither the Publisher nor the authors, contributors, or editors,
assume any liability for any injury and/or damage to persons or property as a matter of products
liability, negligence or otherwise, or from any use or operation of any methods, products,
instructions, or ideas contained in the material herein.

Library of Congress Cataloging-in-Publication Data
A catalog record for this book is available from the Library of Congress

British Library Cataloguing-in-Publication Data
A catalogue record for this book is available from the British Library

ISBN 978-0-12-818685-5

For information on all Academic Press publications
visit our website at https://www.elsevier.com/books-and-journals

Publisher: Nikki Levy
Editorial Project Manager: Barbara Makinster
Production Project Manager: Maria Bernard
Cover Designer: Matthew Limbert

Typeset by SPi Global, India

Working together
to grow libraries in
developing countries

www.elsevier.com • www.bookaid.org

Contents

7. Rehabilitation to improve psychological well-being in people with dementia   111

Lee-Fay Low, Monica Cations, Deborah Koder, and Annaliese Blair

8. Driving and community mobility for people living with dementia   129

Theresa L. Scott, Jacki Liddle, and Nancy A. Pachana

9. Supporting people with dementia in employment   149

David Evans, Carolyn Murray, Angela Berndt, and Jacinta Robertson

10. Can buildings contribute to the rehabilitation of people living with dementia?   171

Richard Fleming

Contributors

Alex Bahar-Fuchs
Department of Psychiatry, Academic Unit for Psychiatry of Old Age, The University of Melbourne, Melbourne, VIC, Australia

Kirrie Ballard
Faculty of Medicine and Health; Brain and Mind Centre, The University of Sydney, Sydney, NSW, Australia

Angela Berndt
University of South Australia, Adelaide, SA, Australia

Annaliese Blair
Aged Care Evaluation Unit, Southern NSW Local Health District, Queanbeyan, NSW, Australia

Michael Bruneau Jr.
Health Sciences Department, Drexel University, Philadelphia, PA, United States

Michele L. Callisaya
Peninsula Clinical School, Monash University; Academic Unit, Peninsula Health, Melbourne, VIC, Australia

Monica Cations
College of Education, Psychology and Social Work, Flinders University, Adelaide, SA, Australia

Lindy Clemson
Faculty of Medicine and Health, The University of Sydney, Sydney, NSW, Australia

Kay Cox
Medical School, Royal Perth Hospital Unit, University of Western Australia, Perth, WA, Australia

Sarah El-Wahsh
Faculty of Medicine and Health, The University of Sydney, Sydney, NSW, Australia

David Evans
University of South Australia, Adelaide, SA, Australia

Richard Fleming
Faculty of Science, Medicine and Health, University of Wollongong, Wollongong, NSW, Australia

Laura N. Gitlin
College of Nursing and Health Professions, Drexel University, Philadelphia, PA, United States

Susan W. Hunter
School of Physical Therapy, University of Western Ontario, London, ON, Canada

Yun-Hee Jeon
Sydney Nursing School, The University of Sydney, Sydney, NSW, Australia

Cassandra Kaizik
Sydney Nursing School, The University of Sydney, Sydney, NSW, Australia

Deborah Koder
Department of Psychological Sciences, Swinburne University of Technology, Melbourne, VIC, Australia

Fiona Kumfor
School of Psychology; Brain and Mind Centre, The University of Sydney, Sydney, NSW, Australia

Susan Kurrle
Faculty of Medicine & Health, University of Sydney, Sydney, NSW, Australia

Nicola T. Lautenschlager
Department of Psychiatry, Academic Unit for Psychiatry of Old Age, The University of Melbourne; Aged Persons Mental Health Program, North Western Mental Health, Melbourne Health, Melbourne, VIC, Australia

Kate Laver
Department of Rehabilitation, Aged and Extended Care, College of Medicine and Public Health, Flinders University, Adelaide, SA, Australia

Jacki Liddle
School of Information Technology & Electrical Engineering, The University of Queensland, St Lucia, QLD, Australia

Lee-Fay Low
Faculty of Medicine and Health, University of Sydney, Sydney, NSW, Australia

Nicole Milne
Sydney Nursing School, The University of Sydney, Sydney, NSW, Australia

Penelope Monroe
Faculty of Medicine and Health, The University of Sydney, Sydney, NSW, Australia

Manuel Montero-Odasso
Division of Geriatric Medicine, Department of Medicine, Parkwood Institute, University of Western Ontario; Lawson Health Research Institute; Gait and Brain Lab, Parkwood Institute, London, ON, Canada

Loren Mowszowski
Faculty of Science, School of Psychology & Healthy Brain Ageing Program, Brain and Mind Centre, The University of Sydney, Sydney, NSW, Australia

Carolyn Murray
University of South Australia, Adelaide, SA, Australia

Claire M.C. O'Connor
Centre for Positive Ageing, HammondCare; School of Population Health, University of New South Wales, Sydney, NSW, Australia

Nancy A. Pachana
School of Psychology, The University of Queensland, St Lucia, QLD, Australia

Catherine Verrier Piersol
Department of Occupational Therapy, Thomas Jefferson University, Philadelphia, PA, United States

Barbara Resnick
School of Nursing, The University of Maryland, Baltimore, MD, United States

Jacinta Robertson
Anglicare South Australia, Adelaide, SA, Australia

Theresa L. Scott
School of Psychology, The University of Queensland, St Lucia, QLD, Australia

Kate Swaffer
School of Nursing, University of Wollongong, Wollongong, NSW, Australia

Jacqueline B. Wesson
Faculty of Medicine and Health, The University of Sydney; Montefiore Residential Care, Sydney, NSW, Australia

Rachel Wiley
Day By Day Home Therapy, Devon, PA, United States

Preface

Rehabilitation is "a set of measures that assist individuals, who experience or are likely to experience disability, to achieve and maintain optimum functioning in interaction with their environments" (World Health Organization, 2011).

A core diagnostic feature of dementia is impairment of function. Ironically, people living with dementia receive very little rehabilitation to achieve and maintain optimum functioning.

People with dementia have been asking for rehabilitation for decades, and lack of rehabilitation is seen as a violation of human rights. In response to its advocacy, national dementia action plans are starting to include provision of rehabilitation as a goal. However, the majority of clinicians and social care professionals working with people with dementia have not entertained the notion that they might benefit from rehabilitation, nor have they received any training on the provision of rehabilitation for people with dementia.

This book is a resource for health and social professionals, service planners, policy makers, and academics bringing together clinical and research knowledge on rehabilitation for people living with dementia. It shows that rehabilitation can improve many aspects of function for people with dementia and provides practical information on delivering rehabilitation. The many gaps in evidence are also articulated, which we hope will stimulate further research.

In Chapter 1, Kate Swaffer opens the book by outlining the arguments that people with dementia have been making for rehabilitation on the grounds of legal, human rights, and personal experience.

Chapters 2–8 focus on different areas of functioning affected by dementia. These have been coauthored by academics and clinicians or clinician-academics and present the current approaches for assessment and intervention with case studies or practical tips to support use in clinical practice. The research evidence, relevant theory, and knowledge gaps are also discussed.

Specifically, in Chapter 2 Bahar-Fuchs, Mowszowski, Lautenschlager, and Cox give an overview of cognitive difficulties in dementia and the impact of cognitive training, cognitive rehabilitation, cognitive stimulation therapy, and physical activity. In Chapter 3, El-Wahsh, Monroe, Kumfor, and Ballard discuss how communication is impacted by dementia and the evidence for word retrieval intervention, script training, memory books, and communication partner training. In Chapter 4, Callisaya, Montero-Odasso, and Hunter explore the decline in physical functioning associated with dementia and pharmacological and non-pharmacological interventions to maintain or improve physical function and prevent falls.

In Chapter 5, Laver, Piersol, and Wiley outline how independence in activities of daily living can be promoted through task modification, environmental adaptation, and working with the person and their care partners. In Chapter 6, O'Connor, Clemson, and Wesson explore promoting leisure activities through task modification, creative therapies, shared activities, and activity prescription. In Chapter 7, Cations, Koder, Blair, and I review how dementia impacts self-identity, friendships and mood, and how to mitigate these through supportive counseling and cognitive behavior therapy and other manualized psychological therapies. In Chapter 8, Scott, Liddle, and Pachana describe supporting people with dementia and their family through giving up driving using strategies such as counseling, education and alternative transport options. In Chapter 9, Evans, Murray, Berndt, and Robertson tackle vocational rehabilitation for workers with dementia and give suggestions on vocational assessment, workplace support, reasonable adjustment, and planned transitions.

Chapters 10–13 cover issues which can facilitate or hinder optimal functioning and delivery of rehabilitation. In Chapter 10, Fleming discusses how architectural aspects, interior and exterior designs, and ambient environment can promote independence and well-being in people with dementia. In Chapter 11, Gitlin and Bruneau Jr. consider the impact of dementia on care partners using the Good Life Model and explore the role of care partners in supporting non-pharmacological interventions through activities, such as exercise, music, art, and pet therapy. Chapter 12 reviews the medical comorbidities in dementia and how these can be managed with a focus on rehabilitation. Finally, in Chapter 13 Jeon, Milne, Kaizik, and Resnick review the evidence, key principles, and elements that contribute to the success of the multicomponent rehabilitation program to improve functional independence for people with dementia.

Please use ideas in this book in your daily work and share them with your colleagues. If you do, please write and let me know how it goes. I'd love to hear about your successes and challenges.

Lee-Fay Low

Reference

World Health Organization. (2011). World report on disability. Retrieved from: https://www.refworld.org/docid/50854a322.html.

Introduction: Rehabilitation as a new way of working with people with dementia

Lee-Fay Low[a] and Kate Laver[b]

[a]Faculty of Medicine and Health, University of Sydney, Sydney, NSW, Australia
[b]Department of Rehabilitation, Aged and Extended Care, College of Medicine and Public Health, Flinders University, Adelaide, SA, Australia

We are transitioning to a new era relating to how we treat, support, and work with people with dementia as clinicians, service providers, policy makers, and researchers.

I (Lee-Fay) began my career 20 years ago as a home care worker for people with dementia with "challenging behaviors," and as a research assistant in a psychogeriatric unit with a drug trials team. In that world people with dementia were clients, patients, and subjects.

My (Kate) first job as an occupational therapy graduate was on an aged care ward at a large hospital. Most of my time was spent assessing and planning for hospital discharge by organizing home supports. Treatment of symptoms of dementia and education of families were not considered to be part of my role.

Our thinking about disease is shaped by culture, professional norms, technological possibilities, and intellectual content (Holstein, 1997). In the 18th century, terms used to describe dementia included amentia, imbecility, morosis, fatuitas, foolishness, stupidity, anoea, simplicity, cams, idiocy, dotage, senility, lethargy, and light-headedness, witlessness (Berrios, 1987). Dementia was originally not defined in terms of cognitive deficit—declines in behavior, personality, and judgment were the symptoms of dementia (Berrios, 1987). In the early 20th century, senile dementia was not distinguishable neuropathologically from normal aging. The discovery of plaques and tangles in Alzheimer's disease suggested a disease entity distinct from senile dementia for which there was potential for cure (Holstein, 1997). This has driven the exponential increase over the last 40 years in dementia research, mostly driven around the concept of Alzheimer's disease as a clinicopathological entity (Boller & Forbes, 1998). In the last 10 years, voices of people with dementia have started to influence our conceptualization of dementia, championing the notion of dementia as a disability, and that people with dementia have human rights to treatment including rehabilitation (see Chapter 2). Some researchers are also starting to think about dementia as partly being a social disease (Vernooij-Dassen & Jeon, 2016).

The lens or frame through which the problem of dementia is viewed has consequences for how the treatment and care of people with dementia is approached (Knifton & Yates, 2019). If problematized as a natural consequence of aging, then we need to prevent aging.; a mental disorder lens may focus on managing behavior and mood, a biomedical disease requires pharmacological treatments, a neurocognitive disorder implies brain treatment and cognitive training, a terminal illness suggests a palliation approach, and as a disability and social disease leads to work in community inclusion and social participation (Knifton & Yates, 2019).

Today, we both work within interdisciplinary research groups with psychology, occupational therapy, physical activity, medical, sociology, anthropology, social marketing, policy, and health systems expertise. People with dementia are our collaborators, colleagues, and friends. While a curative treatment and prevention are eminently desirable, our work relates to supporting people with dementia to live good lives according to their own meaning of "good." One part of having a good life is to receive rehabilitation—i.e., therapies which address their symptoms of dementia and services which support them to be active and participate in their usual roles and communities (Dementia Australia, 2019). They also want to be involved as collaborators on initiatives that promote independence (Dementia Australia, 2019).

During the development of this book, we (the editors) have had many discussions with each other and with our peers about whether we should use the term "rehabilitation" when describing treatments for people with dementia. Alternative terms that are often used when discussing programs that aim to optimize independence and well-being in older people include "reablement," "restorative care," and "reactivation." Such terms seem to be particularly popular with policy makers and service providers in countries such as the United Kingdom, the United States, and Australia. Our decision to use the term "rehabilitation" aligns with the terminology used by the World Health Organization when describing interventions for people with chronic conditions that optimize functioning and reduce disability in individuals with health conditions in interaction with their environment (World Health Organization, 2011). The World Health Organization's global action plan in response to dementia (2017–25) specifically calls for member states to develop pathways of efficient and coordinated care that include rehabilitation (World Health Organization, 2017).

The broad definition of rehabilitation means that it is an inclusive intervention approach; it applies to people with a range of different disabilities, at different times in their illness, and in different settings. The World Health Organization describes how rehabilitation may be needed by anyone with a health condition and difficulties in mobility, vision, hearing, speech, swallow, or cognition (World Health Organization, 2011). This applies to people with dementia who are likely to experience most of these symptoms over the course of the condition. Rehabilitation addresses impairments, activity limitations, and participation restrictions, as well as personal and environmental factors (including assistive technology) that impairs functioning. In contrast, terms such as reablement and restorative care usually refer to one-off short-term programs provided for community-dwelling older people (Sims-Gould, Tong, Wallis-Mayer, & Ashe, 2017).

The field of rehabilitation is relatively young; however, recognition of its importance is growing. People are living longer with disabilities and surviving significant trauma. Medical models of care, particularly acute models of care, do not address the functional consequences of illness or disease. Rehabilitation is a person- and/or family-centered process, with interventions focused on optimizing function and capacity. Evidence from research studies is accumulating and there is now good evidence supporting multidisciplinary rehabilitation programs for people with conditions such as hip fracture (Cameron, 2010) and stroke (Langhorne, Bernhardt, & Kwakkel, 2011).

In the field of dementia care, there is little evidence for programs which are described by research teams as being rehabilitation interventions. However, there is good evidence for interventions such as occupational therapy, exercise programs, psychological therapy, and working with families to optimize independence. We have worked with experts to gather this evidence for this book.

We believe that this book outlines evidence that rehabilitative interventions are possible and efficacious for people with dementia. Our aim is that this evidence will contribute to combating therapeutic nihilism that nothing can be done for people with dementia, and to convincing clinicians, service providers, and policy makers to start delivering rehabilitative interventions that support people with dementia to function optimally and reduce their disability.

References

Berrios, G. E. (1987). Dementia during the seventeenth and eighteenth centuries: a conceptual history. *Psychological Medicine, 17*(04), 829. https://doi.org/10.1017/s0033291700000623.

Boller, F., & Forbes, M. M. (1998). History of dementia and dementia in history: An overview. *Journal of the Neurological Sciences, 158*(2), 125–133. https://doi.org/10.1016/s0022-510x(98)00128-2.

Cameron, I. D. (2010). Models of rehabilitation–commonalities of interventions that work and of those that do not. *Disability and Rehabilitation, 32*(12), 1051–1058.

Dementia Australia. (2019). *Our solution: Quality care for people living with dementia.* Canberra: Dementia Australia. Retrieved from: https://www.dementia.org.au/sites/default/files/documents/DA-Consumer-Summit-Communique.pdf.

Holstein, M. (1997). Alzheimer's disease and senile dementia, 1885–1920: An interpretive history of disease negotiation. *Journal of Aging Studies, 11*(1), 1–13. https://doi.org/10.1016/s0890-4065(97)90008-6.

Knifton, C., & Yates, S. (2019). A 'history of problematizations' for dementia education: A Foucauldian approach to understanding the framing of dementia. *Journal of Research in Nursing, 24,* 212–230. https://doi.org/10.1177/1744987119831737.

Langhorne, P., Bernhardt, J., & Kwakkel, G. (2011). Stroke rehabilitation. *The Lancet, 377*(9778), 1693–1702.

Sims-Gould, J., Tong, C. E., Wallis-Mayer, L., & Ashe, M. C. (2017). Reablement, reactivation, rehabilitation and restorative interventions with older adults in receipt of home care: a systematic review. *Journal of the American Medical Directors Association, 18*(8), 653–663.

Vernooij-Dassen, M., & Jeon, Y.-H. (2016). Social health and dementia: the power of human capabilities. *International Psychogeriatrics, 28*(5), 701–703. https://doi.org/10.1017/S1041610216000260.

World Health Organization. (2011). *World report on disability* Retrieved from: https://www.refworld.org/docid/50854a322.html.

World Health Organization. (2017). *Global action plan on the public health response to dementia 2017 - 2025.* Geneva: World Health Organization. Retrieved from: https://www.who.int/mental_health/neurology/dementia/action_plan_2017_2025/en/.

CHAPTER 1

Rehabilitation: A human right for everyone

Kate Swaffer
School of Nursing, University of Wollongong, Wollongong, NSW, Australia

I keep the patients alive. Rehabilitation gives them Quality of Life.
(Dr. Tagio Tumas, Ministry of Health, Rehabilitation 2030 Forum, Geneva, July 2019).

Dementia is an acquired disability

The World Health Organization (WHO) and Alzheimer's Disease International (ADI) declared dementia a global "public health priority" in 2015 (World Health Organisation, 2015). There are more than 50 million people living with dementia, nearly 10 million cases are diagnosed every year, with a new diagnosis every 3.2 s. Dementia is the fifth leading cause of death globally, and a major cause of disability and dependence in older persons (World Health Organisation, 2019).

Dementia is a progressive and chronic neurodegenerative disorder, characterized by cognitive and functional impairments, including changes to long- and short-term memory recall, reasoning, planning, language, perception, and activities of daily living. It is a terminal condition, which often spans many years from diagnosis to death.

Dementia is also a condition causing disability, i.e., "a physical, mental, cognitive, or developmental condition that impairs, interferes with, or limits a person's ability to engage in certain tasks or actions, or participate in typical daily activities and interactions, or an impairment (such as a chronic medical condition or injury) that prevents someone from engaging in gainful employment" (Miriam–Webster, 2020).

This book on rehabilitation for those living with dementia is timely. There has been increasing pressure to recognize the human and legal rights of people living with dementia due largely to the activism of our representative organizations and allies (Dementia Alliance International, 2016;

Dementia Rehabilitation
https://doi.org/10.1016/B978-0-12-818685-5.00001-5

1

Swaffer, 2015a, 2015b, 2015c, 2018a, 2018b). Dementia was included in the United Nations Report of the Special Rapporteur on the rights of persons with disabilities (Devandas-Aguilar, 2019), which identified human rights concerns faced by both people with disabilities who are aging and older persons who acquire a disability.

Researchers and health professionals have been slow to consider or describe dementia as a disability (Thomas & Milligan, 2018). There has also been a lack of recognition about the importance of rehabilitation for people with dementia (Cations et al., 2019), with the result being that people with dementia are still not offered disability assessment and support, and may be denied rehabilitation.

To elevate the experience and quality of life of people living with dementia, it is important to manage the symptoms of all dementias as acquired disabilities, at the time of diagnosis, and to provide post diagnostic assessment and support for disabilities, including rehabilitation immediately after diagnosis.

If we manage the symptoms as cognitive and other disabilities, rather than only equating dementia to memory loss, which supports the myths and stigma around dementia, then the fear and discrimination may decrease. Symptoms of dementia are not only changes to memory, and many with younger onset dementia report they have few changes to memory when first diagnosed. People with dementia experience many disabilities including aphasia and other language and communication disabilities, acquired dyslexia, spatial and depth perception changes, sensory changes to taste and smell, and many others.

Perhaps most importantly, reframing dementia as a disability reinforces the rights for people with dementia as described in the UN Convention on the Rights of Persons with Disabilities (CRPD; see below for details). These are the standards every human being is entitled to and include the right to the highest attainable standard of universal health coverage with respect to a diagnosis, to its ethical disclosure, to access to rehabilitation services, and to postdiagnostic services including non-pharmacological supports. People with dementia have the same legal rights as others throughout all stages of their life. These legal rights are inviolable and can never be removed no matter how advanced the dementia.

For decades, our human rights, and our legal rights have been ignored, and continue to be breached daily.

The benefits of reframing dementia as a disability

Reframing dementia as a disability will move our approach away from the medical model of care to one that is based on a social and disability pathway of support and care. The UN Convention on the Rights on Persons with Disabilities (CRPD) rejects the medical model, and its treatment of persons with disabilities as "objects" of charity and social protection. It instead embodies a view of all disabled persons as "subjects" with human and legal rights, who should be able to claim their rights as active citizens (Korolkova & Anthony, 2016). For example, Article 26 of the CRPD states that: "States Parties shall take effective and appropriate measures, including through peer support, to enable persons with disabilities to attain and maintain maximum independence, full physical, mental, social and vocational ability, and full inclusion and participation in all aspects of life."

The pathologization of dementia has led to expressions of suffering and defiance toward one's circumstances (Boyle, 2008). This is particularly harmful in a human rights context as behavior *should* be valued as expressions of one's will and choices but instead is perceived as symptoms caused by the pathology of dementia. These "behaviors" are commonly referred to as behavioral and psychological symptoms of dementia (BPSD), and in this context, "challenging behaviors" or BPSD are assumed to be a result of dementia, and lack of insight rather than being seen as an adaptive response to the environments' (Evans et al., 2016; Wigg, 2010) or as "normal human responses" to changes including unmet needs (Barnsness et al., 2018). This pathologization results in a denial of will and choice, and therefore of human rights. Dementia is not a mental health condition, nor is it an intellectual disability or a psychosocial disability. The symptoms caused by dementia are now recognized as cognitive disabilities.

Conceptualizing dementia as a disability also moves us away from the "welfare and charity" approach, which has been widely criticized for being paternalistic and failing to encourage "independence, social integration and participation in the life of the community" (Power, Lord, & Defranco, 2009). Welfare approaches traditionally focused on providing institutional forms of care to persons with disabilities which kept them in a state of dependency, rather than providing them with support and enabling their participation in society. This is currently the case for people with dementia.

Classifying dementia as a disability forces greater consideration of the human and legal rights of people with dementia. Traditional approaches have excluded us from engaging in decision-making about our personal affairs, health needs, and from society more generally (Kayess & French, 2008). The CRPD moves our approach toward a human and legal rights framework, recognizing an extensive obligation of governments to provide support in achieving full equality of rights for all persons with disabilities (Kayess & French, 2008).

The Convention on the Rights of Persons with Disabilities

The Universal Declaration of Human Rights was adopted by the General Assembly of the United Nations on 10 December 1948. This UN Convention was (and still is) meant to protect every single member of civil society in the world, including people diagnosed with any type of dementia, and who have disabilities caused by the symptoms of dementia.

The CRPD and its Optional Protocol was adopted in 2006, and adopts a broad categorization of persons with disabilities, reaffirming that all persons with all types of disabilities must enjoy all human rights and fundamental freedoms. This includes people with dementia.

However, in 2015 the Organization for Economic Co-operation and Development (OECD, 2015) reported that "Dementia receives the worst care in the developed world." This OECD report reinforced to me the importance of my demand for human rights, including rehabilitation at the WHO First Ministerial Conference on Dementia in 2015 (Dementia Alliance International, 2015); an approach which includes full access to the CRPD and therefore full rehabilitation.

CRPD Article 26, Habilitation and Rehabilitation (UN General Assembly, 2007), is of particular relevance as people with dementia have the same right as all others with any other disease or disability to be supported fully and to maintain independence, and to receive rehabilitation. Article 26 states that parties shall "enable persons with disabilities to attain and maintain maximum independence, full physical, mental, social and vocational ability, and full inclusion and participation in all aspects of life" and to "organize, strengthen, and extend comprehensive habilitation and rehabilitation services and programs, particularly in the areas of health, employment, education, and social services."

Rehabilitation plays a key role in enacting the UN Convention on the Rights of Persons with Disabilities (Global Rehabilitation Alliance, 2019). Systematic integration of rehabilitation into health systems, development of sustainable funding mechanisms aiming at universal health coverage, and support for community-based rehabilitation (CBR) have been identified as crucial elements to make the much-needed progress. Other Articles of the CRPD which are being ignored and breached include rights to non-discrimination (Article 5), liberty and security of the person (Article 14), equality before the law (Article 12), accessibility (Article 9), and independent living and community inclusion (Article 19).

Article 21 is also relevant, especially to the notion of management of behavior. "Persons with disabilities enjoy the ability to share thoughts, beliefs, and feelings through all forms of communication." Therefore, to chemically restrain (medicate) or physically restrain someone due to a perceived "behavior" could be interpreted as a violation of their right to expression, especially in the many instances where if a careful investigation is undertaken, it will show the person is simply trying to communicate, communicating differently, or expressing an unmet need such as pain.

The aim of Community Based Rehabilitation (CBR) is to help people with disabilities by establishing community-based programs for social integration, equalization of opportunities, and physical therapy rehabilitation. This broad life approach focus has the potential to change lives, increase well-being, independence, and quality of life. We could potentially see far more tangible changes to people's lives, if we used this approach in dementia-friendly initiatives, rather than just the basic awareness and fundraising campaigns that are currently in place.

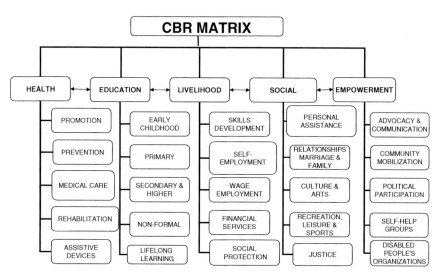

Health-care professionals currently also have a limited view of the value of rehabilitation for dementia (Cations et al., 2019). Defining the symptoms of all dementias as cognitive and functional disabilities will potentially help health-care professionals to understand why rehabilitation is a suitable postdiagnosis option, especially when the person is diagnosed in the earlier stages of dementia, with more cognitive and other capacity to uptake active rehabilitation strategies.

Rehabilitation for people with dementia

The King's Fund (King's Fund 1998, in Squires & Hastings, 2002) determined that the primary objective of rehabilitation involves restoration of function (mental or physical) or a role, requires a multidisciplinary team. The three basic approaches are to reduce disability, acquire new skills and strategies to reduce the impact of the disability, and approaches that help alter the physical and social environment, so that a given disability carries with it as little impairment as possible.

In my blog post Rehabilitation and Dementia (Swaffer, 2018a), it was effortless to provide a list of 50 references on the value of rehabilitation for people with dementia. Rehabilitation does not have to be expensive, nor does it necessarily involve lengthy clinical consultations or attending formally defined and funded rehabilitative programs.

During my Masters studies in 2015, I conducted a case study where I used walking as an intervention for Client H, an 86-year-old lady, diagnosed with "mild dementia" of the Alzheimer's type (Swaffer, 2015a). After 4 weeks of walking in a group she reported reductions in sadness and loneliness, increased feelings of independence, confidence in walking, and physical mobility. Her physiotherapist reported that her balance improved significantly and she more than doubled the length of her walks. She had also been doing gardening again in the last 2 weeks of the program, a sign not only of her confidence but of her improved balance, strength, and mobility. I concluded "The greatest lesson is that rehabilitation is valuable and worthwhile for the frail elderly and for people with dementia, regardless of the amount of evidence-based research to support it."

Our rights to rehabilitation are not being met

Despite the ethical and legal imperatives to ensure quality care, the care provided to people with dementia and their care partners pre- and postdiagnosis is often suboptimal. For example, in Australia there is often a significant delay in the diagnosis of dementia, with symptoms noticed by families an average of 1.9 years prior to seeking any health-care professional advice, and an average of 3.1 years before a firm diagnosis of dementia is made (Speechly, Bridges-Webb, & Passmore, 2008). The physical, psychological, and social concerns of people with dementia are often undetected or undermanaged by health-care professionals and care providers.

Rehabilitation and other allied health-care services are rarely offered at the time of diagnosis, even though rehabilitation focuses on strategies to support people to maintain or improve functional ability and independence through maximizing capacity. Despite a significant body of evidence, health-care providers have continued to ignore rehabilitation for people with dementia.

My postdiagnostic "support" and self-prescribed rehabilitation

Dementia has, quite literally, been the Olympics of my life (Swaffer, 2015b).

Following my diagnosis of the semantic variant of primary progressive aphasia (svPPA) in 2008, I was not referred to any support, including my local dementia advocacy organization. I was advised by my health-care professional there was no medication or other treatment available for my type of dementia, and nothing I could to do to delay the progression. I was also told that typically people with this type of dementia live 8–10 years following a diagnosis, and I was advised by all health-care professionals and organizations around me to give up my paid work and my tertiary studies as soon as possible. Initially, the sense of despair and loss of hope was profound.

Being diagnosed with dementia resulted in me experiencing firsthand that "sense of nobodiness" (King, 1963; Swaffer, 2018b), similar to a social death, which involves the exclusion of a person from society, and where people are stripped of their identity and confined to a state of alienation in the name of submitting to an infallible power [dementia]. It's a form of branding, a reminder of one's "otherness" or inferiority; it often feels like a fate worse than physical death. Harvard sociologist Orlando Patterson provided a racial context for the theory in his book *Slavery and Social Death* (Patterson, 1982). Slavery, Patterson wrote, was not merely about dishonoring or devaluing black people through physical violence, economic exploitation, or political disenfranchisement—it was a wholesale attempt by the white establishment to render black peoples' lives meaningless, unworthy of dignity or respect. For me, living with dementia often feels like that.

When I did find support in 2009, the only advice I was given was to attend a short "Living with memory loss" (now called Living with Dementia) course, which provided some basic information about dementia, but which also focused on getting my end of life affairs in order. I was also advised to attend an aged day care center once a month, to "get used to it." At that time, I was 50. I referred to all of this well meaning advice, i.e., to give up work, give up study, get my end of life affairs in order and prepare for aged care, as prescribed disengagement® (Swaffer, 2015).

This medicalized postdiagnostic pathway, caused in part by a 20th century view of dementia, is no longer appropriate for anyone with dementia, except perhaps those diagnosed in the later stages.

I have contrasted the medical model of care for people with dementia, against a social and disability pathway of support, which I developed specifically for myself with the support of the university where I study and a neurophysiotherapist.

The University of South Australia offered me a disability assessment and has provided support and ongoing assessments since 2008. This helped me continue to live in a way which supports my continued personal goals.

In 2009, my Disability Access Plan devised through the University noted the following:

Kate's disabilities are neurological in nature and are chronic and degenerative. Symptoms include persistent fatigue; acquired dyslexia; Primary Progressive Aphasia (PPA); word finding and comprehension; way finding difficulties, all due to changes in her cognitive functioning, including concentration and recall; chronic (and sometimes severe) pain; intermittent paresthesia, muscle spasms, and speech problems; occasional choking reflex, dizziness, and disorientation. She had a cranial decompression and graft for an Arnold-Chiari Malformation in 2005, a C5/6 Discectomy with a titanium graft in 2005, and was diagnosed with Semantic Dementia in 2008. A letter of confirmation of her condition(s) and symptoms has been received from her neurologist and a letter supporting her ongoing management from her GP.

My 2009 Access Plan included: counseling, more time (e.g., for exams and library loans) technology such as a laptop and dictation software, and professional note-taker and scribe.

Once I was able to better understand the impact of my dementia within the framework of disability, and work on my grief, I was not only more able to manage it, but to live my life again. In returning to positive living, it became obvious that the health-care system, including service providers and advocacy organization, had failed me.

I soon realized if I'd had a stroke aged 49, I would have been provided with stroke rehabilitation, and supported to go back to work in whatever capacity I was capable of, with reasonable accommodations to support me to do so. Then I put my retired nurse's hat back on, and I decided to self-prescribe rehabilitative therapies which included neurophysiotherapy, exercise, mindfulness, meditation, self-hypnosis, and dietary changes.

The experience of others with dementia

Importantly, I don't believe rehabilitation is a cure, but many people with dementia including me believe rehabilitation may slow down the progression of symptoms. Those of us who have self-prescribed rehabilitation, and have the funds to pay for it (most health systems do not fund appropriate or adequate rehabilitation for dementia), find that rehabilitation improves our quality of life and helps us maintain independence, which in turn enables us to have greater opportunities to continue to contribute to society in a meaningful way.

Members of Dementia Alliance International (an organization run by people with dementia for people with dementia) report that Prescribed Disengagement is still happening in 2020 and their experiences with rehabilitative treatments have also been almost nonexistent.

> *Rehabilitation must be part of a compassionate and dignified approach to ensure those living with dementia can maintain, and live an independent life. It must be a comprehensive approach, including all modalities of rehabilitation such as lifestyle changes, physiotherapy, speech pathology, Pilates, yoga, occupational therapy, exercise and support to maintain recreational and professional wants and needs. The person's needs must be assessed on a person-to-person basis and adjusted to meet individual the needs. For myself, my physiotherapy, and Pilates are a very large part of my rehabilitation that helps keep my balance, coordination and strength in tact; without them, I likely would not be able to continue to manage living on my own.*
> **Christine Thelker, living with Dementia in Canada, (August 1, 2019).**

> *After my diagnosis is March 2017, it was 12 months before I could access a post diagnosis support course which meant undertaking a 130 mile round trip once a week for 6 weeks and 14 months to access a Dementia Support Worker. Where I live there were no services provided by the local Council or NHS for people living with Dementia under the age of 65, however, I have now used my universal rights under International Law via the UN CRPD to obtain funding for a Young Onset service to start in April 2020. Subsequently it has taken over 2 years to access a community OT and I am still having to fight to get referrals for services such as rehabilitation, which historically have not been deemed appropriate for people living with Dementia. Even today, people living with dementia are not having their unmet needs and rights met, yet following a later diagnosis of another chronic terminal disease, they find that there unmet needs and rights are suddenly met by that additional diagnosis.*
> **Howard Gordon, living with dementia in England (September 11, 2019).**

As a person living well with Younger Onset Alzheimer's, why am I constantly discrim-inated against by some Doctors in General and Specialty medicine. Why was I told at Diagnosis to just get my affairs in order. At this stage I knew little about Dementia and thought I'd be dead in a short time. There was no referral to Dementia Australia, no hand-out with agencies where I could find support, and no referrals to allied health professionals for occupational therapy, speech pathology or any other forms of rehabilitation to improve my quality of life. What is going on? I feel a deep sense of loss when I'm not treated with respect and dignity. All I ask is for empathy, under-standing and some time, and for adequate post diagnostic support and services.

Phil Hazell, living with dementia in Australia (September 30, 2019).

I asked for psychological support from the team when I was diagnosed but they had no one. So I asked my GP to refer me back to the chronic fatigue service and the CBT therapist. I had 8 sessions but then found I needed to work with her regularly. But the CFS service only allows her to give 8 sessions.

Jacki Bingham, living with dementia in the UK (October 1, 2019).

Self-advocates all around the world themselves provide anecdotal evidence of the power of continuing to live positively with dementia, in spite of being told to go home and prepare to die. A great many are living far longer than they had been told at the time of diagnosis.

We need a new pathway of diagnostic support

For our communities to support people with dementia based on the recognition of human rights and dementia as a disability, we need a new pathway of psychosocial and disability support to live positively and independently with dementia for as long as possible.

My vision is a pathway of support similar to this, provided for all people with dementia:

1. Timely and accurate diagnosis
2. Focus on assets and quality of life
3. Disability assessment and support, immediately postdiagnosis.
4. Community based rehabilitation
5. Rehabilitation immediately postdiagnosis, which includes exercise and other lifestyle changes in line with other chronic diseases such as:
   (a) Occupational therapy
   (b) Physiotherapy and neurophysiotherapy
   (c) Speech therapy—not just a "swallowologist" for the end of life when one is no longer able to swallow
   (d) Walking/mobility rehabilitation
   (e) Dietician

(f) Psychologist

(g) Social worker

(h) Specialized rehabilitation for cognitive impairments

6. Grief and loss counseling, not just information about dying, aged care, and "challenging behaviors"

7. Peer-to-peer support groups for people with dementia, our care partners and families, and for those with younger onset dementia, our older parents, and our children

8. Support to maintain our prediagnosis lifestyle, if our choice

9. Support to continue working if a person with younger onset dementia, again if our choice, or volunteering and remaining active in our communities

10. Support to continue usual activities, socializing, sport, recreation, community engagement, volunteering

11. Inclusive and accessible communities—not dementia-friendly, as too often the awareness-raising initiatives are still based on our deficits

12. Adequate palliative care from the time of diagnosis.

It is also imperative we have educated health-care professionals, including support workers. Everyone would be shocked to be admitted to hospital following a diagnosis of cancer, or a stroke or heart attack, only to discover the staff knew very little about those conditions. Yet we still have staff in the acute, aged care, and community care settings with minimal knowledge about dementia.

What needs to happen in global policy

The WHO Global Dementia Action Plan provides little evidence of using the CRPD Articles, or the WHO Disability Action Plan, apart from the seven cross-cutting principles.

Of the 194 countries that have ratified the CRPD, none have yet implemented it for people with dementia, nor considered the WHO's Global Disability and Development Action Plan, its revised guidelines for CBR and its new Quality Rights Indicators for Mental Health (which includes dementia) as well as full access to the CRPD and other Conventions. By harnessing the CRPD and numerous other Conventions and embedding human rights into dementia plans we will increase independence and reduce the cost to governments and society of dementia.

The WHO Global Disability Action Plan 2014–2021: Better Health For All People With Disability (World Health Organization, 2015) should now also be applied to people with dementia. This plan's vision, goal, objectives, guiding principles, and approaches (p. 3) includes: "A world in which all persons with disabilities and their families live in dignity, with equal rights and opportunities, and are able to achieve their full potential." The overall goal is to contribute to achieving optimal health, functioning, well-being and human rights for all persons with disabilities.

Conclusion

For more than 10 years, I have been campaigning for dementia as a disability and rehabilitation for all people with dementia, immediately following a diagnosis; under Article 26 of the CRPD, there is no doubt it is everyone's right. Similarly, there is no doubt the symptoms of all dementias are acquired disabilities.

It is almost two decades since Marshall edited *Perspectives on Rehabilitation and Dementia* (Marshall, 2004). Since then health-care professionals and advocacy organizations still have not responded to the book, or to the emerging evidence since, in their clinics or within policy and programs.

This book summarizes the evidence that rehabilitation improves outcomes for people with dementia. My hope that it changes attitudes of everyone, especially health-care professionals, and that the diagnosis of dementia is seen and managed as a major cause of disability; rehabilitation will not only delay dependence, it will improve quality of life and increase independence. This will hopefully lead to appropriate disability assessment and support including rehabilitation soon after diagnosis, rather than only an assessment of activities of daily living.

The time is now for tangible change, and for rehabilitation for all people, including people with dementia.

References

Barnsness, S., Bisiani, L., Greenwood, D. C., MacCaulay, S., Power, A., & Swaffer, K. (2018). Rethinking dementia care. *Australian Journal of Dementia Care, 7*(4), 8.

Boyle, G. (2008). Autonomy in long-term care: A need, a right or a luxury? *Discourse & Society, 23*(4), 299–310. https://doi.org/10.1080/09687590802038795.

Cations, M., May, N., Crotty, M., Low, L.-F., Clemson, L., Whitehead, C., … Laver, K. E. (2019). Health professional perspectives on rehabilitation for people with dementia. *The Gerontologist.* https://doi.org/10.1093/geront/gnz007.

Dementia Alliance International. (2015). *WHO First Ministerial Conference on Dementia.* https://www.dementiaallianceinternational.org/dai-update-on-the-first-who-ministerial-conference-on-dementia/.

Dementia Alliance International. (2016). *How the UN protects our rights: An introduction to the Social Forum.* https://www.dementiaallianceinternational.org/un-protects-human-rights/.

Devandas-Aguilar, C. (2019). *Report of the special Rapporteur on the rights of persons with disabilities*. Retrieved from Geneva.

Evans, E. A., Perkins, E., Clarke, P., Haines, A., Baldwin, A., & Whittington, R. (2016). Care home manager attitudes to balancing risk and autonomy for residents with dementia. *Aging & Mental Health*, 1–9. https://doi.org/10.1080/13607863.2016.1244803.

Global Rehabilitation Alliance. (2019). *Rehabilitation for the realisation of human rights and inclusive development*. Retrieved from https://handicap-international.de/sn_uploads/document/Study2019_Rapport_rehab_human_rights_v4_Web.pdf.

Kayess, R., & French, P. (2008). Out of darkness into light? Introducing the convention on the rights of persons with disabilities. *Human Rights Law Review*, *8*(1), 1–34. https://doi.org/10.1093/hrlr/ngm044.

King, M. L., Jr. (1963). Letter from a Birmingham jail. Letter, 16. *April, 1963*. Retrieved from https://www.africa.upenn.edu/Articles_Gen/Letter_Birmingham.html.

Korolkova, J., & Anthony, A. (2016). *Disability human rights clinic: The United Nations convention on the rights of persons with disabilities and the right to support*. Retrieved from Melbourne.

Marshall, M. (2004). *Perspectives on rehabilitation and dementia*. UK: Jessica Kingsley Publishers.

Miriam-Webster. (2020). *Disability*. Retrieved from https://www.merriam-webster.com/dictionary/disability.

The Organisation for Economic Cooperation, & Development's published report of the world's 38 richest countries (OECD). (2015). Addressing Dementia: The OECD Response. In *Health Policy Studies*. Paris: OECD Publishing House.

Patterson, O. (1982). *Slavery and social death: A comparative study*. Cambridge, Mass: Harvard University Press.

Power, A., Lord, J. E., & Defranco, A. S. (2009). *Active citizenship and disability: Implementing the personalisation of support*. Cambridge: Cambridge University Press.

Speechly, C. M., Bridges-Webb, C., & Passmore, E. (2008). The pathway to dementia diagnosis. *Medical Journal of Australia*, *189*(9), 487–489.

Squires, A. J., & Hastings, M. B. (2002). *Rehabilitation of the older person: A handbook for the interdisciplinary team*. Cheltenham: Nelson Thornes.

Swaffer, K. (2015a). Dementia and prescribed disengagement™. *Dementia*, *14*(1), 3–6. https://doi.org/10.1177/1471301214548136.

Swaffer, K. (2015b). *Rehabilitation: A case study*. Retrieved from https://kateswaffer.com/2015/02/26/rehabilitation-a-case-study/.

Swaffer, K. (2015c). *Slowing the progression of dementia*. Retrieved from https://kateswaffer.com/2015/08/17/slowing-the-progression-of-dementia/.

Swaffer, K. (2018a). *Rehabilitation and dementia*. Retrieved from https://kateswaffer.com/2018/06/30/rehabilitation-and-dementia-2/.

Swaffer, K. (2018b). *What the hell happened to my brain: Living beyond dementia*. London: Jessica Kingsley Publishers.

Thomas, C., & Milligan, C. (2018). Dementia, disability rights and disablism: Understanding the social position of people living with dementia. *Disability & Society*, *33*(1), 115–131. https://doi.org/10.1080/09687599.2017.1379952.

UN General Assembly. (2007). *Convention on the rights of persons with disabilities: Resolution/adopted by the general assembly*. Retrieved from https://www.refworld.org/docid/45f973632.html.

Wigg, J. M. (2010). Liberating the wanderers: Using technology to unlock doors for those living with dementia. *Sociology of Health & Illness*, *32*(2), 288–303. https://doi.org/10.1111/j.1467-9566.2009.01221.x.

World Health Organization. (2015). *WHO global disability action plan 2014–2021: Better health for all people with disability*. Geneva: World Health Organization.

World Health Organisation. (2015). *Dementia: a public health priority*. Retrieved from https://www.who.int/mental_health/publications/dementia_report_2012/en/; (2007).

World Health Organisation. (2019). *Dementia*. Retrieved from https://www.who.int/en/news-room/fact-sheets/detail/dementia.

CHAPTER 2

Cognitively oriented treatments in dementia

Alex Bahar-Fuchs[a], Loren Mowszowski[b], Nicola T. Lautenschlager[a,c], and Kay Cox[d]

[a]Department of Psychiatry, Academic Unit for Psychiatry of Old Age, The University of Melbourne, Melbourne, VIC, Australia
[b]Faculty of Science, School of Psychology & Healthy Brain Ageing Program, Brain and Mind Centre, The University of Sydney, Sydney, NSW, Australia
[c]Aged Persons Mental Health Program, North Western Mental Health, Melbourne Health, Melbourne, VIC, Australia
[d]Medical School, Royal Perth Hospital Unit, University of Western Australia, Perth, WA, Australia

Introduction

The process of decline in dementia

Dementia is fundamentally characterized by an insidious decline in cognition and ultimately neurological function due to the progressive death of neurons in various brain regions. A number of processes cause this deterioration, including neurodegeneration, neuroinflammation, oxidative damage, and vascular pathology. Over the last decade, methodological advances in screening and diagnostic techniques, largely focusing on the identification of biomarkers of the pathophysiological processes in Alzheimer's disease (e.g., amyloidopathy and tauopathy), shifted our understanding of the neurodegenerative process (Dubois et al., 2016). Dementia is now viewed along a continuum of neuropathological and cognitive decline, beginning at a much earlier "preclinical" stage when pathophysiological markers (such as elevated tau in cerebrospinal fluid, amyloid deposition in the brain, or disproportionate regional brain atrophy) may be identified through lumbar puncture, magnetic resonance (MR) or positron emission tomography (PET) imaging (Sperling et al., 2011; McKhann, 2011), and may identify people at risk of developing dementia 10–15 years prior to the onset of symptoms (Dubois et al., 2016).

Why is early identification of dementia relevant for rehabilitation?

The use of biomarkers to identify preclinical or "at risk" stages of dementia has largely been limited to research, because of lack of consensus parameters

Dementia Rehabilitation
https://doi.org/10.1016/B978-0-12-818685-5.00002-7

or guidelines for measurement and/or interpretation of biomarkers (e.g., cut-scores), as well as limited access to relevant technology. Clinically, there are concerns around the moral, ethical, and emotional connotations of identifying and disclosing underlying biological factors relating to disease when (a) this may occur years prior to clinical onset, and (b) clinical manifestation of dementia in those with biomarkers of the disease may be mediated by resilience or protective factors such as cognitive reserve, which are not fully understood.

From a rehabilitation perspective, earlier identification may lead to new treatment options, which may delay onset and/or slow cognitive and functional decline, thus maximizing independent functioning and quality of life.

What is the cognitive trajectory of dementia?

Many older people experience some degree of cognitive change as part of normal aging (Harada, Natelson Love, & Triebel, 2013). Normal, age-related changes typically affect the cognitive domains of processing speed and learning/memory. Even older adults without dementia may notice that their thinking is a little slower; it may take a little longer to process information or they may find it more difficult to think of the right word or name during a conversation. Critical signs that a clinical neuropsychologist looks for in determining the significance of subjective cognitive concerns relate to *change* in frequency or severity over time, as well as the *impact* on day-to-day functioning.

Rehabilitation clinicians may become involved when more overt or frequent cognitive changes emerge, and the pattern and impact of such changes should influence the goals or designated outcomes of cognition-oriented treatments. At this point, a person may be identified as having Mild Cognitive Impairment (MCI). In some cases, MCI is an intermediate state between normal aging and dementia, capturing older people who experience cognitive decline that is greater than expected for their age and background, but who function largely independently with only minimal day-to-day functional impact (see Petersen et al., 2018).

Cognitive screening tools, such as the Mini-Mental State Examination (Folstein, Folstein, & McHugh, 1975) tend to be insensitive to mild changes in cognition and function, and more in-depth neuropsychological assessment incorporating appropriate normative (i.e., matched for age and where available, education or other key demographic factors) comparison is required to identify MCI. In people with Alzheimer biomarkers, MCI is thought to indicate progression to a "symptomatic" stage of pre-dementia

(Albert et al., 2011). However, MCI has multiple etiological factors (e.g., depression, cardiovascular disease, etc.) and may not always signify underlying progressive condition. Indeed, around 40% of older people who meet criteria for MCI remain stable or even revert to previous levels of functioning (Mitchell & Shiri-Feshki, 2009).

Cognitive profiles in dementia

Cognitive profiles in dementia are characterized by patterns of impairment, with early changes in specific domains aiding in differential diagnosis by pointing to the site of initial neuropathological damage. While many gold standard diagnostic criteria emphasize the predominance of impairment in key domains, they also recognize concurrent (often milder or later-developing) impairment in other domains, particularly as the underlying process of neurodegeneration continues. Additionally, it is common for a person to present with "mixed" dementias due to underlying comorbid pathologies.

Although there are many diseases that cause dementia, the archetypal clinical picture is of predominant episodic memory impairment, characterized by rapid forgetting, repetition of questions or anecdotes, and "absentmindedness." This pattern of cognitive decline is characteristic of Alzheimer's disease, the most common cause of dementia.

However, the clinical presentation of dementia may vary widely, such as where Alzheimer's disease presents atypically or in other types of dementia. For example, in some of the less common variants of AD, people may initially present with predominant and significant impairment in word-finding (known as logopenic primary progressive aphasia, see Gorno-Tempini et al., 2011); in complex visuospatial processing (known as Posterior Cortical Atrophy, see McMonagle, Deering, Berliner, & Kertesz, 2006); or even in aspects of executive functions such as impaired judgment, reasoning, and problem-solving (McKhann, 2011).

Dementia with Lewy Bodies characteristically presents with visuospatial impairment, executive dysfunction, and poor attention/concentration, often with fluctuations in cognitive performance or alertness throughout the day, as well as other neurological signs (e.g., visual hallucinations and falls, see McKeith et al., 2017).

Vascular dementia presents with a "subcortical" pattern characterized by impairment in processing speed, working memory, executive functions, and encoding/retrieval of new information, and may also be associated with changes in mood (e.g., late-onset depression).

Frontotemporal dementia may lead to significant changes in personality and behavior (behavioral-variant) or in language, affecting speech production, comprehension, and/or understanding/knowledge of words and concepts (progressive non–fluent aphasia or semantic dementia) (see overview by Warren, Rohrer, & Rossor, 2013). This is described further in Chapter 4 on communication.

While beyond the scope of this chapter, we note that there are numerous other rarer causes of dementia, including alcohol-related dementia, Parkinson's disease with dementia, and HIV-associated dementia. Each type is associated with particular patterns of cognitive and other neurological symptoms.

Impact on day-to-day functioning

While impairment in specific cognitive domains can be extremely helpful for diagnostic purposes, from a treatment perspective it is imperative to consider the impact of cognitive difficulties on function. For example, what is the likely impact of working memory impairment on grocery shopping? The World Health Organization's International Classification of Functioning, Disability and Health (World Health Organisation, 2001), emphasizes that problems with functioning are caused by the interconnection between bodily impairment (in this example, working memory impairment), activity limitation (e.g., calculating how much change is owed by the supermarket cashier), and participation restriction (e.g., independent shopping).

Clinicians should attempt to identify specific tasks and activities that are meaningful to the person with dementia and which are affected by cognitive weaknesses by talking to the person with dementia, their care partners, and/or other health care professionals who may have relevant knowledge. It is often helpful to ask about "a typical day" or "activities that you would like to do but feel you are not able" or "tasks that are important to you" to help identify areas of functional impact. Chapters 4 (communication), 6 (activities of daily living), and 7 (leisure activities) discuss goal-based functional assessment further.

Clinicians may observe a discrepancy between neuropsychological test results and the completion of daily tasks (Skidmore, 2017). For example, the person with dementia who performs well on tests of new learning in a quiet, structured assessment environment may nevertheless struggle to recall details of their next doctors' appointment in a loud, bustling reception area. Vice versa, a person may perform poorly on cognitive tests but may remain independent with some complex daily tasks such as preparing a familiar family meal. This is because completion of day-to-day activities (particularly more cognitively complex instrumental activities of daily living, or IADLs), relies on a sophisticated interplay between multiple cognitive processes, physical skills, environmental resources, and task-specific demands in order to effectively plan, execute, and appraise an activity. This has been described as "functional cognition," a concept that attempts to integrate the intricate relationship between cognitive processing itself and the application of cognitive processes to enabling or underpinning everyday function (Wesson, Clemson, Brodaty, & Reppermund, 2016).

Targets and aims of nonpharmacological treatments (NPTs) for people with dementia

Unlike drug-based treatments, that target biological systems, the targets of NPT (i.e., outcomes that are expected to change as a direct reaction to the treatment) are cognitive, physical, functional, or psychosocial. NPTs are often associated with "downstream" aims (Hart et al., 2019), or outcomes beyond those directly targeted by the intervention. Such aims may include the alleviation of depression or anxiety as an indirect outcome of improved global cognition following a cognition-oriented treatment (COT). The current chapter is concerned with cognitive and other outcomes associated with cognition-oriented treatments and physical exercise treatments.

Cognition-oriented treatments

Cognition-oriented treatments (COTs) is an umbrella term referring to a group of NPTs in which a range of techniques are applied to engage thinking and cognition with various degrees of breadth and specificity and in which goals include improving or maintaining cognitive processes or addressing the impact of impairment in cognitive processes on associated functional ability in daily life (Bahar-Fuchs, Martyr, Goh, Sabates, & Clare, 2019). Clare and Woods (2004) propose a distinction between cognitive "stimulation," "training," and "rehabilitation" in classifying COT (see Table 1). However, these terms have been and continue being used interchangeably in the literature (e.g., Fernández-Prado, Conlon, Mayán-Santos, & Gandoy-Crego, 2012; Giordano et al., 2010), which led to some confusion.

The practice known as "reality orientation" originated in nursing homes in the 1950s. During reality orientation basic personal and current

Table 1 Characteristics of the main COT approaches.

	Cognitive training	Cognitive rehabilitation	Cognitive stimulation
Target	Impairment	Participation restriction	Participation restriction
Context	Structured tasks and environments	In the person's natural environment	Usually in a clinic/residential care, or daycare setting
Focus of intervention	Specific cognitive abilities and processes. Psychoeducation and strategy training sometimes included	Groups of cognitive abilities and processes required to perform individually relevant everyday tasks. Behavior, environment and everyday activity. Psychoeducation and strategy training sometimes included	Orientation, global cognitive status
Format	Individualized or group	Individualized	Typically group
Proposed mechanism of action	Mainly restorative; mechanisms related to neuroplasticity	A combination of restorative and compensatory approaches; reduction of "excess disability"	Improved orientation, general activation
Goals	Improved or maintained ability in specific cognitive domains	Performance and functioning in relation to collaboratively set behavioral or functional goals	Improve overall orientation and engagement in pleasant abilities

From Bahar-Fuchs, A., Martyr, A., Goh, A., Sabates, J., & Clare, L. (2019). Cognitive training for people with mild to moderate dementia. *Cochrane Database of Systematic Reviews* , *2019*(3), CD013069. https://doi.org/10.1002/14651858.CD013069.pub2.

information is repeatedly presented (usually using external cues indicating time, date, place, person, and key events) in a structured classroom format. Reality orientation has some positive impacts on the cognition and behavior of residents with dementia (Spector, Orrell, Davies, & Woods, 2000). Cognitive stimulation therapy (CST) built on reality orientation, centered on "engagement in a range of activities and discussions (usually in a group) aimed at general enhancement of cognitive and social functioning" (Clare & Woods, 2004). This engagement is assumed to implicitly stimulate memory, executive functioning, and language skills, and to enhance overall cognitive function, as well as the quality of life (QoL) and mood (Woods, Aguirre, Spector, & Orrell, 2012). CST is built upon theories including learning theory and brain plasticity; which suggest that appropriate and targeted mental stimulation can lead to the development of new neuronal pathways. CST sessions follow a set of guiding principles which include "new ideas, thoughts, and associations" and "opinions rather than facts" (Gibbor, Yates, Volkmer, & Spector, 2020). CST is not to be confused with the related Reminiscence Therapy approach, which involves discussion of distant autobiographical events and experiences (individually or in small groups), usually with the aid of prompts, including music, photos, and familiar objects, and which has been associated with modest benefits for quality of life, communication, mood, and cognition immediately after the intervention (O'Philbin, Woods, Farrell, Spector, & Orrell, 2018).

A structured and manualized, 7-week, 14 session CST program was developed and evaluated in a pilot study (Spector, Orrell, Davies, & Woods, 2001), and subsequently in a randomized controlled trial (RCT) (Spector et al., 2003). CST was associated with benefits in global cognition and quality of life. Maintenance CST including 24 additional weekly sessions was later developed and evaluated in a multicenter pragmatic RCT, which found that sustained effects on quality of life at 6-months, as well as improved cognition in participants who were also on anti-dementia medications (Orrell et al., 2014). Maintenance CST included 45-min small group sessions which involved a warm-up orientation activity, prompts to recall recent activities and a brief discussion of a current affair.

A meta-analysis of 718 participants included in 15 RCTs of cognitive stimulation (of which two were manualized CST) found clear benefits for overall cognition and self-rated quality of life (Woods et al., 2012). The manualized UK CST protocol has been since adapted and evaluated in several countries including the United States, Japan, and Portugal. A recent systematic review which evaluated the effects of manualized CST identified

12 eligible trials and found consistent benefits for cognition and frequently also for the quality of life and depression (Lobbia et al., 2018). Taken together, CST is associated with meaningful benefits for people with mild-to-moderate dementia.

In contrast to cognitive stimulation, which is relatively nonspecific and tends to be delivered in small groups, cognitive rehabilitation (CR) is a highly individualized approach, centered around the identification and focus on personally meaningful goals related to everyday activities. CR involves the person with dementia and close others (e.g., family and friends) working collaboratively with a therapist to identify goals and develop strategies to reduce the impact of cognitive impairment on the person's capacity to carry out relevant everyday activities independently. Potential goals are defined based on comprehensive assessment of the person's cognitive and behavioral functioning, their psychological adjustment and coping styles, and available support (Bahar-Fuchs, Kudlicka, & Clare, 2016). Making the most of residual and unimpaired cognitive abilities, therapists use a combination of external (e.g., notes and calendars) and internal (e.g., mnemonics) strategies, as well as evidence-based learning principles (e.g., vanishing cues and spaced retrieval), to support the performance of relevant functional goals. For example, a person with dementia may have difficulty learning how to use a mobile banking application. During CR, they may be taught strategies and given the opportunity to practice ways to learn how to use the application. In CR there is no assumption that underlying cognitive impairment can be improved, or that gains will transfer to untrained tasks and activities, the emphasis is on the performance of meaningful daily activities, not cognitive function. Wherever possible, CR should be offered in the milder stages, as early intervention provides an opportunity for advanced planning, and to capitalize on the person's residual cognitive strengths and relatively circumscribed functional limitations. Goals need to change to accommodate changes in function as dementia progresses (Clare & Woods, 2004).

Building on the encouraging findings from the first pilot RCT of CR (Clare et al., 2010), a large UK-based multisite RCT of people with mild-to-moderate dementia found those who received CR, as well as their care partners rated their performance of individualized goals much higher than participants who received treatment as usual (Clare et al., 2019). Notably, CR did not lead to objective improvements on cognitive tests, and goal performance was subjectively rated and not corroborated with a formal rating of actual goal performance. A small trial in Australia ($N = 40$), involving participants with either mild cognitive impairment (MCI) or mild dementia, also found that relative to treatment, as usual, those receiving CR were more satisfied with their performance of personally defined goals (Regan, Wells, Farrow, O'Halloran, & Workman, 2017). Hence, a small but growing body of evidence suggests that the goal-oriented CR approach may lead to greater satisfaction with one's capacity to perform meaningful daily activities, but more research is needed. A systematic review of CR is currently underway (Kudlicka, Martyr, Bahar-Fuchs, Woods, & Clare, 2019). Cognitive training (CT), sometimes described in the literature as "brain training," "retraining," or "remediation," targets specific cognitive domains and processes (e.g., divided attention, processing speed, etc.). CT has a relatively long history of research in clinical and nonclinical populations, with early studies applying CT to people with dementia spanning more than 30 years (e.g., Beck, Heacock, Mercer, Thatcher, & Sparkman, 1988). CT typically involves guided practice of a set of standardized and structured tasks usually of an increasing level of difficulty (Bahar-Fuchs, Woods, & Clare, 2013; Mowszowski, Batchelor, & Naismith, 2010). CT can be divided into cognitive exercise and strategy training (Gates, Sachdev, Singh, & Valenzuela, 2011), the latter involves instruction and practice in using specific cognitive strategies to enhance performance (e.g., method of loci). Computerized CT has become the dominant approach, as technology allows for ever more flexible tailoring of training. A central assumption of CT is training targets an underlying process or ability, and gains made during training should be evident in the performance of tasks relying on similar cognitive processes as those trained. Although there is consensus among researchers in this area that cognitive training leads to improved performance on trained tasks, it has been much harder to demonstrate that gains transfer beyond the training context. The most recent Cochrane Review on CT found moderate quality evidence, based on 33 studies, of modest effects of CT on global cognition in people with mild-to-moderate dementia (Kudlicka et al., 2019).

The evidence for COTs across the continuum from cognitively healthy older people to those with dementia has been summarized in a systematic overview. Fig. 1 shows Forest Plots that summarize the evidence for outcomes associated with COTs for people with dementia, showing that CST and CT have been found beneficial for cognition in people with mild-to-moderate dementia (Malmberg-Gavelin, Lampit, Hallock, Sabates, & Bahar-Fuchs, 2020).

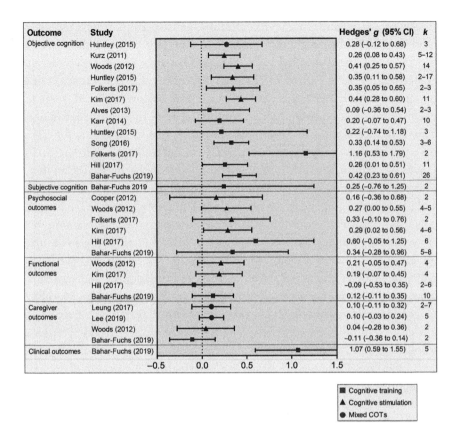

Fig. 1 Forest plot depicting effect sizes of COTs for people with dementia. *(Adapted from Malmberg-Gavelin, H., Lampit, A., Hallock, H., Sabates, J., & Bahar-Fuchs, A. (2020). Cognition-oriented treatments for older adults: A systematic overview of systematic reviews. Neuropsychology Review. Advance online publication. https://doi.org/10.1007/s11065-020-09434-8.)*

Physical activity treatments

Regular physical activity (PA), if prescribed appropriately, can be associated with health benefits for people with dementia, such as supporting physical health, falls risk reduction (see Chapter 5), supporting functional independence, quality of life, and mental health. However, the evidence on the benefits of physical exercise on cognition in people with dementia is inconsistent. A meta-analysis of 18 RCTs ($N = 802$) investigating the effect of PA with people with AD and non-AD dementia reported positive effects on cognition for aerobic exercise and combined aerobic and non–aerobic exercise (Groot et al., 2016). However, a more recent systematic review of eight RCTs concluded that while there was some evidence that aerobic exercise is associated with benefits in global cognition, there was little evidence of benefits in specific cognitive domains (Cammisuli, Innocenti, Fusi, Franzoni, & Pruneti, 2018). Nonetheless, these reviews provide at least some evidence that physical exercise improves cognition in AD and dementia. The reviews also highlight variations in study design and measurement, a need for greater treatment specifications for exercise, carefully defined exercise regimes, and well-designed studies that are adequately powered.

Challenges and enablers to adoption and clinical implementation of behavioral interventions including cognition-oriented and physical activity treatments

Here, we outline common challenges and enablers relating both to clinicians and people with dementia.

Clinician-related factors
Clinician knowledge, competence, and confidence

Many clinicians would like to incorporate cognitive or physical activity interventions in their practice but do not know where to start. Common challenges include:

- feeling overwhelmed by the breadth of techniques, programs, and resources available;
- questioning their competence in providing instruction or guidance in unfamiliar strategies;
- low confidence in knowing which techniques to utilize for particular people with dementia or in particular situations.

Clinician competence and knowledge can be improved through training and engaging with instructive materials and evidence-based guidelines to clarify specific procedures and resource requirements to conduct a particular type of COT. Although there is no existing "manual" for cognitive interventions specific to dementia, clinicians can find useful and practical information in resources addressing acquired brain injury populations, such as the Cognitive Rehabilitation Manual by the Brain Injury Interdisciplinary Special Interest Group of the American Congress of Rehabilitation Medicine (Haskins, 2012) or the INCOG guidelines for best practices in cognitive rehabilitation following traumatic brain injury (Bayley et al., 2014).

Key considerations for the design and evaluation of COTs for older people with and without dementia have been addressed by the cognition-oriented interventions design, evaluation, and reporting (CIDER) international working group (Bahar–Fuchs, Kudlicka, & Clare, 2016), and relevant recommendations were developed on the basis of a recent survey of experts (Simon et al., 2020). Clinicians may also keep up to date with the latest evidence through resources such as the Cognition-oriented treatments article library and evaluation (CogTale; www.cogtale.org), an online platform for the evaluation, synthesis and dissemination of evidence related to COTs in older adults with and without dementia (Bahar–Fuchs et al., 2018).

Many professional and research organizations have special interest subgroups relating to cognition, rehabilitation, and/or dementia, which provide opportunities to keep up to date with current evidence and practice while simultaneously expanding professional networks with like-minded colleagues. This may occur on an international scale (e.g., the Alzheimer's Association International Society to Advance Alzheimer's Research and Treatment (ISTAART), locally such as via professional registration or advocacy groups, or informally via peer support. Engaging with these networks increases accessibility to conferences, workshops, lectures, or other events that may offer knowledge and skill building in relation to COTs.

A structured approach to determining whether COT is appropriate

Clinicians may also benefit from a structured approach to determining whether and which COT is appropriate. We have found the rubric in Box 1 to be a helpful tool in guiding our decision-making and approach in clinical practice.

Person with dementia- and care partner-related factors

Person with dementia engagement

Like any treatment program, the success of cognitive intervention is greatly attributable to the person's level of engagement and motivation, as this impacts their ability to internalize, apply and generalize the skills, strategies, and exercises practiced through the intervention. Additionally, cognitive impairment may create a potential barrier to engagement. For example, a person presenting with deficits in attention may have difficulty engaging in intervention sessions due to wavering concentration and susceptibility to fatigue. A person with executive dysfunction may be somewhat apathetic about participating in intervention sessions or may miss appointments due to reduced drive or poor initiation of activities required to get them to the intervention location. A person with marked deficits in new learning may have trouble absorbing the information presented during the intervention. Clinicians should account for the potential impact of these difficulties (e.g., by selectively setting a location or time of day for the sessions; by utilizing

Box 1 Indicators of suitability of a cognitively oriented treatment for people with dementia.

For this person with dementia?
- Has the person with dementia's cognition been assessed?
- What is the functional impact of any cognitive deficits or weaknesses?
  Prompts: "a typical day" / "activities you would like to do but are no longer able to" / "tasks that are important to you"
- Is there evidence for using COTs in people with these cognitive deficits?
- Are the persons motivated and likely to engage?
- What are the treatment goals? Who has set them? Are they:
  Specific Measurable Achievable Realistic/Relevant Time-based?
- Can the outcomes be maintained over time?
- Can the outcomes be generalized to other situations?
- Does the person have support to implement skills/strategies outside of the intervention?

At this time?
- What is the person's stage of disease severity?
- Are there other medical, lifestyle, or environmental factors that may need to be?
- What else is the person involved in currently (e.g., other allied health interventions, respite activities, etc.)—might the person be overwhelmed, or can the activities work synergistically?
- Is there enough time to address the person's goals during the available intervention period?

In this context?
- Where is the person with dementia residing, and will this affect their access to the intervention? (e.g., inpatient who may be discharged at any time; homebound, etc.)
- Is your clinical environment conducive to offering cognitive interventions (i.e., do you have the necessary time and resources to devote to intervention activities; does this fit within the scope of your role or service)?
  Are there other options for intervention that may have cognitive or functional benefits?

family, residential care staff or others to assist the person in attending the intervention, and by choosing to use appropriate methods such as errorless learning or chaining).

Even in people without marked executive dysfunction, motivation is frequently problematic. This may particularly relate to insight in people with dementia. Awareness of cognitive deficits is not unitary and may vary across different cognitive domains and tasks; additionally, insight into cognitive deficits may not lead to insight regarding the consequences or functional impact of the impairment (see Zanetti et al., 1999). Hence the person may not see the need to participate in rehabilitative activities.

Beliefs and emotions in relation to the treatment are also important. Stubbs et al. (2014) showed that motivation for physical activity is increased when the person believes it is important or wants to maintain physical and mental health when they can appreciate and see the benefits, when the exercise itself is meaningful and enjoyable, and when they experience positive feelings about being active.

Engagement may also be impacted by medical comorbidities such as depression, physical limitations, frailty, or infection. Other medical needs should be adequately treated or managed prior to commencing a cognitive or physical activity intervention if improvement in those symptoms is likely to facilitate greater engagement in the intervention. Lifestyle and environmental factors may also play a role in engagement. For example, compared to people with dementia in residential care, those living in the community may have additional barriers to attending a series of recurring intervention appointments respect to transport and assistance.

Two recent reviews have reported on barriers and enablers to physical activity treatments which could reasonably also apply to COTs in people with dementia living in the community (Stubbs et al., 2014; van Alphen, Hortobágyi, & van Heuvelen, 2016). Interestingly, age and global cognition did not appear to affect participation. These reviews have shown that key facilitators include:
- better physical health and quality of life,
- greater social functioning and social support from family and professionals,
- practical strategies to assist while exercising and focusing on "what works," and
- access to appropriate, personalized, and convenient exercise programs; while key barriers include:
- poorer physical and mental health,
- cognitive difficulties specifically in attention and memory (but not lower global cognition), and
- concerns regarding safety.

Care partner involvement
Care partners are a significant resource for rehabilitation clinicians. Especially in cases where the person with dementia's insight is reduced, care partners can help to identify areas of functional impact as these are often activities or tasks where they have to provide additional support. Additionally, care partners can be invaluable in facilitating or ensuring practice, adherence, generalization,

and maintenance of cognitive strategies or techniques and/or physical activities/exercises outside of the therapeutic setting. Care partners are optimally engaged with the intervention when they are recognized as "care partners," making a direct and meaningful contribution to the rehabilitation process.

From a "person-centered care" perspective, clinicians need to be mindful of avoiding situations where the care partner "overtakes" the person with dementia in providing background information and inadvertently ends up setting the agenda for treatment, driving the goal-setting process, and selectively directing which strategies, techniques or exercises are adhered to. The clinician, therefore, needs to be mindful of and balance carefully, the need for care partner input and support, while simultaneously ensuring a person-centered approach and maximizing intrinsic motivation from the person with dementia themselves.

Examples of strategies for optimizing care partner support and engagement include:

- Explaining the "person-centered approach" to the care partner and person with dementia at the outset of treatment in order to clarify each person's role in the intervention and provide a framework and ground rules to enhance communication.
- Demonstrating methods and techniques and giving <u>both</u> the person with dementia and care partner opportunities to practice in session in order to troubleshoot any challenges and provide feedback as needed.
- Illustrating to the care partner how to simplify or modify day-to-day tasks so that the person with dementia can be involved and contribute effectively.
- Teaching the care partner how to recognize signs of frustration or agitation while carrying out new techniques, strategies or exercises (e.g., verbalizations, facial expressions, avoidance, and restlessness) and how to manage this. For example, they might suggest taking a break, modifying the task again, or redirecting the person with dementia (e.g., distracting them, changing the topic, and introducing a new task).

Conclusions and future directions

In summary, mounting evidence suggests that COTs, particularly cognitive stimulation and training, are associated with modest benefits for cognition in people with mild-to-moderate dementia, and that benefits often extend beyond cognition to include mood, quality of life, goal satisfaction, and overall well-being. Physical activity treatments are associated with a range of clinically meaningful benefits for people with dementia, but the direct benefit for cognition is unclear. Clinician knowledge, competence and confidence, the appropriateness of the intervention for that person, person with dementia engagement, and care partner involvement should be considered when implementing interventions.

To support the development of practice guidelines, research in this area is now shifting toward pragmatic community healthcare implementation trials. There is also growing interest in the potential synergistic effects of combination trials, in which COTs are combined with another treatment, such as physical exercise (Karssemeijer, Aaronson, Bossers, Smits, & Kessels, 2017) or Transcranial Direct Current Stimulation (tDCS; Hampstead, Sathian, Bikson, & Stringer, 2017). There is also growing interest in improving our understanding of the various moderators of treatment efficacy so that interventions can be better tailored to the needs and circumstances of the individual person with dementia (Lampit, Hallock, & Valenzuela, 2014).

A key challenge for future research on COTs and related treatments for people with dementia concerns the impact of ethnoracial factors on recruitment, retention, and outcomes (Mabulal et al., 2019), as such factors influence participant and care partner behavior in other chronic health conditions (Gavin, Fox, & Grandy, 2011), and care partners (Graham-Phillips, Roth, Huang, Dilworth-Anderson, & Gitlin, 2016). Cultural factors play a role in information processing and learning preferences (e.g., Yang, Chen, Ng, & Fu, 2013), suggesting that the design of COTs should take this into account (e.g., Wong et al., 2015).

Existing and rapidly emerging technologies such as mobile health applications, virtual and augmented reality, wearables, artificial intelligence, and tele-health are revolutionizing the ways in which nonpharmacological interventions are delivered. These technologies can overcome traditional barriers and are expected to lead to groundbreaking improvements in the support available for people with dementia and their care partners. A key challenge is the major gap between the rapid pace of technology development and the relatively slow changes in relevant policy and practice (Astell et al., 2019).

Acknowledgments

The authors would like to acknowledge the assistance of Dr. Hanna Malmberg-Gavelin in preparing Fig. 1 which is adapted from Malmberg-Gavellin et al. (2020, In Press).

References

Albert, M. S., DeKosky, S. T., Dickson, D., Dubois, B., Feldman, H. H., Fox, N. C., … Phelps, C. H. (2011). The diagnosis of mild cognitive impairment due to Alzheimer's disease: Recommendations from the NIA-AA workgroups on diagnostic guidelines for Alzheimer's disease. *Alzheimer's & Dementia*, 7(3), 270–279.

Astell, A. J., Bouranis, N., Hoey, J., Lindauer, A., Mihailidis, A., Nugent, C., & Robillard, J. M. (2019). Technology and dementia: The future is now. *Dementia and Geriatric Cognitive Disorders*, 47(3), 131–139.

Bahar-Fuchs, A., Kudlicka, A., & Clare, L. (2016). Cognitive rehabilitation for people with dementia: What is it and does it work? *Australian Journal of Dementia Care*, 5(5), 37–40.

Bahar-Fuchs, A., Martyr, A., Goh, A., Sabates, J., & Clare, L. (2019). Cognitive training for people with mild to moderate dementia. *Cochrane Database of Systematic Reviews*, 2019(3). https://doi.org/10.1002/14651858.CD013069.pub2.

Bahar-Fuchs, A., Mota Marques, D., Mancuso, S., Cong, Z., Hampstead, B. M., Belleville, S., … Sinnott, R. (2018). Cognition-oriented treatments article library and evaluation (CogTale): A novel online platform for cognitive intervention research evaluation, synthesis, and translation. *Alzheimer's & Dementia*, 14(7S-25), P3–605.

Bahar-Fuchs, A., Woods, R. T., & Clare, L. (2013). Cognitive training and cognitive rehabilitation for mild to moderate Alzheimer's disease and vascular dementia. *Cochrane Database of Systematic Reviews*, 2013(6). https://doi.org/10.1002/14651858.

Bayley, M. T., et al. (2014). INCOG guidelines for cognitive rehabilitation following traumatic brain injury: Methods and overview. *Journal of Head Trauma Rehabilitation*, 29(4), 290–306.

Beck, C., Heacock, P., Mercer, S., Thatcher, R., & Sparkman, C. (1988). The impact of cognitive skills remediation training on persons with Alzheimer's disease or mixed dementia. *Journal of Geriatric Psychiatry*, 21(1), 73–88.

Cammisuli, D. M., Innocenti, A., Fusi, J., Franzoni, F., & Pruneti, C. (2018). Aerobic exercise effects upon cognition in Alzheimer's disease: A systematic review of randomized controlled trials. *Archives Italiennes de Biologie*, 156(1–2), 54–63.

Clare, L., Kudlicka, A., Oyebode, J. R., Jones, R. W., Bayer, A., Leroi, I., … Brand, A. (2019). Individual goal-oriented cognitive rehabilitation to improve everyday functioning for people with early-stage dementia: A multicentre randomised controlled trial (the GREAT trial). *International Journal of Geriatric Psychiatry*, 34(5), 709–721.

Clare, L., Linden, D. E., Woods, R. T., Whitaker, R., Evans, S. J., Parkinson, C. H., … Rugg, M. D. (2010). Goal-oriented cognitive rehabilitation for people with early-stage Alzheimer disease: A single-blind randomized controlled trial of clinical efficacy. *The American Journal of Geriatric Psychiatry*, 18(10), 928–939.

Clare, L., & Woods, R. T. (2004). Cognitive training and cognitive rehabilitation for people with early-stage Alzheimer's disease: A review. *Neuropsychological Rehabilitation*, 14(4), 385–401.

Dubois, B., Hampel, H., Feldman, H. H., Scheltens, P., Aisen, P., Andrieu, S., … Washington, D. C. (2016). Preclinical Alzheimer's disease: Definition, natural history, and diagnostic criteria. *Alzheimer's & Dementia*, 12(3), 292–323. https://doi.org/10.1016/j.jalz.2016.02.002.

Fernández-Prado, S., Conlon, S., Mayán-Santos, J. M., & Gandoy-Crego, M. (2012). The influence of a cognitive stimulation program on the quality of life perception among the elderly. *Archives of Gerontology and Geriatrics*, 54(1), 181–184.

Folstein, M. F., Folstein, S. E., & McHugh, P. R. (1975). Mini mental state: A practical method for grading the cognitive state of patients for the clinician. *Journal of Psychiatric Research*, 12, 189–198. https://doi.org/10.1016/0022-3956(75)90026-6.

Gates, N. J., Sachdev, P. S., Singh, M. A. F., & Valenzuela, M. (2011). Cognitive and memory training in adults at risk of dementia: A systematic review. *BMC Geriatrics, 11*(1), 55.

Gavin, J. R., Fox, K. M., & Grandy, S. (2011). Race/ethnicity and gender differences in health intentions and behaviors regarding exercise and diet for adults with type 2 diabetes: A cross-sectional analysis. *BMC Public Health, 11*(1), 533.

Gibbor, L., Yates, L., Volkmer, A., & Spector, A. (2020). Cognitive stimulation therapy (CST) for dementia: A systematic review of qualitative research. *Aging & Mental Health*, 1–11.

Giordano, M., Dominguez, L. J., Vitrano, T., Curatolo, M., Ferlisi, A., Di Prima, A., ... Barbagallo, M. (2010). Combination of intensive cognitive rehabilitation and donepezil therapy in Alzheimer's disease (AD). *Archives of Gerontology and Geriatrics, 51*(3), 245–249.

Gorno-Tempini, M. L., Hillis, A. E., Weintraub, S., Kertesz, A., Mendez, M., Cappa, S. F., ... Grossman, M. (2011). Classification of primary progressive aphasia and its variants. *Neurology, 76*(11), 1006–1014. https://doi.org/10.1212/WNL.0b013e31821103e6.

Graham-Phillips, A., Roth, D. L., Huang, J., Dilworth-Anderson, P., & Gitlin, L. N. (2016). Racial and ethnic differences in the delivery of the resources for enhancing Alzheimer's caregiver health II intervention. *Journal of the American Geriatrics Society, 64*(8), 1662–1667.

Groot, C., Hooghiemstra, A. M., Raijmakers, P. G. H. M., van Berckel, B. N. M., Scheltens, P., Scherder, E., ... Ossenkoppele, R. (2016). The effect of physical activity on cognitive function in patients with dementia: A meta-analysis of randomized control trials. *Ageing Research Reviews, 25*, 13–23.

Hampstead, B. M., Sathian, K., Bikson, M., & Stringer, A. Y. (2017). Combined mnemonic strategy training and high-definition transcranial direct current stimulation for memory deficits in mild cognitive impairment. *Alzheimer's & Dementia: Translational Research & Clinical Interventions, 3*(3), 459–470.

Harada, C. N., Natelson Love, M. C., & Triebel, K. L. (2013). Normal cognitive aging. *Clinics in Geriatric Medicine, 29*(4), 737–752. https://doi.org/10.1016/j.cger.2013.07.002.

Hart, T., Dijkers, M. P., Whyte, J., Turkstra, L. S., Zanca, J. M., Packel, A., ... Chen, C. (2019). A theory-driven system for the specification of rehabilitation treatments. *Archives of Physical Medicine and Rehabilitation, 100*(1), 172–180.

Haskins, E. C. (Ed.). (2012). *Cognitive rehabilitation manual: Translating evidence-based recommendations into practice.* Virginia: ACRM Publishing.

Karssemeijer, E. E., Aaronson, J. J., Bossers, W. W., Smits, T. T., & Kessels, R. R. (2017). Positive effects of combined cognitive and physical exercise training on cognitive function in older adults with mild cognitive impairment or dementia: A meta-analysis. *Ageing Research Reviews, 40*, 75–83.

Kudlicka, A., Martyr, A., Bahar-Fuchs, A., Woods, B., & Clare, L. (2019). Cognitive rehabilitation for people with mild to moderate dementia. *Cochrane Database of Systematic Reviews, 2019*(7). https://doi.org/10.1002/14651858.CD013388.

Lampit, A., Hallock, H., & Valenzuela, M. (2014). Computerized cognitive training in cognitively healthy older adults: A systematic review and meta-analysis of effect modifiers. *PLoS Medicine, 11*(11).

Lobbia, A., Carbone, E., Faggian, S., Gardini, S., Piras, F., Spector, A., & Borella, E. (2018). The efficacy of cognitive stimulation therapy (CST) for people with mild to moderate dementia: A review. *European Psychologist, 24*(3), 257–277.

Mabulal, G. M., Quiroz, Y. T., Albensi, B. C., Arezana-Urquijo, E., Astell, A. J., Babiloni, C., ... International Society to Advance Alzheimer's Research and Treatment, Alzheimer's Association. (2019). Perspectives on ethnic and racial disparities in Alzheimer's disease and related dementias: Update and areas of immediate need. *Alzheimer's & Dementia, 15*(2), 292–312. https://doi.org/10.1016/j.jalz.2018.09.009.

Malmberg-Gavelin, H., Lampit, A., Hallock, H., Sabates, J., & Bahar-Fuchs, A. (2020). Cognition-oriented treatments for older adults: A systematic overview of systematic reviews. *Neuropsychology Review*. https://doi.org/10.1007/s11065-020-09434-8. Advance online publication.

McKeith, I. G., Boeve, B. F., Dickson, D.W., Halliday, G., Taylor, J.-P., Weintraub, D., ... Kosaka, K. (2017). Diagnosis and management of dementia with Lewy bodies. Fourth consensus report of the DLB Consortium. *Neurology*, *89*(1), 88–100. https://doi.org/10.1212/wnl.0000000000004058.

McKhann, G. M. (2011). Changing concepts of Alzheimer disease. *Journal of the American Medical Association*, *305*(23), 2458–2459. https://doi.org/10.1001/jama.2011.810.

McMonagle, P., Deering, F., Berliner, Y., & Kertesz, A. (2006). The cognitive profile of posterior cortical atrophy. *Neurology*, *66*(3), 331–338. https://doi.org/10.1212/01.wnl.0000196477.78548.db.

Mitchell, A. J., & Shiri-Feshki, M. (2009). Rate of progression of mild cognitive impairment to dementia—Meta-analysis of 41 robust inception cohort studies. *Acta Psychiatrica Scandinavica*, *119*, 252–265. https://doi.org/10.1111/j.1600-0447.2008.01326.x.

Mowszowski, L., Batchelor, J., & Naismith, S. L. (2010). Early intervention for cognitive decline: Can cognitive training be used as a selective prevention technique? *International Psychogeriatrics*, *22*(4), 537–548.

O'Philbin, L., Woods, B., Farrell, E. M., Spector, A. E., & Orrell, M. (2018). Reminiscence therapy for dementia: An abridged Cochrane systematic review of the evidence from randomized controlled trials. *Expert Review of Neurotherapeutics*, *18*(9), 715–727. https://doi.org/10.1080/14737175.2018.1509709.

Orrell, M., Aguirre, E., Spector, A., Hoare, Z., Woods, R. T., Streater, A., ... Russell, I. (2014). Maintenance cognitive stimulation therapy for dementia: Single-blind, multicentre, pragmatic randomised controlled trial. *The British Journal of Psychiatry*, *204*(6), 454–461.

Petersen, R. C., Lopez, O., Armstrong, M. J., Getchius, T. S. D., Ganguli, M., Gloss, D., ... Rae-Grant, A. (2018). Practice guideline update summary: Mild cognitive impairment. Report of the guideline development, dissemination, and implementation subcommittee of the American academy of neurology. *Neurology*, *90*, 126–135. https://doi.org/10.1212/WNL.0000000000004826.

Regan, B., Wells, Y., Farrow, M., O'Halloran, P., & Workman, B. (2017). MAXCOG—Maximizing cognition: A randomized controlled trial of the efficacy of goal-oriented cognitive rehabilitation for people with mild cognitive impairment and early Alzheimer disease. *The American Journal of Geriatric Psychiatry*, *25*(3), 258–269.

Simon, S. S., Castellani, M., Belleville, S., Dwolatzky, T., Hampstead, B. M., & Bahar-Fuchs, A. (2020). The design, evaluation, and reporting on non-pharmacological, cognition-oriented treatments for older adults: Results of a survey of experts. *Alzheimer's & Dementia: Translational Research & Clinical Interventions*, *6*(1), e12024.

Skidmore, E. R. (2017). Functional cognition: Implications for practice, policy, and research. *The American Journal of Geriatric Psychiatry*, *25*(5), 483–484.

Spector, A. E., Orrell, M., Davies, S. P., & Woods, B. (2000). Reality orientation for dementia. *Cochrane Database of Systematic Reviews*, *2000*(3), CD001119.

Spector, A., Orrell, M., Davies, S., & Woods, B. (2001). Can reality orientation be rehabilitated? Development and piloting of an evidence-based programme of cognition-based therapies for people with dementia. *Neuropsychological Rehabilitation*, *11*(3–4), 377–397.

Spector, A., Thorgrimsen, L., Woods, B., Royan, L., Davies, S., Butterworth, M., & Orrell, M. (2003). Efficacy of an evidence-based cognitive stimulation therapy programme for people with dementia: Randomised controlled trial. *The British Journal of Psychiatry*, *183*(3), 248–254.

Sperling, R. A., Aisen, P. S., Beckett, L. A., Bennett, D. A., Craft, S., Fagan, A. M., ... Phelps, C. H. (2011). Toward defining the preclinical stages of Alzheimer's disease: Recommendations from the National Institute on Aging-Alzheimer's Association workgroups on diagnostic guidelines for Alzheimer's disease. *Alzheimer's & Dementia, 7*(3), 280–292. https://doi. org/10.1016/j.jalz.2011.03.003.

Stubbs, B., Eggermont, L., Soundy, A., Probst, M., Vandenbulcke, M., & Vancampfort, D. (2014). What are the factors associated with physical activity (PA) participation in community dwelling adults with dementia? A systematic review of PA correlates. *Archives of Gerontology and Geriatrics, 59*(2), 195–203.

van Alphen, H. J. M., Hortobágyi, T., & van Heuvelen, M. J. G. (2016). Barriers, motivators, and facilitators of physical activity in dementia patients: A systematic review. *Archives of Gerontology and Geriatrics, 66*, 109–118.

Warren, J. D., Rohrer, J. D., & Rossor, M. N. (2013). Frontotemporal dementia. *British Medical Journal, 347*, f4827. https://doi.org/10.1136/bmj.f4827.

Wesson, J., Clemson, L., Brodaty, H., & Reppermund, S. (2016). Estimating functional cognition in older adults using observational assessments of task performance in complex everyday activities: A systematic review and evaluation of measurement properties. *Neuroscience & Biobehavioral Reviews, 68*, 335–360. https://doi.org/10.1016/j. neubiorev.2016.05.024.

World Health Organisation. (2001). *International classification of functioning, disability and health: ICF.* Geneva: World Health Organization.

Wong, G. H., Ng, C. K., Lai, C. K., Lee, M. N., Lum, T. Y., Jiang, N., … Dai, D. L. (2015). Development of six arts, a culturally appropriate multimodal nonpharmacological intervention in dementia. *The Gerontologist, 55*(5), 865–874.

Woods, B., Aguirre, E., Spector, A. E., & Orrell, M. (2012). Cognitive stimulation to improve cognitive functioning in people with dementia. *Cochrane Database of Systematic Reviews, 2012*(2). https://doi.org/10.1002/14651858.CD005562.pub2.

Yang, L., Chen, W., Ng, A. H., & Fu, X. (2013). Aging, culture, and memory for categorically processed information. *The Journals of Gerontology. Series B, Psychological Sciences and Social Sciences, 68*(6), 872–881. https://doi.org/10.1093/geronb/gbt006.

Zanetti, O., Vallotti, B., Frisoni, G. B., Geroldi, C., Bianchetti, A., Pasqualetti, P., & Trabucchi, M. (1999). Insight in dementia: when does it occur? Evidence for a nonlinear relationship between insight and cognitive status. *The Journals of Gerontology Series B: Psychological Sciences and Social Sciences, 54*(2), P100–P106.

CHAPTER 3

Communication interventions for people with dementia and their communication partners

Sarah El-Wahsh[a], Penelope Monroe[a], Fiona Kumfor[b,c], and Kirrie Ballard[a,c]
[a]Faculty of Medicine and Health, The University of Sydney, Sydney, NSW, Australia
[b]School of Psychology, The University of Sydney, Sydney, NSW, Australia
[c]Brain and Mind Centre, The University of Sydney, Sydney, NSW, Australia

Introduction

The ability to communicate allows us to interact with the world, have conversations, build relationships, and participate in work. Effective communication fosters psychosocial well-being and quality of life (Tompkins, 2012). In many dementia types, a decline in communication and language is among the first symptoms (Forbes-McKay & Venneri, 2005). These changes are a major contributor to loss of independence, carer burden, and stress (Mioshi et al., 2013). This chapter provides an outline of the communication changes typically experienced in dementia; specifically, the communication profiles of different dementia types and an overview of assessment and intervention options for people with dementia and their care partners.

The relation between memory and communication

Communication is a reciprocal to-and-fro act that involves exchange of information, ideas, needs, and wants. Communication involves linguistic and motor speech skills, as well as general cognitive functions, including memory and attention. Memory can be broken down into explicit memory and implicit memory. Explicit memory (declarative, conscious memory of facts) is involved across most stages of communication. Implicit memory (procedural memory), specifically, motor memory of how to articulate speech sounds, is also required in communication.

Fig. 1 shows a theoretical model of the relationship between memory and communication (Levelt, 1989). In order to express an idea, the speaker must first conceptualize their idea by accessing explicit memory (e.g., facts and what has already been said in the conversation). Next, words that best

Dementia Rehabilitation
https://doi.org/10.1016/B978-0-12-818685-5.00003-9

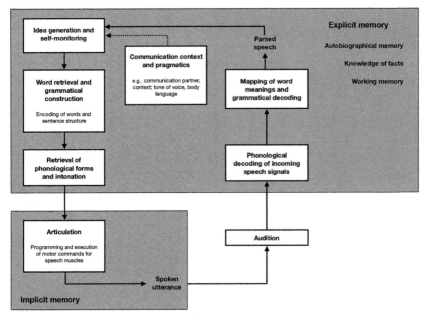

Fig. 1 Model of language production and comprehension. *(Modified from Levelt, W. J. (1989). Speaking: From intention to articulation. Cambridge, MA: The MIT Press.)*

correspond to the intended message are retrieved from the *lexicon* (word store). Subsequently, the most appropriate *syntax* (sentence structure) and *morphology* (word structure e.g., affixes, pluralization, tense markers) are selected to construct a grammatical utterance. While developing the utterance, the speaker takes into account the communication context and modifies their communication depending on the nature of their communication partner (e.g., familiar versus unfamiliar, friend versus person of higher authority) and the situation (e.g., group versus one-on-one, happy versus sad event). *Pragmatics* refers to this system of rules that governs the interpretation and use of language in social contexts. Next, to produce the spoken utterance, the utterance has to be prepared for articulation. First, the phonological form of each word (i.e., its sound sequence and correct number of syllables) is activated. The correct verbal prosody is also selected to match the function of the sentence (e.g., rising intonation at the end of a yes/no question). Implicit memories of speech sounds are activated to initiate coordinated movement within the respiratory, laryngeal, and supralaryngeal systems, as well as adjusting articulation to account for the communication context (e.g., background noise or the hearing level of the communication partner).

To make sense of the spoken language of others, a person's phonological system decodes the incoming speech signal into *phonemes* (individual sounds), syllables, and words. The speech comprehension system maps these incoming words onto their meaning and decodes the syntactic relationships between them to ensure correct interpretation of the meaning of the sentence (e.g., "the cat chased the dog" versus "the cat was chased by the dog"). The extracted meaning is then integrated with the preceding conversational narrative.

Communication changes based on dementia type

The communication changes experienced by people with dementia can occur across different components of the communication system and are influenced by dementia etiology, location and extent of neuropathology, and disease stage. Different dementia types present with different distributions of neuropathology and, therefore, characteristic profiles of communication are observed in the early stages of disease. Here, we review communication impairment that can result from three common dementia types: Alzheimer's disease (AD), vascular dementia (VaD), and frontotemporal dementia (FTD) (see Table 1).

AD is the most common cause of dementia. It is characterized by the formation of amyloid plaques and neurofibrillary tangles, which typically start in the medial temporal lobes, posterior cingulate cortex, and the inferior parietal lobe (Zhou et al., 2008) and give rise to the hallmark clinical feature of episodic or explicit memory loss. Language impairment is often observed in AD, typically beginning with word-finding difficulties in everyday conversational speech (Fraser, Meltzer, & Rudzicz, 2016). This inability to find words results in circuitous and empty speech, having a semblance of fluency but lacking in completeness and coherence, which can result in communication breakdowns (Fraser et al., 2016). Other changes in conversation include a loss of spontaneity (Forbes-McKay & Venneri, 2005). In the middle stage, communication impairment in AD becomes more severe across spoken and nonverbal modalities (e.g., increased word-finding difficulties, fragmented sentences, decreased comprehension of concrete and nonliteral language, incoherent discourse, and reduced facial expression) (Banovic, Zunic, & Sinanovic, 2018). In advanced AD, comprehension becomes exceedingly limited and speech is largely noncommunicative, with many people becoming partially or completely mute.

Logopenic variant primary progressive aphasia (lvPPA) has been considered an atypical early form of AD, with predominately initial

Table 1 Key communication impairments in the early stages of the main dementia types.

Type of dementia		Key communication impairments in the early stages of dementia
Alzheimer's disease (AD)	Typical presentation	Word finding difficulties Semantic paraphasias (substitution of words) (e.g., "TV" instead of "remote") Circumlocutory language (talking around a word) (e.g., "can you hand me the *clicker*" instead of "remote") Use of vague or empty words (e.g., "you know what I mean" instead of the right word) Difficulty understanding or following a conversation despite adequate hearing Repetition and digression in conversations, including difficulties maintaining the topic of conversation
	Logopenic variant PPA (lvPPA)	Word finding difficulties Phonemic paraphasias Circumlocutory language Shorter and simpler sentences Difficulty understanding more complex sentences Difficulty repeating longer sentences
Vascular dementia (VaD)		Shorter and simpler sentences Difficulty with motor speech skills (e.g., precision and rate of speaking, volume, intonation)
Frontotemporal dementia: (FTD)	Behavioral-variant frontotemporal dementia (bvFTD)	Repetition and digression in conversations, including difficulties maintaining the topic of conversation Difficulty understanding nonliteral language that requires inferencing such as sarcasm, proverbs, humor, metaphors, and ambiguous language

Table 1 Key communication impairments in the early stages of the main dementia types—cont'd

Type of dementia		Key communication impairments in the early stages of dementia
	Semantic variant primary progressive aphasia (svPPA)	Word finding difficulties Semantic paraphasias Circumlocutory language Difficult comprehending the meanings of words Difficulty understanding or following a conversation despite adequate hearing
	Non-fluent variant PPA (nfvPPA)	Word finding difficulties Phonemic paraphasias (use of words that are mispronounced) (e.g., "rebote" for "remote") Shorter and simpler sentences Sentences with grammatical mistakes (e.g., words in the wrong order, grammatical words like "the" omitted, use of wrong tense) Difficulty understanding or following a conversation despite adequate hearing Difficulty understanding more complex sentences

language-related symptoms (Gorno-Tempini et al., 2011). Although sharing similar neuropathology, namely amyloid plaques and neurofibrillary tangles, the symptoms of lvPPA differ from AD due to involvement of different brain regions. In the early stages of the disease, brain atrophy in AD preferentially affects the mesial temporal lobes, while in lvPPA there is early involvement of the posterior parietal gray matter (Beber, Kochhann, da Silva, & Chaves, 2014).

VaD results from cerebrovascular pathologies, such as ischemic, hypoperfusive, or hemorrhagic brain lesions (O'Brien & Thomas, 2015). Neural damage in VaD varies depending on the extent and location of infarcted tissue and cortical and/or subcortical pathology, hence the communication impairment profile of VaD differs across individuals. Typically, frontal and subcortical brain regions are affected, which can give rise to syntax impairment, including grammatical errors and simplified sentence structures (Hier, Hagenlocker, & Shindler, 1985; Vuorinen, Laine, & Rinne,

2000). Involvement of frontal brain regions also increases the possibility of articulatory-based motor speech impairment (i.e., dysarthria or apraxia of speech, characterized by slurred, effortful, and/or halting speech) (Banovic et al., 2018). Moreover, a key feature of VaD is slowed processing speed, which impacts communication (Karantzoulis, Galvin, Braak, Mckhann, et al., 2011), making it difficult to keep up with fast-paced conversations, follow multistep instructions, and interpret nuances and multiple meanings in conversation (Pichora-Fuller, 2003).

There are three clinical variants of FTD—behavioral variant FTD (bvFTD) and two language variants: semantic variant primary progressive aphasia (svPPA) and non-fluent variant PPA (nfvPPA) (Gorno-Tempini et al., 2011). BvFTD is characterized by communication changes related to pragmatics (e.g., impaired comprehension of nonliteral language, poor social inhibition) (Kumfor, Hazelton, Rushby, Hodges, & Piguet, 2019). SvPPA and nfvPPA are characterized by a decline in language and/or motor speech abilities early in the disease with other cognitive deficits emerging later. For a detailed description of the patterns of language deterioration in svPPA and nfvPPA, see Leyton et al. (2011) and refer to Table 1. In the remainder of this chapter, the three subtypes of primary progressive aphasia (PPA), lvPPA, svPPA, and nfvPPA, will be grouped together and referred to using the umbrella term PPA, unless otherwise specified.

Impact of communication impairment on the person with dementia and the carer

Reduced communication in people with dementia can lead to poorer quality interactions and withdrawal from social contact, leading to loss of friendships, reduced social activities, social isolation, depression, higher burden of care, and overall reduced quality of life (Mioshi et al., 2013; Small, Geldart, & Gutman, 2000). Family members of people with dementia also report frequent communication breakdowns that can result in loss of intimacy and quality interactions (Perry, Galloway, Bottorff, & Nixon, 2005; Small et al., 2000). This contributes to care partner burden and increased risk of early institutionalization (Potkins et al., 2003). This highlights the critical need for care partner interventions that support communication and help maintain and foster positive relationships. Accordingly, the communication abilities and needs of individuals with dementia should be evaluated and addressed early to inform care planning (Potkins et al., 2003).

Current approaches and evidence on communication assessment and intervention

Communication assessment and intervention is an essential part of a multi-disciplinary approach to dementia management. Management of communication impairment should be holistic in nature, taking into consideration personal goals, life stage, dementia type, disease stage, and psychosocial factors such as resilience, support networks, and personality.

Assessment and goal setting

No single gold standard assessment is available to assess spoken communication in dementia. A comprehensive communication assessment aims to cover all levels of the World Health Organization's (WHO) International Classification of Functioning, Disability and Health framework (ICF), including impairment, environmental factors, activity, participation, and personal factors (Hopper, 2007). Communication assessment is typically conducted by a speech-language pathologist and/or a clinical neuropsychologist. Specific tasks chosen for a communication assessment should initially be informed by the individual's/care partner's specific complaints and goals. Information gathering should rely on a variety of data sources including case history and discussion with the person with dementia and family members, neurological examination, behavioral assessment tasks, and consideration of concomitant health conditions (e.g., vision and hearing status) [American Speech-Language-Hearing Association (ASHA), 2003]. Table 2 lists examples of assessment measures that can be used to assess communication skills in dementia.

Intervention

In line with WHO's ICF model, a person-centered approach to communication intervention focuses on co-designing the specific goals that address the individual's unique needs and context and embraces collaboration with the person with dementia and their family (Tippett, Niparko, & Hillis, 2014). Through behavioral interventions, clinicians can target body structure and function to restore lost function or slow decline of communication behaviors in the person with dementia. These impairment-based interventions can involve repeated practice of targeted skills, such as word retrieval intervention, in daily drill-type exercises or embedded within daily activities that can assist in improving social participation. To date, there has been a stronger focus on impairment-based interventions for individuals

Table 2 Examples of assessment tools available to evaluate different aspects of communication across the dementia types.

Assessment	Areas and skills assessed
Impairment-focused assessments	
Arizona Battery for Communication Disorders of Dementia (ABCD) (Bayles & Tomoeda, 1993)	Primary language processes, including linguistic expression, linguistic comprehension, verbal episodic memory, visuospatial construction, and mental status
Western Aphasia Battery (WAB) (Kertesz, 1982)	Linguistic and nonlinguistic skills, including content of verbal expression, fluency, auditory comprehension, repetition, naming, reading, writing, drawing, and calculation
Picture description tasks (e.g., cookie theft, refused umbrella, cat rescue, flowerpot incident)	Quality and quantity of connected speech, word retrieval and errors, sentence formulation and complexity, discourse structure, and cohesion
Boston Naming Test (BNT) (Kaplan, Goodglass, & Weintraub, 1983)	Word retrieval and errors
The Sydney Language Battery (SydBat) (Savage, Hsieh, et al., 2013; Savage, Ballard, Piguet, & Hodges, 2013)	Word retrieval, word repetition, word comprehension, and semantic associations between words
Cognitive Linguistic Quick Test (Helm-Estabrooks, 2001)	Attention, memory, executive functions, language, and visuospatial skills
Addenbrooke's Cognitive Examination (ACE) (Eneida Mioshi, Dawson, Mitchell, Arnold, & Hodges, 2006)	Orientation/attention, memory, verbal fluency, language, and visuospatial skills
Frenchay Dysarthria Assessment (Enderby, 1980)	Integrity of respiratory, phonatory, and articulatory systems for speaking, speech precision, and intelligibility
Participation-focused assessments	
Assessment of Language-Related Functional Activities (ALFA) (Baines, Martin, & Heeringa, 1999)	Telling time, counting money, solving daily math problems, understanding medicine labels, using a calendar, and writing a phone message
Communication Activities of Daily Living (CADL-3) (Holland, Frattali, & Fromm, 1999)	Social interactions, humor and other nonliteral language contexts, reading, writing, and using numbers
Self/other-report measures	
Assessment for Living with Aphasia (Simmons-Mackie et al., 2014)	Pictographic self-report measure of communication impairment-related quality-of-life

Table 2 Examples of assessment tools available to evaluate different aspects of communication across the dementia types—cont'd

Assessment	Areas and skills assessed
Communicative Effectiveness Index (CETI) (Donovan, Kendall, Young, & Rosenbek, 2008)	Effectiveness of communication across eight speaking contexts (e.g., familiar person in quiet place, stranger on phone, someone at a distance, in a group), assessed through self-report using a four-point rating scale
Inpatient Functional Communication Interview Staff Questionnaire (IFCI SQ) (O'Halloran, Coyle, & Lamont, 2017)	The IFCI SQ is completed by a nurse who has cared for the patient for at least one shift and is a measure of how well an inpatient can communicate in relevant hospital situations assessed on a three-point rating scale
The Pragmatics Profile of Everyday Communication Skills in Adults (Dewart & Summers, 1996)	Communication in everyday interactions, assessed through informal interview with guided questions

in the milder stages of dementia or with PPA (Hinshelwood, Henry, & Fromm, 2016). Their success for PPA demonstrates that language skills can be improved and possibly sustained for longer in these earlier disease stages (Croot et al., 2019; Hinshelwood et al., 2016). Behavioral interventions may also focus on compensatory strategies that either circumvent the damaged system and recruit intact systems or skills (Hopper, 2007), or assist communication partners in better supporting successful communication interactions (O'Rourke, Power, O'Halloran, & Rietdijk, 2018). These approaches primarily address improving participation in daily activities and interactions. While they can be introduced at any stage of the disease process, they are often applied in the later stages of dementia (Hinshelwood et al., 2016).

We review four evidence-based communication interventions used in dementia to illustrate the different approaches: word retrieval intervention and script training, which are impairment based; and memory books and communication partner training, which compensate for damaged systems.

Word retrieval intervention
Word retrieval intervention aims to improve a person's ability to retain or regain access to vocabulary in their explicit memory. The person with dementia, clinician, and care partner identify target words that are salient,

personally relevant, and drawn from everyday vocabulary so that they can be practiced regularly and in context (Jokel, Graham, Rochon, & Leonard, 2014). Practice exercises can include confrontational naming (i.e., "Tell me what this picture shows"), sorting pictures and words by semantic category, using the word in functional phrases (e.g., "Use the word [target] in a sentence/question/to describe this picture"), feature description (e.g., "Show me the one that you drink with"), phonemic evaluation (e.g., "Show me something starting with /s/"), and association/comprehension (e.g., "Show me the picture that goes with bread" or "Show me butter") (Jokel et al., 2014; Krajenbrink, Croot, Taylor-Rubin, & Nickels, 2018; Savage, Ballard, Piguet, & Hodges, 2013; Savage, Piguet, & Hodges, 2015). Materials can include real objects, color photographs, and/or pictures (Cadório, Lousada, Martins, & Figueiredo, 2017). The complexity of the task can be adapted to the person's capacity, including the number of pictures/items practiced, the semantic or phonological similarity of options, and the level of frequency of pictures/items (i.e., high versus low frequency in everyday use). When word retrieval attempts fail, a person is provided with either a model for imitation or a cue to support gradually more independent retrieval (i.e., semantic, phonemic first sound, and/or orthographic first letter cues).

Currently, there is no consensus about the ideal intervention length, intensity, or dose for word retrieval intervention in dementia (Cadório et al., 2017). Practice of the target words in a naturalistic context is recommended to facilitate longer-term improvements (Croot et al., 2019). Maintenance studies have been equivocal reporting maintenance of gains ranging from 4 weeks to 6 months posttreatment (Cadório et al., 2017; Savage et al., 2015). Personal factors such as motivation, memory, insight and awareness, and strength of support networks play a large role in the person's ability to engage with and benefit from intensive word retrieval intervention (Taylor-Rubin, Croot, & Nickels, 2019).

Word retrieval intervention has mainly been investigated in PPA (Jokel et al., 2014). People with PPA with mild, moderate, or severe word-finding difficulties can benefit from word retrieval intervention to maintain access to vocabulary (Savage, Hsieh, et al., 2013; Savage, Ballard, et al., 2013). To date, the majority of research investigating the efficacy of word retrieval intervention in PPA comes from case studies or small controlled within-participant experiments (Cadório et al., 2017; Jokel et al., 2014; Savage et al., 2015). Despite the low level of supporting evidence for this communication intervention, clinicians report word retrieval intervention as the most used intervention for people with PPA (Croot et al., 2019). The efficacy of word retrieval intervention for word-finding difficulties in other dementia types remains relatively unexplored. However, this technique may be useful when word-finding difficulties occur.

Script training

Script training involves developing a monologue or a dialogue script that represents a common or important sequence of utterances used in a person's real-life activities. The main aim is to practice the script(s) to the point of overlearning, or inducing automatic retrieval so that the script can be used in social situations to improve participation (e.g., delivering a speech at a child's wedding, independently ordering takeout over the phone, making an appointment at the doctors) (Kaye & Cherney, 2016).

In script training, a person selects their script topic with support from the clinician and the care partner. The script is collaboratively produced and written down. When developing the script, it is important to consider the interests and needs of the person, the complexity of vocabulary and grammar, the number of conversational turns, and the length of the script (Khayum, Wieneke, Rogalski, Robinson, & O'Hara, 2012). The script is then practiced repeatedly with the person, advancing through the script lines with cueing support from the clinician or the carer (e.g., from phrase repetition to choral reading to independent production) (Holland, Milman, Munoz, & Bays, 2002). Therapy sessions can be filmed to help with feedback and can be used as a point of discussion to identify successful communication, communication breakdowns, and strategies to facilitate effective communication (Khayum et al., 2012). Software has been developed to provide a "virtual" communication partner so that the person can practice alone (Henry et al., 2018). To improve transfer of skill to other contexts, practice can be varied by changing the order of script lines, varying the communication partner, and/or modifying the script lines in the dialogue (Goldberg, Haley, & Jacks, 2012). The number of weeks of intervention, session length and frequency, and the number of practices for each script line can be variable and tailored based on the person's needs and rate of progress. Consistent and intensive practice in a short amount of time is essential to achieve script automaticity (Kaye & Cherney, 2016).

Positive outcomes of script therapy include increased speaking rate and decreased revisions, repetitions, and hesitations of target phrases in the treated script (Goldberg et al., 2012). To date, in the dementias, script training has only been empirically evaluated in PPA, where the individual has no/minimal memory impairment. While it has not been empirically evaluated yet, script training may also be appropriate for persons with VaD with predominant aphasia. Research in PPA and other groups, such as poststroke-induced aphasia, suggests that script training can also generalize to improvements in untreated communication activities, including natural conversation, formal communication testing, and individual and care partner perceptions of communication abilities (Goldberg et al., 2012; Henry et al., 2018).

Memory books

Memory books, also known as "communication books" or "a book about me," involve developing a memory aid containing a collection of labeled pictures and photographs and any other materials, such as poems, letters, postcards, and memorabilia, that are of personal significance (Bourgeois, 1992, 1993). These visual and written aids serve as a reminder of places, people, and hobbies important to the person, for the purpose of stimulating and maintaining conversational interactions (Dijkstra, Bourgeois, Burgio, & Allen, 2002; Spilkin & Bethlehem, 2003). This intervention approach is not designed to change the underlying impairment, rather, it is designed to encourage and support more structured, meaningful, successful, and rewarding communicative interactions for the person with dementia and their communication partner.

In developing a memory book, the person with dementia, clinician, care partners, and other key people help determine the information and the general themes that should be included in the book (e.g., personal/biographical facts, family members, hobbies, everyday objects around the home, places traveled, food and beverages, clothing, and favorite restaurants). The clinician should consider how to best lay out and organize the book to meet the person's needs and linguistic, motor, sensory, perceptual, and cognitive abilities. This will influence the size of the book, pictures, and written stimuli—the vocabulary and grammatical complexity of any written material and the amount of information on a page. Examples of different formats include a small wallet-sized book, a ring-binder folder with protective sleeves to enable the addition and removal of pages, a visual art diary, or computerized memory books (De Leo, Brivio, & Sautter, 2011; Meiland et al., 2012). If the person with dementia presents with concomitant motor, sensory, perceptual, and/or cognitive impairment, multidisciplinary input should be considered. For example, an occupational therapist may be consulted on strategies to optimize access and organization of the memory book to accommodate for an individual's impaired upper limb function. The clinician(s) then guides the person with dementia and the care partner how to use the book (Bourgeois et al., 2003). Individuals are shown how the book can support their word-finding difficulties and how it can help them compensate for communication problems. Care partners can be taught how to use the book to support and prompt conversations with the person (e.g., making comments instead of asking excessive questions).

Memory books have been empirically shown to be effective for people with dementia types such as AD and VaD, and across mild to moderate disease stages (Bourgeois, Dijkstra, Burgio, & Allen-Burge, 2001; Subramaniam, Woods, & Whitaker, 2014). Randomized trials comparing memory book intervention to a control condition for people with mild to moderate dementia found benefits in language (e.g., increase in informativeness of verbal output, increase in the duration of speaking time and frequency of utterances), emotional well-being (e.g., reduced frustration, confusion, depression, aggressive behaviors, and anxiety symptoms related to memory and communication problems), and engagement in meaningful social interactions (Bourgeois et al., 2001; Subramaniam et al., 2014). In addition, memory books have been shown to increase closeness between the carer and the person with dementia, reduce stress, and improve knowledge and attitudes to support interactions between care partners and the person with dementia (e.g., reducing the number of questions and pointing to pictures in the memory book to stimulate conversation) (Bourgeois et al., 2001; Subramaniam et al., 2014).

Communication partner training

Communication partner training aims to teach the communication partner(s) skills and strategies to improve communication between them and the person with dementia. To date, this approach has received the most attention in higher-level experimental studies in dementia. This intervention has been examined most commonly in AD, VaD, and mixed dementia as a primary compensatory approach during the middle to late stages of the disease. Despite the current lack of evidence for PPA, it was reported in a survey study (Volkmer et al., 2019) as the most common intervention approach used by UK-based speech pathologists.

Communication partner training can be provided as a multi-session program for communication dyads (e.g., an individual and a partner), in a group (e.g., multiple people with dementia and/or partners), or as a shorter professional development module for health professionals who are directly caring for persons with dementia at home or in residential facilities (O'Rourke et al., 2018). It is typically delivered and facilitated by a speech pathologist and/or a psychologist. Key components include: (1) education on the etiology and symptoms of communication impairment and breakdown, as well as discussing the prognosis and progression of communication symptoms in dementia and (2) teaching communication partners meaningful skills and strategies to enhance communication, such as language-based skills (e.g., reducing sentence length and structure and complexity of vocabulary, collaboration—working together in conversations, elaboration—extending the conversation), non-language-based communication skills (e.g., tone of voice, time allowed for turn-taking, eye contact, gesturing, positive reinforcement), and environmental modification strategies (e.g., minimizing distractions, choosing the best time of day for a conversation) (Burgio et al., 2001; O'Rourke et al., 2018).

All the three communication partner training programs that have the highest level of evidence in dementia reported improved quality of life and communication effectiveness. The programs are (1) MESSAGE (Smith et al., 2011), which has supportive evidence from one randomized cohort trial (Conway & Chenery, 2016), (2) TANDEM, supported by one randomized controlled trial (Haberstroh, Neumeyer, Krause, Franzmann, & Pantel, 2011), and (3) FOCUSED (Ripich, Ziol, & Lee, 1998), supported by one nonrandomized controlled trial (Ripich, Ziol, Fritsch, & Durand, 2000). In these studies, dementia severity ranged from mild to severe and included participants with AD, VaD, and mixed dementia. For people with PPA, Volkmer, Spector, and Beeke (2018) have developed a communication partner training program called Better Conversations with Primary Progressive Aphasia (BCPPA), which is currently being evaluated in a single-blind randomized controlled pilot study. Troche, Willis, and Whiteside (2019) also explored the efficacy of the Supported Conversations with Aphasia (SCA) progam (Kagan, 1998), which combined SCA with elements of the TANDEM and FOCUSED programs. A pilot study found that the participants percieved benefit from the program (Troche et al., 2019).

Summary of communication changes and intervention

A theoretical model of the relationship between memory and communication, and the different components of the communication system in a box-and-arrow diagram was described earlier in this chapter. We will now revisit this figure (see Fig. 2).

Mapping of communication impairments

AD is commonly associated with impaired idea generation and spontaneity (A), word retrieval (B)(i), and working memory (G). LvPPA is commonly

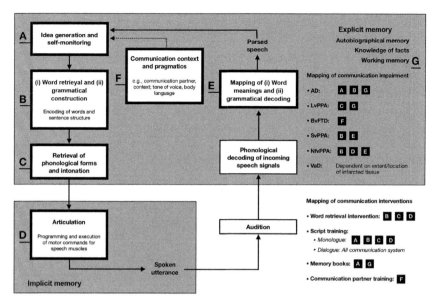

Fig. 2 In conjunction with the description below, this figure shows (1) a mapping of the breakdowns that are suggested to occur in the communication system across different dementia types and (2) a mapping of how the different interventions outlined in this chapter are understood to target different components of the communication system.

associated with impaired retrieval of phonological forms (C) and working memory (G). BvFTD is commonly associated with impaired pragmatics (F) (i.e., social language and interactional skills). SvPPA is commonly associated with impaired word retrieval (B)(i) and comprehension of word meanings (E)(i). NfvPPA is commonly associated with impaired grammatical construction of sentences (B)(ii), conversion of phonological forms into articulatory commands (D), and grammatical decoding (E)(ii) (e.g., understanding complex sentences). The communication profile of VaD is dependent on the extent and location of infarcted tissue, and hence "typical" communication impairments seen in VaD cannot be mapped onto this figure.

Mapping of communication interventions

Word retrieval intervention primarily targets word retrieval (B)(i) and can also target retrieval of phonological forms and intonation (C) and articulation (D) if the task requires production. For svPPA, word retrieval intervention also targets mapping of word meanings (E)(i). Script training can be done as a recitation/monologue, which targets the production component of the communication system: idea generation (A), word retrieval (B)(i), grammatical construction (B)(ii), retrieval of phonological forms and intonation (C), and articulation (D). Script training can also be done as a dialogue, which targets the whole communication system, both production and comprehension components. Memory books primarily target idea generation (A) by compensating for reduced explicit memory capacity (G). Communication partner training primarily targets the communication context (F) (i.e., communication partner skills and the communication context) to maximize the communication skills of the person with dementia.

Gaps in clinical and research knowledge

While communication impairments may be observed across the dementia types discussed in this chapter, referral to speech pathology services is relatively uncommon. In the most transparent of cases, PPA, people in Germany stated that they are "more isolated from [SLP] services than from any other allied health discipline" (Riedl, Last, Danek, & Diehl-Schmid, 2014). Referral rates, for PPA at least, are increasing as awareness of this primary language impairment spreads (Henry & Grasso, 2018; Volkmer, Spector, & Beeke, 2018).

Support for communication impairment in the dementias is hindered by the lack of a formal agreed upon care pathway (Taylor, Kingma, Croot, & Nickels, 2009; Volkmer et al., 2019; Volkmer, Spector, Warren, & Beeke, 2018). Care pathways ensure that families living with dementia have access to information about communication support services that can help with (a) prolonging independence and engagement in social networks during the early stages of the disease and (b) gradually introducing compensatory methods/devices such as communication partner training during the middle to late stages of the disease. In a survey study of UK-based speech pathologists, Volkmer et al. (2019) reported that only 9.4% of those surveyed reported a systematic care pathway for people with PPA at their workplace. Similarly, for Australia, Taylor et al. (2009) noted the absence of a formal single care pathway for speech pathology management of PPA. This reflects the relative lack of well-controlled studies of communication interventions across (a) different dementia types, (b) severities of impairment, and (c) intervention type.

There is wide scope for future research to explore the efficacy and effectiveness of a range of intervention types that target specific skills (e.g., word retrieval, narrative and discourse skills, pragmatics of language) at different disease stages, and determine whether treatment effects are modified by dementia type. Critical to this effort is assessment of the magnitude and longevity of any treatment effects and how these may be influenced by individual factors such as concomitant impairments, severity, level of family support, education, and social network size. Such detailed and systematic research will identify a care pathway that lessens the burden of the disease on both people with dementia and their care partners and ensures cost effectiveness. Central to this will be evaluation of how intervention can be delivered both through face-to-face, telehealth, and self/carer-administered programs to ensure adequate frequency and intensity of practice and practice within naturalistic contexts to improve potential for use within routine daily activities, as well as control accessibility and cost.

There is a notable lack of patient-reported outcome measures (PROMs) specifically developed and validated to assess communication and language function across the dementia types. PROMs can be valuable tools to screen and monitor symptom evolution, evaluate intervention outcomes via pre- and post-implementation, facilitate patient-centered care by acknowledging patient and carer perceptions, and guide service provision and public policy (Field, Holmes, & Newell, 2019). Moving forward, Khayum and Rogalski (2018) remind us that a person-centered approach is critical so that, as individuals move along the pathway, their care plans are tailored to their specific needs and contexts to maximize independence and active participation in daily life.

Clinical and research recommendations

Below is a list of recommendations that can serve to guide clinical practice and stimulate future translational and implementation research efforts toward formal clinical guidelines.

Clinical recommendations

1. Health professionals with expertise in the assessment and management of communication (e.g., speech pathologist, clinical neuropsychologist) are an integral part of the multidisciplinary care team of people with dementia to provide specialist support with communication impairment (Speech Pathology Australia [SPA], 2014; Volkmer, Spector, Warren, & Beeke, 2018). While additional evidence for specific communication intervention is urgently needed to guide practice and develop care pathways, clinical speech pathologists are ideally suited to consult on any aspect of communication impairment as well as challenges arising due to breakdowns in communicative interaction between the person with dementia and the network of care partners (Morhardt et al., 2015). They

also serve as advocates for ensuring people with dementia continue to be socially included and stimulated through meaningful and respectful communicative interaction, into the latest stages of their disease (ASHA, 2003; Higdon, 2004; SPA, 2014).

2. The goals of communication intervention for a person with dementia will change over the course of the disease (Hinshelwood et al., 2016), and therefore communication intervention should be dynamic and adapt to meet the person's changing communication needs (Khayum & Rogalski, 2018). Accordingly, health professionals with expertise in the assessment and management of communication impairment should be involved across the disease course.

3. Communication intervention for people with dementia should extend beyond the affected individual to include active collaboration with care partners (e.g., family members, nursing stuff) for goal setting, development of intervention resources, and communication partner training.

4. Examples of evidence-based communication interventions used with people with dementia that address spoken communication include word retrieval intervention, script training, memory books, and communication partner training.

Research recommendations

1. To build a stronger evidence base for intervention approaches targeting word retrieval, narrative and discourse, and effective communicative interactions for the purpose of sustaining meaningful participation of person's with dementia across a range of daily contexts. In particular, larger-scale experimental group studies are called for in both institutional and community settings using established design and reporting standards

2. To develop and validate PROMs specifically designed to assess communication function in the dementias. These outcome measures may consist of multiforms to enable information gathering from various sources, including self-perceptions of the person with dementia as well as the perceptions of the care partner(s). This information can help drive patient-centered care and shared decision-making (Field et al., 2019).

3. To develop clinical and research manuals for effective communication interventions to ensure high fidelity in core treatment principles and strategies, while allowing flexibility and tailoring person-centered care.

4. To investigate the theoretical and neural mechanisms of communication impairment across dementia types to aid the development of therapeutic communication interventions.

5. To examine different communication and language interventions across dementia types to determine clinical and demographic factors influencing effectiveness and suitability, such as disease severity, sex, cognitive capacity, insight, and communication partner availability.

6. To evaluate whether the range of existing communication interventions are meeting the needs of persons with dementia and their families, to examine their feasibility in the field, and barriers to use.

References

American Speech-Language-Hearing Association. (2003). *Evaluating and treating communication and cognitive disorders: Approaches to referral and collaboration for speech-language pathology and clinical neuropsychology.* Available at: https://www.asha.org/policy/TR2003-00137/.

Baines, K. A., Martin, A. W., & Heeringa, H. M. (1999). ALFA: Assessment of language-related functional activities. *Archives of Clinical Neuropsychology, 19,* 708.

Banovic, S., Zunic, L. J., & Sinanovic, O. (2018). Communication difficulties as a result of dementia. *Materia Socio-Medica, 30*(3), 221.

Bayles, K. A., & Tomoeda, C. K. (1993). *Arizona battery for communication disorders of dementia.* Tucson, AZ: Canyonlands Publishing.

Beber, B. C., Kochhann, R., da Silva, B. M., & Chaves, M. L. (2014). Logopenic aphasia or Alzheimer's disease: Different phases of the same disease? *Dementia & Neuropsychologia, 8*(3), 302.

Bourgeois, M. S. (1992). Evaluating memory wallets in conversations with persons with dementia. *Journal of Speech, Language, and Hearing Research, 35*(6), 1344–1357.

Bourgeois, M. S. (1993). Effects of memory aids on the dyadic conversations of individuals with dementia. *Journal of Applied Behavior Analysis, 26*(1), 77–87.

Bourgeois, M. S., Camp, C., Rose, M., White, B., Malone, M., Carr, J., & Rovine, M. (2003). A comparison of training strategies to enhance use of external aids by persons with dementia. *Journal of Communication Disorders, 36*(5), 361–378.

Bourgeois, M. S., Dijkstra, K., Burgio, L., & Allen-Burge, R. (2001). Memory aids as an augmentative and alternative communication strategy for nursing home residents with dementia. *Augmentative and Alternative Communication, 17*(3), 196–210.

Burgio, L. D., Allen-Burge, R., Roth, D. L., Bourgeois, M. S., Dijkstra, K., Gerstle, J., … Bankester, L. (2001). Come talk with me: Improving communication between nursing assistants and nursing home residents during care routines. *The Gerontologist, 41*(4), 449–460.

Cadório, I., Lousada, M., Martins, P., & Figueiredo, D. (2017). Generalization and maintenance of treatment gains in primary progressive aphasia (PPA): A systematic review. *International Journal of Language & Communication Disorders, 52*(5), 543–560.

Conway, E. R., & Chenery, H. J. (2016). Evaluating the message communication strategies in dementia training for use with community-based aged care staff working with people with dementia: A controlled pretest–post-test study. *Journal of Clinical Nursing, 25*(7–8), 1145–1155.

Croot, K., Raiser, T., Taylor-Rubin, C., Ruggero, L., Ackl, N., Wlasich, E., … Hodges, J. R. (2019). Lexical retrieval treatment in primary progressive aphasia: An investigation of treatment duration in a heterogeneous case series. *Cortex, 115,* 133–158.

De Leo, G., Brivio, E., & Sautter, S. W. (2011). Supporting autobiographical memory in patients with Alzheimer's disease using smart phones. *Applied Neuropsychology, 18*(1), 69–76.

Dewart, H., & Summers, S. (1996). *The pragmatics profile of everyday communication skills in adults*. NFER-Nelson.

Dijkstra, K., Bourgeois, M., Burgio, L., & Allen, R. (2002). Effects of a communication intervention on the discourse of nursing home residents with dementia and their nursing assistants. *Journal of Medical Speech-Language Pathology, 10*(2), 143–158.

Donovan, N. J., Kendall, D. L., Young, M. E., & Rosenbek, J. C. (2008). The communicative effectiveness survey: Preliminary evidence of construct validity. *American Journal of Speech-Language Pathology, 17*, 335–347.

Enderby, P. (1980). Frenchay dysarthria assessment. *British Journal of Disorders of Communication, 15*(3), 165–173.

Field, J., Holmes, M. M., & Newell, D. (2019). PROMs data: Can it be used to make decisions for individual patients? A narrative review. *Patient Related Outcome Measures, 10*, 233.

Forbes-McKay, K., & Venneri, A. (2005). Detecting subtle spontaneous language decline in early Alzheimer's disease with a picture description task. *Neurological Sciences, 26*, 243–254.

Fraser, K. C., Meltzer, J. A., & Rudzicz, F. (2016). Linguistic features identify Alzheimer's disease in narrative speech. *Journal of Alzheimer's Disease, 49*(2), 407–422.

Goldberg, S., Haley, K. L., & Jacks, A. (2012). Script training and generalization for people with aphasia. *American Journal of Speech-Language Pathology, 21*, 222–238.

Gorno-Tempini, M. L., Hillis, A. E., Weintraub, S., Kertesz, A., Mendez, M., Cappa, S. F., ... Boeve, B. F. (2011). Classification of primary progressive aphasia and its variants. *Neurology, 76*(11), 1006–1014.

Haberstroh, J., Neumeyer, K., Krause, K., Franzmann, J., & Pantel, J. (2011). TANDEM: Communication training for informal caregivers of people with dementia. *Aging & Mental Health, 15*(3), 405–413.

Helm-Estabrooks, N. (2001). *Cognitive linguistic quick test: CLQT*. Psychological Corporation.

Henry, M. L., & Grasso, S. M. (2018). Assessment of individuals with primary progressive aphasia. In *Paper presented at the seminars in speech and language*.

Henry, M. L., Hubbard, H. I., Grasso, S. M., Mandelli, M. L., Wilson, S. M., Sathishkumar, M.T., ... Miller, B. L. (2018). Retraining speech production and fluency in non-fluent/agrammatic primary progressive aphasia. *Brain, 141*(6), 1799–1814.

Hier, D. B., Hagenlocker, K., & Shindler, A. G. (1985). Language disintegration in dementia: Effects of etiology and severity. *Brain and Language, 25*(1), 117–133.

Higdon, C. W. (2004). The role of speech-language pathologists and audiologists in life care planning. In *Pediatric life care planning and case management* (pp. 225–324). CRC Press.

Hinshelwood, H., Henry, M., & Fromm, D. (2016). Helping them hold on: Through phased treatment, speech-language pathologists can help clients with primary progressive aphasia function as normally as possible—For as long as they can. *The ASHA Leader, 21*(10), 44–51.

Holland, A. L., Frattali, C., & Fromm, D. (1999). *Communication activities of daily living: CADL-2*. Pro-Ed.

Holland, A., Milman, L., Munoz, M., & Bays, G. (2002). Scripts in the management of aphasia. In *Paper presented at the world federation of neurology, aphasia and cognitive disorders section meeting, Villefranche, France*.

Hopper, T. (2007). The ICF and dementia. In *Paper presented at the seminars in speech and language*.

Jokel, R., Graham, N. L., Rochon, E., & Leonard, C. (2014). Word retrieval therapies in primary progressive aphasia. *Aphasiology, 28*(8–9), 1038–1068.

Kagan, A. (1998). Supported conversation for adults with aphasia: Methods and resources for training conversation partners. *Aphasiology, 12*(9), 816–830.

Kaplan, E., Goodglass, H., & Weintraub, S. (1983). *The Boston naming test*. Philadelphia, PA: Lea & Febiger.

Karantzoulis, S., Galvin, J. E., Braak, S., Mckhann, M. K., ... Butters. (2011). Distinguishing Alzheimer's disease from other major forms of dementia. *Expert Review of Neurotherapeutics, 11*(11), 1579–1591.

Kaye, R. C., & Cherney, L. R. (2016). Script templates: A practical approach to script training in aphasia. *Topics in Language Disorders*, *36*(2), 136.

Kertesz, A. (1982). *Western aphasia battery (WAB)*. San Antonio, TX: The Psychological Corporation.

Khayum, B., & Rogalski, E. (2018). Toss the workbooks! Choose treatment strategies for clients with dementia that address their specific life-participation goals. *The ASHA Leader*, *23*(4), 40–42.

Khayum, B., Wieneke, C., Rogalski, E., Robinson, J., & O'Hara, M. (2012). Thinking outside the stroke: Treating primary progressive aphasia (PPA). *Perspectives on Gerontology*, *17*(2), 37–49.

Krajenbrink, T., Croot, K., Taylor-Rubin, C., & Nickels, L. (2018). Treatment for spoken and written word retrieval in the semantic variant of primary progressive aphasia. *Neuropsychological Rehabilitation*, *30*, 1–33.

Kumfor, F., Hazelton, J. L., Rushby, J. A., Hodges, J. R., & Piguet, O. (2019). Facial expressiveness and physiological arousal in frontotemporal dementia: Phenotypic clinical profiles and neural correlates. *Cognitive, Affective, & Behavioral Neuroscience*, *19*(1), 197–210.

Levelt, W. J. (1989). *Speaking: From intention to articulation*. Cambridge, MA: The MIT Press.

Leyton, C. E., Villemagne, V. L., Savage, S., Pike, K. E., Ballard, K. J., Piguet, O., … Hodges, J. R. (2011). Subtypes of progressive aphasia: Application of the international consensus criteria and validation using β-amyloid imaging. *Brain*, *134*(10), 3030–3043.

Meiland, F. J., Bouman, A. I., Sävenstedt, S., Bentvelzen, S., Davies, R. J., Mulvenna, M. D., … Bengtsson, J. E. (2012). Usability of a new electronic assistive device for community-dwelling persons with mild dementia. *Aging & Mental Health*, *16*(5), 584–591.

Mioshi, E., Dawson, K., Mitchell, J., Arnold, R., & Hodges, J. R. (2006). The Addenbrooke's cognitive examination revised (ACE-R): A brief cognitive test battery for dementia screening. *International Journal of Geriatric Psychiatry*, *21*(11), 1078–1085.

Mioshi, E., Foxe, D., Leslie, F., Savage, S., Hsieh, S., Miller, L., … Piguet, O. (2013). The impact of dementia severity on caregiver burden in frontotemporal dementia and Alzheimer disease. *Alzheimer Disease and Associated Disorders*, *27*, 68–73.

Morhardt, D., Weintraub, S., Khayum, B., Robinson, J., Medina, J., O'Hara, M., … Rogalski, E. J. (2015). The CARE pathway model for dementia: Psychosocial and rehabilitative strategies for care in young-onset dementias. *Psychiatric Clinics*, *38*(2), 333–352.

O'Halloran, R., Coyle, J., & Lamont, S. (2017). Screening patients for communication difficulty: The diagnostic accuracy of the IFCI staff questionnaire. *International Journal of Speech-Language Pathology*, *19*(4), 430–440.

O'Brien, J., & Thomas, A. (2015). Vascular dementia. *The Lancet*, *386*(10004), 1698–1706.

O'Rourke, A., Power, E., O'Halloran, R., & Rietdijk, R. (2018). Common and distinct components of communication partner training programmes in stroke, traumatic brain injury and dementia. *International Journal of Language & Communication Disorders*, *53*(6), 1150–1168.

Perry, J., Galloway, S., Bottorff, J. L., & Nixon, S. (2005). Nurse-patient communication in dementia: Improving the odds. *Journal of Gerontological Nursing*, *31*(4), 43–52.

Pichora-Fuller, M. K. (2003). Processing speed and timing in aging adults: Psychoacoustics, speech perception, and comprehension. *International Journal of Audiology*, *42*(sup1), 59–67.

Potkins, D., Myint, P., Bannister, C., Tadros, G., Chithramohan, R., Swann, A., … Ballard, C. (2003). Language impairment in dementia: Impact on symptoms and care needs in residential homes. *International Journal of Geriatric Psychiatry*, *18*(11), 1002–1006.

Riedl, L., Last, D., Danek, A., & Diehl-Schmid, J. (2014). Long-term follow-up in primary progressive aphasia: Clinical course and health care utilisation. *Aphasiology*, *28*(8–9), 981–992.

Ripich, D. N., Ziol, E., Fritsch, T., & Durand, E. J. (2000). Training Alzheimer's disease caregivers for successful communication. *Clinical Gerontologist*, *21*(1), 37–56.

Ripich, D. N., Ziol, E., & Lee, M. M. (1998). Longitudinal effects of communication training on caregivers of persons with Alzheimer's disease. *Clinical Gerontologist, 19*(2), 37–55.

Savage, S. A., Ballard, K. J., Piguet, O., & Hodges, J. R. (2013). Bringing words back to mind–improving word production in semantic dementia. *Cortex, 49*(7), 1823–1832.

Savage, S., Hsieh, S., Leslie, F., Foxe, D., Piguet, O., & Hodges, J. R. (2013). Distinguishing subtypes in primary progressive aphasia: Application of the Sydney language battery. *Dementia and Geriatric Cognitive Disorders, 35*(3–4), 208–218.

Savage, S. A., Piguet, O., & Hodges, J. R. (2015). Cognitive intervention in semantic dementia: Maintaining words over time. *Alzheimer Disease & Associated Disorders, 29*(1), 55–62.

Simmons-Mackie, N., Kagan, A., Victor, J. C., Carling-Rowland, A., Mok, A., Hoch, J. S., … Streiner, D. L. (2014). The assessment for living with aphasia: Reliability and construct validity. *International Journal of Speech-Language Pathology, 16*(1), 82–94.

Small, J. A., Geldart, K., & Gutman, G. (2000). Communication between individuals with dementia and their caregivers during activities of daily living. *American Journal of Alzheimer's Disease, 15*(5), 291–302.

Smith, E. R., Broughton, M., Baker, R., Pachana, N. A., Angwin, A. J., Humphreys, M. S., … Gallois, C. (2011). Memory and communication support in dementia: Research-based strategies for caregivers. *International Psychogeriatrics, 23*(2), 256–263.

Speech Pathology Australia. (2014). Submission to the inquiry into the prevalence of different types of speech, language and communication disorders and speech pathology services in Australia. Speech Pathology Australia (SPA), Melbourne, Australia.

Spilkin, M.-L., & Bethlehem, D. (2003). A conversation analysis approach to facilitating communication with memory books. *International Journal of Speech-Language Pathology, 5*(2), 105–118.

Subramaniam, P., Woods, B., & Whitaker, C. (2014). Life review and life story books for people with mild to moderate dementia: A randomised controlled trial. *Aging & Mental Health, 18*(3), 363–375.

Taylor, C., Kingma, R. M., Croot, K., & Nickels, L. (2009). Speech pathology services for primary progressive aphasia: Exploring an emerging area of practice. *Aphasiology, 23*(2), 161–174.

Taylor-Rubin, C., Croot, K., & Nickels, L. (2019). Adherence to lexical retrieval treatment in primary progressive aphasia and implications for candidacy. *Aphasiology, 33*(10), 1182–1201.

Tippett, D. C., Niparko, J. K., & Hillis, A. E. (2014). Aphasia: Current concepts in theory and practice. *Journal of Neurology & Translational Neuroscience, 2*(1), 1042.

Tompkins, C. A. (2012). Rehabilitation for cognitive-communication disorders in right hemisphere brain damage. *Archives of Physical Medicine and Rehabilitation, 93*(1), S61–S69.

Troche, J., Willis, A., & Whiteside, J. (2019). Exploring supported conversation with familial caregivers of persons with dementia: A pilot study. *Pilot and Feasibility Studies, 5*(1), 10.

Volkmer, A., Rogalski, E., Henry, M., Taylor-Rubin, C., Ruggero, L., Khayum, R., … Rohrer, J. D. (2019). Speech and language therapy approaches to managing primary progressive aphasia. *Practical Neurology, 20*. practneurol-2018-001921.

Volkmer, A., Spector, A., & Beeke, S. (2018). Better conversations with primary progressive aphasia (BCPPA): Asking people with PPA and their families how speech and language therapists could support them to live well and maintain relationships. *Aphasiology, 32*(sup1), 239–240.

Volkmer, A., Spector, A., Warren, J. D., & Beeke, S. (2018). Speech and language therapy for primary progressive aphasia: Referral patterns and barriers to service provision across the UK. *Dementia, 1–15.

Vuorinen, E., Laine, M., & Rinne, J. (2000). Common pattern of language impairment in vascular dementia and in Alzheimer disease. *Alzheimer Disease & Associated Disorders, 14*(2), 81–86.

Zhou, Y., Dougherty, J. H., Jr., Hubner, K. F., Bai, B., Cannon, R. L., & Hutson, R. K. (2008). Abnormal connectivity in the posterior cingulate and hippocampus in early Alzheimer's disease and mild cognitive impairment. *Alzheimer's & Dementia, 4*(4), 265–270.

CHAPTER 4

Maintaining and improving physical function in dementia

Michele L. Callisaya[a,b], Susan W. Hunter[c], and
Manuel Montero-Odasso[d,e,f]

[a]Peninsula Clinical School, Monash University, Melbourne, VIC, Australia
[b]Academic Unit, Peninsula Health, Melbourne, VIC, Australia
[c]School of Physical Therapy, University of Western Ontario, London, ON, Canada
[d]Division of Geriatric Medicine, Department of Medicine, Parkwood Institute, University of Western Ontario, London, ON, Canada
[e]Lawson Health Research Institute, London, ON, Canada
[f]Gait and Brain Lab, Parkwood Institute, London, ON, Canada

Introduction

Research in the area of dementia has traditionally concentrated on interventions to improve or maintain cognitive function. It is now recognized that physical functioning is also affected in people with dementia. Strength, coordination, balance, and mobility are worse, and along with cognitive impairment, contribute to increased risk of adverse events such as falls and fractures. Concurrent diseases of aging, lower levels of physical activity, and the loss of neurons and pathways underlying both cognition and motor control are all likely to contribute poorer functioning in people living with dementia.

This chapter will outline the common physical impairments found in people living with dementia. A review of the evidence for treatments to maintain or improve physical function and prevent falls, in both community and residential settings will be provided.

Current approaches and evidence

Physical function and dementia

Although cognition and sensorimotor functions decline with age, people with dementia have greater levels of impairment than those who are not cognitively impaired. Impairments include poorer reaction time, weaker muscle strength, less coordination, and reduced static and dynamic balance (Taylor, Delbaere, Lord, Mikolaizak, & Close, 2013). Walking ability may also be affected, as cognitive processes are required to integrate incoming sensory information and execute appropriate motor outputs so that

Dementia Rehabilitation
https://doi.org/10.1016/B978-0-12-818685-5.00004-0
57

balance can be maintained (Allan, Ballard, Burn, & Kenny, 2005). Walking is not an automatic activity and relies on both physical and cognitive abilities (Martin et al., 2013). Interestingly, walking speed slows, and step-to-step variability increases, many years before the symptoms of dementia are recognized (Ceïde, Ayers, Lipton, & Verghese, 2018; Montero-Odasso et al., 2017; Verghese, Wang, Lipton, Holtzer, & Xue, 2007), suggesting it is an early indicator of underlying pathology.

The type of dementia and cognitive domains affected may influence the extent of mobility limitation. Greater changes in mobility are found in those with Parkinson's disease, vascular and Lewy body dementia than in those with Alzheimer's disease-type dementia (AD) (Allan et al., 2005). The non-amnestic domains of executive function (e.g., attention, inhibitory control, task switching, and working memory), visual-spatial function and processing speed appear to be particularly important in maintaining adequate mobility (Martin, Blizzard, Wood, et al., 2013). In-line with this, gait speed is slower in those with nonamnestic mild cognitive impairment (MCI) and non-AD compared with amnestic MCI and AD, respectively (Allali et al., 2016) (Callisaya et al., 2017). In a multicountry study, gait speed was found to be progressively slower with increasing cognitive impairment—e.g., speeds ranged from cognitively normal (1.05 ± 0.22 m/s), mild AD (0.74 ± 0.19 m/s), mild non-AD (0.72 ± 0.20 m/s), and moderate AD (0.68 ± 0.21 m/s) to the slowest speeds in moderate non-AD (0.62 ± 0.20 m/s) (Allali et al., 2016). Other related gait measures such as shorter steps, longer stance and double support times, and greater step-to-step variability showed a similar pattern of decline across groups (Allali et al., 2016).

Specific cognitive domains may be important in limiting an individual's ability to navigate over uneven surfaces or complex environments (Fig. 1). For example, a poor judgment regarding one's own abilities or decision-making regarding the safety of the external environment could lead to falls. Poor visuospatial function or central slowing may lead to a cautious gait pattern, difficulty negotiating uneven or changing surfaces, and general slowing of walking, respectively.

The role of attention during walking is evident while performing a secondary task, a skill that is required in many activities such as carrying a cup of coffee or walking and talking with friends. In people diagnosed with cognitive impairment or dementia, gait speed slows under dual-task to a greater extent than in people with normal cognitive function (Camicioli, Howieson, Lehman, & Kaye, 1997; Muir et al., 2012). This can be explained by two tasks competing for limited attentional resources, which may in turn

Fig. 1 Examples of environments requiring the cognitive domains of executive function, processing speed, attention, and visuospatial function.

impact on walking safety. Individuals without cognitive impairment tend to prioritize walking rather than the secondary cognitive task for safety (the posture first theory); however, those with neurological conditions have been shown to do the opposite, compromising safety and potentially increasing the risk of falls (Bloem, Grimbergen, van Dijk, & Munneke, 2006).

Recently, studies have assessed the effect of cognition on walking using an obstacle negotiation experiment in cognitively impaired older adults. Specifically, in older adults with a diagnosis of mild cognitive impairment, there was less deceleration and distance adjustment before avoiding an obstacle when walking and performing a cognitively demanding task. These studies suggest that deficits in higher-order cognitive processing may limit obstacle negotiation capabilities in cognitively impaired older adults, potentially increasing the risk of falls (Pieruccini-Faria, Sarquis-Adamson, & Montero-Odasso, 2019).

In summary, balance, strength, reaction time, coordination, and aspects of mobility, including the ability to dual-task and negotiate obstacles, are more impaired in people with dementia than those that are not cognitively impaired. The following section will outline the success or otherwise of interventions to improve or maintain physical function in people with dementia.

Interventions to improve physical function
Nonpharmacological interventions

A systematic review published by Zeng et al. (2016), which only included participants with dementia, suggested exercise can improve balance and mobility (Zeng et al., 2016). Improvements were noted for the Timed Get

Up and Go (TUG) (3 trials, $n = 206$; MD $= -2.87$ s, 95% CI $-3.25, -2.5$), Functional Reach Test (2 trials $n = 80$; MD $= 4.25$ cm, 95% CI 3.52, 4.98), Berg Balance Scale (BBS) (2 trials; $n = 356$; MD $= 3.62$, 95% CI 1.51, 5.73), and walking cadence (2 trials; $n = 183$; MD $= 12$ steps/min, 95% CI 6.92, 18.51) (Zeng et al., 2016). However, there was no improvement found for walking speed (3 trials; $n = 211$; MD $= 13.21$, 95% CI $-8.01, 34.43$) (Zeng et al., 2016). A further meta-analyses published by Lam et al. (2018), which included both people with MCI and dementia, reported exercise was able to improve functional strength, balance, and mobility as measured by the 30 s sit-to-stand test (4 trials, $n = 278$; MD 2.1 repetitions 95% CI 0.3, 3.9), BBS (6 trials, $n = 722$; MD 3.6 95% CI 0.3–7.0), functional reach test (6 trials; $n = 242$; MD 3.9 cm 95% CI 2.2, 5.5), TUG (11 trials; $n = 606$; MD 1 s 95% CI $-2, 0$), walking speed (7 trials; $n = 568$; MD 0.13 m/s 95% CI 0.03, 0.24), and step length (5 trials, $n = 296$ MD 5 cm 95% CI 2, 8) (Lam et al., 2018).

Exercise is a broad term that encompasses type (aerobic, resistance, balance, flexibility, etc.) and dose (frequency, intensity, and length) of an intervention. Furthermore, programs carried out in community versus residential aged care settings may differ in terms of delivery, level of participant dependence, and institutional factors (Zeng et al., 2016). Therefore, the following section elaborates on some of the key studies and outlines the type and dose of exercise by setting.

Community settings

Multimodal exercise interventions greater than 3 months in length have been shown to improve performance in balance, functional strength, and mobility in people living with dementia in the community (Lewis, Peiris, & Shields, 2017; Zeng et al., 2016) although sample sizes of the included studies were mostly small. One study ($n = 40$) randomized participants from a memory disorder clinic into either 4-months of home-based exercise or usual care. The exercise program was the Home Support Exercise program for frail older people (Canadian Centre for Activity and Aging), which involved 30 min of walking, strength, and balance exercises daily. The Functional Reach Test, sit-to-stand test and the TUG improved compared to the usual care group (Vreugdenhil, Cannell, Davies, & Razay, 2012). Another small study ($n = 40$) found that 6 months of the Otago exercise program performed 5 days per week at home combined with six visits by a physiotherapist improved performance on the Functional Reach Test compared with an education control, but not for a number of other mobility and balance tests (Suttanon et al., 2013). In a larger three-arm study ($n = 210$) both a home and group exercise programs were more effective in slowing progression of the motor FIM, but not the short physical performance battery (SPPB) (Pitkala et al., 2013).

Although adherence, and even some outcomes, might be better for home versus group programs (Pitkala et al., 2013), care may need to be taken when selecting participants, as caregiver burden is a major consideration (Suttanon et al., 2013; Taylor et al., 2017). Small group training may be preferable for some, with aerobic, resistance, and functional training all showing some benefit if delivered at moderate to high intensity. Three months of group-based progressive resistance and functional training (2 h/twice per week) was more effective than a low intensity seated exercise (1 h/twice per week) in improving muscle strength, the five-chair-stand test, stair-climbing ability, and measures of balance and mobility (SPPB, the Performance Oriented Mobility Assessment, and TUG) (Hauer et al., 2012). The same program also improved quantitative gait measures (gait speed, cadence, stride length, stride time, and double support time) (Schwenk et al., 2014). Simple instructions, haptic support, empathy, reassurance, and use of a mirror were used to support the exercise program (Hauer et al., 2012). Moderate to high-intensity aerobic training might also be beneficial, as 1 h three times per week of aerobic bike, cross-trainer, and treadmill training for 4 months was effective in improving 400 m walk time, the TUG test, 10-m walk time, and a dual-task numbers test (counting backwards in 1 s from 50), but only in those who adhered to at least 66.6% of sessions (Sobol et al., 2016). Dual-task training targets both physical and cognitive impairments, and there is preliminary evidence that it might be beneficial. Twelve weeks (2 h/twice per week) of concurrent motor (e.g., throwing or catching a ball) or cognitive (e.g., arithmetic tasks and repeating names of animals) tasks combined with strength and balance training improved dual-task walking counting backwards in 3 s in a small study of 61 people with dementia (Schwenk, Zieschang, Oster, & Hauer, 2010).

Nursing home settings

Short-term (2.5–4 months; 30–60 min/2–4 times per week) multimodal exercise programs delivered in groups appear effective in improving balance and muscle strength in people with dementia living in nursing homes (Bossers et al., 2015; Telenius, Engedal, & Bergland, 2015; Toots et al., 2016). Interestingly, in one study exercise resulted in better balance outcomes only in those with non-AD, highlighting potential differences in responses to exercise in different dementia subtypes (Toots et al., 2016).

Multimodal exercise interventions might be more beneficial than single-type exercise interventions. A program that included only walking did not improve functional mobility or endurance over 4 months (5 times per week), although the study ($n = 82$) may have lacked power (Roach, Tappen, Kirk-Sanchez, Williams, & Loewenstein, 2011). The specificity of exercise should also be considered, as walking and strength training were more effective in improving muscle strength than walking alone over 9 weeks (30 min/4 times per week) (Bossers et al., 2015).

Despite improvements in strength and balance in people living in nursing home settings, the effectiveness of exercise on mobility is less certain and may reflect the severity of disease in people residing in nursing homes. In people with severe disease, a 12-month multimodal exercise program (1 h /twice per week delivered in groups) of walking, strength, flexibility, and balance training improved walking speed but not performance on the TUG (Rolland et al., 2007). Shorter strength and balance programs of 9 weeks (Bossers et al., 2015) or 12 weeks (Telenius et al., 2015) training were also not effective in improving walking speed, the Figure 8 Test, the Groningen Meander Walking Test, or the TUG (Telenius et al., 2015).

Delivery of exercise interventions to improve physical performance

Although strategies to maintain adherence to exercise are similar to those who are cognitively normal (van der Wardt et al., 2017) there may also be differences. Poor memory may require greater effort and provision of written material or reminders. Ability to maintain attention, or reduced capacity to store or work with information (working memory), may require shorter but more frequent sessions. Executive dysfunction may require greater attention to safety and assistance with planning exercise. Visuospatial deficits may require changes to the environment and extra attention to delivering an intervention safely. Motivation and behavior may also impact on exercise adherence. Observing an individual's daily routine and incorporating exercise into everyday activities might be more successful. Asking about hobbies and incorporating these into exercise may also assist in improving participation. People with dementia themselves identify specific barriers to exercise including "memory," "lack of companionship," and "accessibility" (Chong et al., 2014). Strategies that could be tailored to the person living with dementia are listed in Table 1.

Due to the inclusion criteria of studies, findings are based on people able to walk independently without the assistance of another person and who

Table 1 Considerations for delivery of exercise programs for people living with dementia.

Instructions	• Large font for written material
	• One-step instructions or breaking down instructions into components rather than multistage commands or complex sentences
	• Repeating instructions, demonstrating, and/or writing them down
	• Using touch, facilitation, or visual cues
	• Giving time for a response and sufficient time for the session
	• Speaking clearly and slowly to the person at eye level
	• Do not raise voice unless needed for hearing
Sessions	• Short but frequent to allow for any reduction in attention
Environment	• Reduce noise/distractions
	• Increase lighting and reduce glare
	• Reduce shadows and patterns
	• Color contrast doors or other objects
Exercises	• Functional
	• Start with single tasks
	• Tap into activities enjoyed in the past
	• Consider music to facilitate exercises
	• Specific to target, e.g., balance exercises to improve balance
Delivery	• Group classes ratios 1:3 or 1:4 instructors to participants
	• Engage care partner but consider burden if at home
Safety	• An increased risk for adverse events does not appear to be present for people with dementia participating in an exercise program, but due to the high background risk for falls, safety precautions should be used to limit possible occurrence.
Other	• Respect, empathy, and involvement of family, and care partners
	• Treat the person as an individual
	• Be aware of comorbidies such as hearing or visual impairments
	• Be aware of nonverbal signs of pain

have not experienced major changes in behaviors that interfere with their ability to follow instructions.

In summary, there is preliminary evidence from mostly small RCT that multimodal exercise programs can improve balance and strength in people with dementia living in nursing homes or the community. Multimodal, dual-task, or aerobic training may improve mobility from programs delivered in the community, but evidence for such programs is uncertain in nursing homes. People living with dementia in the community should be provided with the option of home or group-based programs, with consideration for care partner burden. Exercise trainers should be trained in dementia-specific communication and exercise delivery techniques that are specific to the function to be improved.

Pharmacological approaches to improve physical function

Table 2 summarizes studies that have specifically evaluated the effects of cognitive pharmacological interventions to improve mobility. Due to the small number of studies in the area, those in cognitively normal individuals have also been included.

Methylphenidate (MPH). Methylphenidate, an attention–enhancer drug, has been tested to improve motor and physical function in older adults. A pilot RCT study conducted in 26 community-living older adults without dementia (Ben Itzhak et al., 2008) showed that MPH improved executive function, gait speed, and reduced gait variability. Similarly, a RCT showed that a single dose of MPH improved gait and postural stability in 30 healthy older adults and reduced the number of step errors and step error rate on gait in both single and dual-tasks. Despite the barriers to using MPH in older adults (short half-life and unsafe adverse events profile) these findings support the role of drugs designed to enhance attention as a therapeutic option for reducing fall risk.

Cholinesterase inhibitors (ChEI). Cognitive function and gait regulation share a number of neurotransmitters that have been targeted to improve motor performance, specifically gait, and to reduce fall risk (for a review, see Montero-Odasso, Verghese, Beauchet, & Hausdorff, 2012). Central cholinergic neurotransmission controls selective attention, memory, and regulates gait motor control and balance. Cholinergic brain neurons are found in the hippocampus, nucleus basalis of Meynert, basal ganglia, thalamus, and the pedunculopontine nucleus. Thalamic cholinergic activity, which derives mainly from terminals of pedunculopontine nucleus neurons, controls the generation of movement patterns during gait performance. Cholinesterase inhibitors (ChEI) (e.g., donepezil, galantamine, and rivastigmine) are currently used for symptomatic treatment in mild-to-moderate AD and vascular dementia. Two small pilot studies indicated the potential effects of galantamine (Assal et al., 2008) and donepezil (Montero-Odasso et al., 2009) in improving gait performance in older adults with mild AD. A subsequent trial of participants with mild AD found significant improvements in gait speed and dual-task gait speed after 4 months of treatment with donepezil (Montero-Odasso et al., 2015). Changes in stride time variability were in the expected direction although not statistically significant. Participants also experienced improvements in executive function, supporting the premise that gait improvements can be cognitively mediated. In a 6 month double-blind, placebo-controlled randomized trial of 60 older adults with MCI, the donepezil group experienced a significant improvement in dual-task gait cost (but not speed) in counting backward by 1 and 7, compared with placebo in the intention-to-treat analysis (Montero-Odasso et al., 2019). Per-protocol analyses showed a nonsignificant reduction in the rate of falls. These positive results need to be viewed with caution since this trial was originally powered for 120 participants but due to recruitment challenges, only 60 participants were included. Finally, in an open label memory clinic study conducted in older participants with AD, memantine, a cognitive enhancer that reduces glutamate neurotransmission, decreased stride time variability (Beauchet et al., 2011).

In summary, pharmacological cognitive enhancement in MCI and AD is a promising avenue to improve physical function, particularly gait, but these preliminary studies need to be treated with caution due to their small samples, and proof-of-principle nature. Definitive RCTs are still needed.

Falls and dementia

Almost 70% of people with dementia will fall at least once, and many will fall more than once (40%) over a 1-year period (Allan, Ballard, Rowan, & Kenny, 2009; Taylor et al., 2013). This is approximately double that of people without cognitive impairment or dementia (Campbell, Borrie, & Spears, 1989; Taylor et al., 2013). A fall can result in a range of adverse outcomes including loss of confidence, injury, reduced mobility, and the need for nursing homes. Around a quarter of patients admitted to hospital with hip fracture also have dementia (Scandol, Toson, & Close, 2013), and although people with dementia have poorer mobility and outcomes, their hospital stays are shorter and they receive less rehabilitation despite their ability to improve (Allen et al., 2012; Muir & Yohannes, 2009). This may be partly due to comorbidities or complications such as delirium, but also to beliefs that people with dementia cannot learn or benefit from rehabilitation (Isbel & Jamieson, 2017).

Understanding the risk factors for falls in people with dementia is the first step to prevention. Poorer cognition alone is a risk factor (Muir, Gopaul, & Montero Odasso, 2012; Tinetti, Speechley, & Ginter, 1988; Whitney, Close, Jackson, & Lord, 2012), and impairments in the domains of executive function and processing speed especially increase risk (Martin et al., 2013; Muir, Gopaul, & Montero Odasso, 2012; Whitney et al., 2012). The poorer

Table 2 Pharmacological cognitive interventions for gait and balance and fall risk.

Study (year)	Study design	Type of intervention	Duration	Participants	Summary of findings
Cognitively normal population					
Ben Itzhak, Giladi, Gruendlinger, and Hausdorff (2008)	RCT, double-blind, placebo-controlled	Before and 2 h after taking 20 mg MPH or a placebo	2 h	26 Participants without dementia with subjective memory complaints (age: 73.8 ± 1.2 years, mean MMSE: 27.8 ± 1.4)	MPH improved Timed Up and Go ($P=0.004$), stride time variability ($P=0.03$), and EF ($P=0.03$); effects not observed after treatment with the placebo
Shorer, Bachner, Guy, and Melzer (2013)	RCT, double-blind, placebo-controlled	Before and 1.5 h after taking 10 mg MPH or a placebo	2 h	30 Participants without dementia (age: 74.9 ± 5.6 years, MMSE > 24)	MPH improved narrow base walking by reducing number of step errors ($P=0.040$) in single and dual tasks; effects not observed in placebo group

MCI and AD populations

Assal, Allali, Kressig, Herrmann, and Beauchet (2008)	Before–after design	Galantamine mean dose of 17.8 ± 3.5 mg/day	6 months	9 Participants with mild-to-moderate AD (age: 77.9 ± 2.1 years; MMSE: 26.4 ± 5.2) compared with 18 no-treatment control subjects (age: 78.1 ± 1.0 years; MMSE: 29.4 ± 0.8)	Stride time was shorter under dual tasking after treatment ($P = 0.01$). There was no change in the controls
Montero-Odasso, Wells, and Borrie (2009)	Open-label study with controls	5 mg/day of donepezil for 1 month, and another 3 months with 10 mg/day. MCI group with no treatment	4 months	6 Participants with mild AD (age: 79.9 ± 4.8 years; MMSE: 22.3 ± 1.2; MoCA: 15 ± 1.4) compared with 8 participants with MCI (age: 75.6 ± 6.2 years; MMSE: 27.9 ± 1.7; MoCA: 22.9 ± 1.7)	Participants with mild AD increased their single– ($P = 0.045$) and dual-task gait velocity ($P = 0.047$) after 1 month. Stride time variability decreased (improved). Control group declined in gait velocity and variability
Beauchet, Launay, Fantino, Annweiler, and Allali (2011)	Before–after design	Memantine mean dose of 20 mg/day, titrated in 5 mg increments over 4 weeks	4.4 to 8 months	17 Participants with AD (age 83.8 ± 5.8 years; 52.9% women; MMSE: 14.5 ± 4.2) and 32 age-sex-matched controls with AD without any antidementia drug (age: 0.0 ± 6.6 years; MMSE: 23.2 ± 5.3)	Stride time variability decreased (improved) during follow-up in the memantine group (6.3 ± 6.1 versus 3.6 ± 1.3, $P = 0.038$)

Continued

Table 2 Pharmacological cognitive interventions for gait and balance and fall risk.—cont'd

Study (year)	Study design	Type of intervention	Duration	Participants	Summary of findings
Montero-Odasso et al. (2015)	Before-after design	5 mg/day of donepezil for 1 month, and 5 months with 10 mg/day	5 months	43 Patients with mild AD (age: 76.9 ± 8 years; MMSE: 24.63 ± 2; MoCA: 18.5 ± 4)	Gait velocity improved from 108.4 ± 18.6 to 113.3 ± 19.5 cm/s ($P=0.01$); dual-task gait velocity from 80.6 ± 23.0 to 85.3 ± 22.3 cm/s ($P=0.03$). Trail Making Tests A ($P=0.030$), B ($P=0.001$) and B–A ($P=0.042$) improved after intervention
Montero-Odasso et al. (2018)	RCT, double-blind, placebo-controlled	First month with 5 mg/day of donepezil, and next 5 months with 10 mg/day	6 months	60 Patients with MCI (age: 75.3 ± 7 years; MMSE: 27.5 ± 2; MoCA: 23.6 ± 2.5)	Gait velocity improved only under dual-task conditions, and there was a reduction in falls, albeit not significant.

Note: AD, Alzheimer's disease; *EF*, executive function; *MCI*, mild cognitive impairment; *MMSE*, Mini Mental State Examination; *MoCA*, Montreal Cognitive Assessment; *MPH*, methylphenidate.
Modified and updated from Montero-Odasso, M., & Speechley, M. (2018). Falls in cognitively impaired older adults: Implications for risk assessment and prevention. *Journal of the American Geriatrics Society, 66*(2), 367–375. https://doi.org/10.1111/jgs.15219.

Table 3 Risk factors for falls in people with cognitive impairment and dementia.

Cognition/dementia	Severity of dementia; Lewy Body or Parkinson's-type dementia; poorer executive function, processing speed and visuospatial function
Medications	Greater total number; centrally acting medications
Psychological	Depression; anxiety; impulsivity and verbally disruptive behavior
Physical	Poorer balance; reaction time; coordination; higher or lower levels of physical activity
Mobility	Greater gait variability in double support time and step length; higher scores on the Unified Parkinson's Disease Rating Scale; greater amounts of outdoor walking; use of mobility aids; lower average walking bouts in 24 h
Medical	Hypotension; autonomic dysfunction
Other	Past history of falls; white matter hyperintensities on brain scans

executive function may contribute to falls through unsafe decision-making, inappropriate assessment of risk for level of function (e.g., walking too fast for one's ability or environment conditions), poor planning or inability to sustain, switch or divide attention. Slowed processing speed may reduce the time to make decisions and react to internal or external perturbations resulting in a slip or a trip where balance cannot be recovered. Other risk factors for falls are outlined in Table 3 and include cognitive, psychological, physical, and medical factors (Allan et al., 2009; Fernando, Fraser, Hendriksen, Kim, & Muir-Hunter, 2017; Modarresi, Divine, Grahn, Overend, & Hunter, 2018; Montero-Odasso & Speechley, 2018; Taylor et al., 2014). Interestingly, both higher and lower physical activity levels are associated with falls potentially reflecting that those with better functional ability are exposed to higher risk (e.g., greater number of steps or situations where falls are likely to occur) or those with low levels of activity who have more impairments associated with greater falls risk (Allan et al., 2009; Taylor et al., 2014).

Interventions to prevent falls
Community
Multifactorial (targeting more than one risk factors), multicomponent (fixed combinations of interventions), and exercise interventions (particularly those that include balance and functional training) may be effective in reducing falls in cognitively normal older adults living in the community (Hopewell et al., 2018; Sherrington et al., 2017, 2019). However, few studies have specifically included people with dementia.

The American and British Geriatric Society guidelines from, 2011 state that "…there is insufficient evidence to recommend, for or against, single or multifactorial interventions in community-living older adults with known cognitive impairment" ("Summary of the Updated American Geriatrics Society/British Geriatrics Society clinical practice guideline for prevention of falls in older persons,", 2011). Since then meta-analyses of two studies that included only people living with dementia, reported exercise decreased the number of falls (MD = − 1.06 [− 1.67 to − 0.46]; $n = 271$) and reduced the risk of being a faller by 32% (RR 0.68 [0.55–0.85]; $n = 271$) (Burton et al., 2015). In a more recent meta-analysis that included one further study, exercise also reduced falls (pooled rate ratio 0.55, 95% CI 0.37–0.83) (Sherrington et al., 2017). However, two of the included studies were small or did not include falls as a primary outcome. Wesson et al. randomized participants with mild dementia ($n = 22$ dyads) into a 12-week exercise (balance and strength) and home hazard reduction (e.g., changing footwear, rearranging furniture, securing mats, fluorescent tape to highlight step edges, and sensor lights) intervention versus a control group. Both the rate of falling and the risk of falls were lower in the intervention group, but findings were not significant (Wesson et al., 2013). Suttanon et al. randomized participants ($n = 40$) into either a 6-months Otago exercise program or an education group. Both groups received six physio visits and five phone calls. No differences were observed for falls between groups (Suttanon et al., 2013). A three-arm study by Pitkala et al. was both larger ($n = 210$) and longer (12 months) and compared home-based exercise, community-based exercise, and a control group. In secondary analyses, the control group had a higher rate of falls than the other groups (Pitkala et al., 2013). In the secondary analysis, the risk of falling was higher among patients with advanced dementia, and exercise did reduce falls in this subset of participants [IRR 0.47 (95% CI 0.37–0.60); Ohman et al., 2016]. One recent study of people with mild-to-moderate dementia ($n = 110$), not included in the previous meta-analyses, compared a 12-weeks intervention of strength and functional training to controls. Although the intervention did not influence falls rates overall, the number of falls per 1000 h of activity was significantly lower in the intervention group who suffered multiple falls (Zieschang et al., 2017). Finally, the technology that incorporated a night light path and an electronic bracelet to detect falls may also be useful in reducing falls (Tchalla et al., 2013).

Nursing homes
A recent Cochrane review found no strong evidence to guide falls prevention strategies in nursing homes. Moderate-quality evidence indicated that

vitamin D supplementation might reduce the rate of falls (Cameron et al., 2018). Since the review, an Australian study reported promising findings that 6 months of progressive resistance and balance training for 1 h/twice per week followed by a maintenance phase of 6 months reduced the rate of falls by 55% (IRR 0.45, 0.17, 0.74) (Hewitt, Goodall, Clemson, Henwood, & Refshauge, 2018), but only half the participants had cognitive impairment. In contrast, exercise studies including only people with dementia have been largely unsuccessful. High-intensity functional training (https://www.hifeprogram.se/en) for 4 months two to three times per week did not reduce the rate of falls at 6 or 12 months (Toots et al., 2018) and a multimodal exercise program (based on the Otago exercise program) twice a week for 12 months also did not reduce falls (Kovacs, Sztruhar Jonasne, Karoczi, Korpos, & Gondos, 2013). Differences in findings of the studies based in the community may reflect the severity of dementia and its effect on falls risk factors. Alternatively, falls risk factors may be different in people living with dementia in nursing homes.

A few trials examining multifactorial interventions have included falls as a secondary outcome. One intervention included a falls–risk assessment followed by a 6-month tailored intervention including dementia care mapping, a comprehensive geriatric assessment, medication review, occupational therapy assessment, hip protectors, bed and chair sensors, and 45 min/twice per week of balance training. Adherence to recommendations and exercise was poor (<45%) and the secondary outcome of falls was negative. However, the study was probably also underpowered ($n = 191$) (Whitney, Jackson, & Martin, 2017). A multifactorial intervention implemented after the presentation to the emergency department for a fall (78% from nursing homes) was also unsuccessful in preventing falls (Shaw et al., 2003).

The importance of the severity of cognitive impairment is not yet clear. Secondary analysis of a large trial (6 facilities; $n = 725$) found an environmental hazard check, risk factor assessment, hip protectors, progressive balance, and resistance training, and monthly feedback on falls rates did reduce time to first fall in people with cognitive impairment compared to those that were cognitively normal (Rapp et al., 2008). In contrast, secondary analyses of another trial of a similar multifactorial intervention found there was a significant effect of the intervention for those with a higher MMSE, but not lower MMSE (divided at a score of 19; Jensen, Nyberg, Gustafson, & Lundin-Olsson, 2003).

A novel approach was used in a further study (15 nursing homes; $n = 289$) which examined the effect of (1) education for staff about dementia and implementation of person-centered care; (2) dementia care mapping

(6 h/day for 2 days) to identify factors related to well-being, particularly positive and negative care delivery, or (3) usual care. Compared with usual care, agitation decreased in both interventions and the secondary outcome of falls was fewer in sites that used mapping (0.24, 0.08–0.40). A surprising and difficult to explain finding was that there were more falls with person-centered care (0.15, 0.02–0.28) (Chenoweth et al., 2009).

In summary, there is preliminary evidence that exercise and the use of technology (such as a night light path) might reduce falls for people living with dementia in the community. Surprisingly, considering the wide range of risk factors for falls, multifactorial interventions have largely been ignored in this group in the community. In residential settings, it is unclear if multifactorial interventions can prevent falls, but there is some preliminary support for dementia care mapping. Larger adequately powered definitive trials with falls as the primary outcome are required in both community and nursing home settings.

Gaps and recommendations in clinical and research knowledge

There is preliminary evidence that exercise can improve physical function in people with dementia. However, the ability to develop exercise recommendations for people with dementia and to facilitate knowledge translation to clinicians working with this population is limited by a lack of detail provided regarding programs in many studies. While the terms of "moderate" or "high" intensity are used there is often an inadequate description for assessment of intensity or how exercises were progressed. Studies delivering resistance training need to provide information on intensity (e.g., repetition max), rest period, and the number of sets. Likewise, studies of aerobic training should specify and monitor intensity through heart rate monitors or, if feasible, perceived exertion. Furthermore, some outcomes measures such as the Berg Balance Scale can be difficult for people with more severe dementia and therefore clinicians will need to carefully choose outcome measures depending on abilities. Overall, study replication is currently difficult and would leave many aspects of developing an exercise program unclear for clinicians wanting to achieve successful outcomes reported in the literature.

Gaps in knowledge include whether targeting both impairments in physical and cognitive functions (e.g., dual-task training or pharmacological interventions combined with physical exercise) might be beneficial in improving function or reducing falls. Further work might also look at ways to enrich the environment to allow people with dementia to safely access their community and maintain physical activity. The needs of people with younger onset dementia have largely been ignored, and programs would need to consider that their physical capabilities and goals may be different from older adults.

In terms of delivery, there is little known if there is a differential benefit between providing classes in a group format versus an individualized session and client factors that may support the provision of one over the other. An understanding of the facilitators and barriers to participation in an exercise program for people with dementia needs to be better defined, and whether people with dementia will increase their physical activity level if service providers undertake specific dementia training, become more familiar with the health benefits of exercises, and the features of a successful physical activity program.

For falls prevention, there is preliminary evidence in the community that exercise and use of technology may reduce falls. However, whether falls can be prevented in nursing homes is less clear. Importantly, most studies were small and did not include falls as a primary outcome measure. Lack of success may also be due to different underlying mechanisms for falls in people with dementia, where many interventions have been designed based on factors that increase risk in cognitively normal older people. Designs addressing specific behaviors or cognitive functions are required, and may need to consider the type of dementia, disease severity and need to modify interventions due to specific behavioral and psychological symptoms of the disease. Addressing multifactorial dementia and person-specific factors in future trials will most likely provide the best chance of success.

Finally, there are still negative attitudes to rehabilitation and its benefit in people with dementia. Further education at an undergraduate and graduate level is required across medical, nursing, and allied health staff.

Clinical and research recommendations

In summary, there is preliminary evidence that exercise can improve physical function in people with dementia in both community and nursing home settings. The type of exercise should target assessed deficits and be of sufficient frequency and intensity to facilitate improvement. People living with dementia in the community should be provided with the option of home or group-based programs. Exercise trainers and allied health staff should be trained in dementia-specific communication and exercise delivery techniques.

For falls prevention, a comprehensive risk assessment should be undertaken. There is preliminary evidence in the community that exercise and use of technology may reduce falls. Whether falls can be prevented in nursing homes is less clear, but people with dementia should not be denied preventative treatments. Addressing multifactorial dementia and person-specific factors in future trials will most likely provide the best chance of success.

References

Allali, G., Annweiler, C., Blumen, H. M., Callisaya, M. L., De Cock, A. M., Kressig, R. W., ... Beauchet, O. (2016). Gait phenotype from mild cognitive impairment to moderate dementia: Results from the GOOD initiative. *European Journal of Neurology*, *23*(3), 527–541.

Allan, L. M., Ballard, C. G., Burn, D. J., & Kenny, R. A. (2005). Prevalence and severity of gait disorders in Alzheimer's and non-Alzheimer's dementias. *Journal of the American Geriatrics Society*, *53*(10), 1681–1687. https://doi.org/10.1111/j.1532-5415.2005.53552.x.

Allan, L. M., Ballard, C. G., Rowan, E. N., & Kenny, R. A. (2009). Incidence and prediction of falls in dementia: A prospective study in older people. *PLoS One*, *4*(5). https://doi.org/10.1371/journal.pone.0005521.

Allen, J., Koziak, A., Buddingh, S., Liang, J., Buckingham, J., & Beaupre, L. A. (2012). Rehabilitation in patients with dementia following hip fracture: A systematic review. *Physiotherapy Canada*, *64*(2), 190–201. https://doi.org/10.3138/ptc.2011-06BH.

Assal, F., Allali, G., Kressig, R. W., Herrmann, F. R., & Beauchet, O. (2008). Galantamine improves gait performance in patients with Alzheimer's disease. *Journal of the American Geriatrics Society*, *56*(5), 946–947.

Beauchet, O., Launay, C., Fantino, B., Annweiler, C., & Allali, G. (2011). Does memantine improve the gait of individuals with Alzheimer's disease? *Journal of the American Geriatrics Society*, *59*(11), 2181–2182. https://doi.org/10.1111/j.1532-5415.2011.03648.x.

Ben-Itzhak, R., Giladi, N., Gruendlinger, L., & Hausdorff, J. M. (2008). Can methylphenidate reduce fall risk in community-living older adults? A double-blind, single-dose cross-over study. *Journal of the American Geriatrics Society*, *56*(4), 695–700.

Bloem, B. R., Grimbergen, Y. A., van Dijk, J. G., & Munneke, M. (2006). The "posture second" strategy: A review of wrong priorities in Parkinson's disease. *Journal of the Neurological Sciences*, *248*(1–2), 196–204. https://doi.org/10.1016/j.jns.2006.05.010.

Bossers, W. J., van der Woude, L. H., Boersma, F., Hortobagyi, T., Scherder, E. J., & van Heuvelen, M. J. (2015). A 9-week aerobic and strength training program improves cognitive and motor function in patients with dementia: A randomized, controlled trial. *The American Journal of Geriatric Psychiatry*, *23*(11), 1106–1116. https://doi.org/10.1016/j.jagp.2014.12.191.

Burton, E., Cavalheri, V., Adams, R., Browne, C. O., Bovery-Spencer, P., Fenton, A. M., ... Hill, K. D. (2015). Effectiveness of exercise programs to reduce falls in older people with dementia living in the community: A systematic review and meta-analysis. *Clinical Interventions in Aging*, *10*, 421–434. https://doi.org/10.2147/CIA.S71691.

Callisaya, M. L., Launay, C. P., Srikanth, V. K., Verghese, J., Allali, G., & Beauchet, O. (2017). Cognitive status, fast walking speed and walking speed reserve—The gait and Alzheimer interactions tracking (GAIT) study. *GeroScience*, *39*(2), 231.

Cameron, I. D., Dyer, S. M., Panagoda, C. E., Murray, G. R., Hill, K. D., Cumming, R. G., & Kerse, N. (2018). Interventions for preventing falls in older people in care facilities and hospitals. *Cochrane Database of Systematic Reviews*, *9*. https://doi.org/10.1002/14651858.CD005465.pub4.

Camicioli, R., Howieson, D., Lehman, S., & Kaye, J. (1997). Talking while walking the effect of a dual task in aging and Alzheimer's disease. *Neurology*, *48*(4), 955–958.

Campbell, A. J., Borrie, M. J., & Spears, G. F. (1989). Risk factors for falls in a community-based prospective study of people 70 years and older. *Journal of Gerontology, 44*(4), M112–M117.

Ceïde, M. E., Ayers, E., Lipton, R., & Verghese, J. (2018). Walking while talking and risk of incident dementia. *The American Journal of Geriatric Psychiatry, 26*(5), 580–588.

Chenoweth, L., King, M. T., Jeon, Y. H., Brodaty, H., Stein-Parbury, J., Norman, R., … Luscombe, G. (2009). Caring for aged dementia care resident study (CADRES) of person-centred care, dementia-care mapping, and usual care in dementia: A cluster-randomised trial. *Lancet Neurology, 8*(4), 317–325. https://doi.org/10.1016/S1474-4422(09)70045-6.

Chong, T. W., Doyle, C. J., Cyarto, E. V., Cox, K. L., Ellis, K. A., Ames, D., … AIBL Research Group. (2014). Physical activity program preferences and perspectives of older adults with and without cognitive impairment. *Asia-Pacific Psychiatry, 6*(2), 179–190. https://doi.org/10.1111/appy.12015.

Fernando, E., Fraser, M., Hendriksen, J., Kim, C. H., & Muir-Hunter, S. W. (2017). Risk factors associated with falls in older adults with dementia: A systematic review. *Physiotherapy Canada, 69*(2), 161–170. https://doi.org/10.3138/ptc.2016-14.

Hauer, K., Schwenk, M., Zieschang, T., Essig, M., Becker, C., & Oster, P. (2012). Physical training improves motor performance in people with dementia: A randomized controlled trial. *Journal of the American Geriatrics Society, 60*(1), 8–15. https://doi.org/10.1111/j.1532-5415.2011.03778.x.

Hewitt, J., Goodall, S., Clemson, L., Henwood, T., & Refshauge, K. (2018). Progressive resistance and balance training for falls prevention in long-term residential aged care: A cluster randomized trial of the sunbeam program. *Journal of the American Medical Directors Association, 19*(4), 361–369. https://doi.org/10.1016/j.jamda.2017.12.014.

Hopewell, S., Adedire, O., Copsey, B. J., Boniface, G. J., Sherrington, C., Clemson, L., … Lamb, S. E. (2018). Multifactorial and multiple component interventions for preventing falls in older people living in the community. *Cochrane Database of Systematic Reviews, 7.* https://doi.org/10.1002/14651858.CD012221.pub2.

Isbel, S. T., & Jamieson, M. I. (2017). Views from health professionals on accessing rehabilitation for people with dementia following a hip fracture. *Dementia (London), 16*(8), 1020–1031. https://doi.org/10.1177/1471301216631141.

Jensen, J., Nyberg, L., Gustafson, Y., & Lundin-Olsson, L. (2003). Fall and injury prevention in residential care—Effects in residents with higher and lower levels of cognition. *Journal of the American Geriatrics Society, 51*(5), 627–635.

Kovacs, E., Sztruhar Jonasne, I., Karoczi, C. K., Korpos, A., & Gondos, T. (2013). Effects of a multimodal exercise program on balance, functional mobility and fall risk in older adults with cognitive impairment: A randomized controlled single-blind study. *European Journal of Physical and Rehabilitation Medicine, 49*(5), 639–648.

Lam, F. M., Huang, M. Z., Liao, L. R., Chung, R. C., Kwok, T. C., & Pang, M. Y. (2018). Physical exercise improves strength, balance, mobility, and endurance in people with cognitive impairment and dementia: A systematic review. *Journal of Physiotherapy, 64*(1), 4–15. https://doi.org/10.1016/j.jphys.2017.12.001.

Lewis, M., Peiris, C. L., & Shields, N. (2017). Long-term home and community-based exercise programs improve function in community-dwelling older people with cognitive impairment: A systematic review. *Journal of Physiotherapy, 63*(1), 23–29. https://doi.org/10.1016/j.jphys.2016.11.005.

Martin, K. L., Blizzard, L., Srikanth, V. K., Wood, A., Thomson, R., Sanders, L. M., & Callisaya, M. L. (2013). Cognitive function modifies the effect of physiological function on the risk of multiple falls—A population-based study. *The Journals of Gerontology. Series A, Biological Sciences and Medical Sciences.* https://doi.org/10.1093/gerona/glt010.

Martin, K. L., Blizzard, L., Wood, A. G., Srikanth, V., Thomson, R., Sanders, L. M., & Callisaya, M. L. (2013). Cognitive function, gait, and gait variability in older people: A population-based study. *The Journals of Gerontology. Series A, Biological Sciences and Medical Sciences, 68*(6), 726–732. https://doi.org/10.1093/gerona/gls224gls224.

Modarresi, S., Divine, A., Grahn, J. A., Overend, T. J., & Hunter, S. W. (2018). Gait parameters and characteristics associated with increased risk of falls in people with dementia: A systematic review. *International Psychogeriatrics, 31*(9), 1287–1303. https://doi.org/10.1017/S1041610218001783.

Montero-Odasso, M., Muir-Hunter, S. W., Oteng-Amoako, A., Gopaul, K., Islam, A., Borrie, M., … Speechley, M. (2015). Donepezil improves gait performance in older adults with mild Alzheimer's disease: A phase II clinical trial. *Journal of Alzheimer's Disease, 43*(1), 193–199. https://doi.org/10.3233/JAD-140759.

Montero-Odasso, M., & Speechley, M. (2018). Falls in cognitively impaired older adults: Implications for risk assessment and prevention. *Journal of the American Geriatrics Society, 66*(2), 367–375. https://doi.org/10.1111/jgs.15219.

Montero-Odasso, M., Speechley, M., Chertkow, H., Sarquis-Adamson, Y., Wells, J., Borrie, M., … Muir-Hunter, S. W. (2018). Donepezil for gait and falls in mild cognitive impairment: A randomized controlled trial. *European Journal of Neurology*. https://doi.org/10.1111/ene.13872.

Montero-Odasso, M., Speechley, M., Chertkow, H., Sarquis-Adamson, Y., Wells, J., Borrie, M., … Muir-Hunter, S. W. (2019). Donepezil for gait and falls in mild cognitive impairment: A randomized controlled trial. *European Journal of Neurology, 26*(4), 651–659. https://doi.org/10.1111/ene.13872.

Montero-Odasso, M., Verghese, J., Beauchet, O., & Hausdorff, J. M. (2012). Gait and cognition: A complementary approach to understanding brain function and the risk of falling. *Journal of the American Geriatrics Society, 60*(11), 2127–2136. https://doi.org/10.1111/j.1532-5415.2012.04209.x.

Montero-Odasso, M., Wells, J., & Borrie, M. (2009). Can cognitive enhancers reduce the risk of falls in people with dementia? An open-label study with controls. *Journal of the American Geriatrics Society, 57*(2), 359–360. https://doi.org/10.1111/j.1532-5415.2009.02085.x.

Montero-Odasso, M. M., Sarquis-Adamson, Y., Speechley, M., Borrie, M. J., Hachinski, V. C., Wells, J., … Muir-Hunter, S. (2017). Association of Dual-Task Gait with Incident Dementia in mild cognitive impairment: Results from the gait and brain study. *JAMA Neurology, 74*(7), 857–865. https://doi.org/10.1001/jamaneurol.2017.0643.

Muir, S. W., Gopaul, K., & Montero Odasso, M. M. (2012). The role of cognitive impairment in fall risk among older adults: A systematic review and meta-analysis. *Age Ageing, 41*(3), 299–308. https://doi.org/10.1093/ageing/afs012.

Muir, S. W., Speechley, M., Wells, J., Borrie, M., Gopaul, K., & Montero-Odasso, M. (2012). Gait assessment in mild cognitive impairment and Alzheimer's disease: The effect of dual-task challenges across the cognitive spectrum. *Gait & Posture, 35*(1), 96–100. https://doi.org/10.1016/j.gaitpost.2011.08.014.

Muir, S. W., & Yohannes, A. M. (2009). The impact of cognitive impairment on rehabilitation outcomes in elderly patients admitted with a femoral neck fracture: A systematic review. *Journal of Geriatric Physical Therapy (2001), 32*(1), 24–32.

Ohman, H., Savikko, N., Strandberg, T., Kautiainen, H., Raivio, M., Laakkonen, M. L., … Pitkala, K. H. (2016). Effects of exercise on functional performance and fall rate in subjects with mild or advanced Alzheimer's disease: Secondary analyses of a randomized controlled study. *Dementia and Geriatric Cognitive Disorders, 41*(3–4), 233–241. https://doi.org/10.1159/000445712.

Pieruccini-Faria, F., Sarquis-Adamson, Y., & Montero-Odasso, M. (2019). Mild cognitive impairment affects obstacle negotiation in older adults: Results from "gait and brain study". *Gerontology, 65*(2), 164–173. https://doi.org/10.1159/000492931.

Pitkala, K. H., Poysti, M. M., Laakkonen, M. L., Tilvis, R. S., Savikko, N., Kautiainen, H., & Strandberg, T. E. (2013). Effects of the Finnish Alzheimer disease exercise trial (FINALEX): A randomized controlled trial. *JAMA Internal Medicine, 173*(10), 894–901. https://doi.org/10.1001/jamainternmed.2013.359.

Rapp, K., Lamb, S. E., Buchele, G., Lall, R., Lindemann, U., & Becker, C. (2008). Prevention of falls in nursing homes: Subgroup analyses of a randomized fall prevention trial. *Journal of the American Geriatrics Society*, *56*(6), 1092–1097. https://doi.org/10.1111/j.1532-5415.2008.01739.x.

Roach, K. E., Tappen, R. M., Kirk-Sanchez, N., Williams, C. L., & Loewenstein, D. (2011). A randomized controlled trial of an activity specific exercise program for individuals with Alzheimer disease in long-term care settings. *Journal of Geriatric Physical Therapy (2001)*, *34*(2), 50–56. https://doi.org/10.1519/JPT.0b013e31820aab9c.

Rolland, Y., Pillard, F., Klapouszczak, A., Reynish, E., Thomas, D., Andrieu, S., … Vellas, B. (2007). Exercise program for nursing home residents with Alzheimer's disease: A 1-year randomized, controlled trial. *Journal of the American Geriatrics Society*, *55*(2), 158–165. https://doi.org/10.1111/j.1532-5415.2007.01035.x.

Scandol, J. P., Toson, B., & Close, J. C. (2013). Fall-related hip fracture hospitalisations and the prevalence of dementia within older people in New South Wales, Australia: An analysis of linked data. *Injury*, *44*(6), 776–783. https://doi.org/10.1016/j.injury.2012.11.023.

Schwenk, M., Zieschang, T., Englert, S., Grewal, G., Najafi, B., & Hauer, K. (2014). Improvements in gait characteristics after intensive resistance and functional training in people with dementia: A randomised controlled trial. *BMC Geriatrics*, *14*, 73. https://doi.org/10.1186/1471-2318-14-73.

Schwenk, M., Zieschang, T., Oster, P., & Hauer, K. (2010). Dual-task performances can be improved in patients with dementia: A randomized controlled trial. *Neurology*, *74*(24), 1961–1968.

Shaw, F. E., Bond, J., Richardson, D. A., Dawson, P., Steen, I. N., McKeith, I. G., & Kenny, R. A. (2003). Multifactorial intervention after a fall in older people with cognitive impairment and dementia presenting to the accident and emergency department: Randomised controlled trial. *BMJ*, *326*(7380), 73.

Sherrington, C., Fairhall, N. J., Wallbank, G. K., Tiedemann, A., Michaleff, Z. A., Howard, K., … Lamb, S. E. (2019). Exercise for preventing falls in older people living in the community. *Cochrane Database of Systematic Reviews*, *1*. https://doi.org/10.1002/14651858.CD012424.pub2.

Sherrington, C., Michaleff, Z. A., Fairhall, N., Paul, S. S., Tiedemann, A., Whitney, J., … Lord, S. R. (2017). Exercise to prevent falls in older adults: An updated systematic review and meta-analysis. *British Journal of Sports Medicine*, *51*(24), 1750–1758. https://doi.org/10.1136/bjsports-2016-096547.

Shorer, Z., Bachner, Y., Guy, T., & Melzer, I. (2013). Effect of single dose methylphenidate on walking and postural stability under single- and dual-task conditions in older adults--a double-blind randomized control trial. *The Journals of Gerontology. Series A, Biological Sciences and Medical Sciences*, *68*(10), 1271–1280. https://doi.org/10.1093/gerona/glt035.

Sobol, N. A., Hoffmann, K., Frederiksen, K. S., Vogel, A., Vestergaard, K., Braendgaard, H., … Beyer, N. (2016). Effect of aerobic exercise on physical performance in patients with Alzheimer's disease. *Alzheimers Dement*, *12*(12), 1207–1215. https://doi.org/10.1016/j.jalz.2016.05.004.

Summary of the Updated American Geriatrics Society/British Geriatrics Society clinical practice guideline for prevention of falls in older person clinical practice guideline for prevention of falls in older persons. (2011). *Journal of the American Geriatrics Society*, *59*(1), 148–157. https://doi.org/10.1111/j.1532-5415.2010.03234.x.

Suttanon, P., Hill, K. D., Said, C. M., Williams, S. B., Byrne, K. N., LoGiudice, D., … Dodd, K. J. (2013). Feasibility, safety and preliminary evidence of the effectiveness of a home-based exercise programme for older people with Alzheimer's disease: A pilot randomized controlled trial. *Clinical Rehabilitation*, *27*(5), 427–438. https://doi.org/10.1177/0269215512460877.

Taylor, M. E., Delbaere, K., Lord, S. R., Mikolaizak, A. S., Brodaty, H., & Close, J. C. (2014). Neuropsychological, physical, and functional mobility measures associated with falls in cognitively impaired older adults. *The Journals of Gerontology. Series A, Biological Sciences and Medical Sciences*, *69*(8), 987–995. https://doi.org/10.1093/gerona/glt166.

Taylor, M. E., Delbaere, K., Lord, S. R., Mikolaizak, A. S., & Close, J. C. (2013). Physical impairments in cognitively impaired older people: Implications for risk of falls. *International Psychogeriatrics*, *25*(1), 148–156. https://doi.org/10.1017/S1041610212001184.

Taylor, M. E., Lord, S. R., Brodaty, H., Kurrle, S. E., Hamilton, S., Ramsay, E., … Close, J. C. (2017). A home-based, carer-enhanced exercise program improves balance and falls efficacy in community-dwelling older people with dementia. *International Psychogeriatrics*, *29*(1), 81–91. https://doi.org/10.1017/S1041610216001629.

Tchalla, A. E., Lachal, F., Cardinaud, N., Saulnier, I., Rialle, V., Preux, P. M., & Dantoine, T. (2013). Preventing and managing indoor falls with home-based technologies in mild and moderate Alzheimer's disease patients: Pilot study in a community dwelling. *Dementia and Geriatric Cognitive Disorders*, *36*(3–4), 251–261. https://doi.org/10.1159/000351863.

Telenius, E. W., Engedal, K., & Bergland, A. (2015). Effect of a high-intensity exercise program on physical function and mental health in nursing home residents with dementia: An assessor blinded randomized controlled trial. *PLoS One*, *10*(5). https://doi.org/10.1371/journal.pone.0126102.

Tinetti, M. E., Speechley, M., & Ginter, S. F. (1988). Risk factors for falls among elderly persons living in the community. *The New England Journal of Medicine*, *319*(26), 1701–1707.

Toots, A., Littbrand, H., Lindelof, N., Wiklund, R., Holmberg, H., Nordstrom, P., … Rosendahl, E. (2016). Effects of a high-intensity functional exercise program on dependence in activities of daily living and balance in older adults with dementia. *Journal of the American Geriatrics Society*, *64*(1), 55–64. https://doi.org/10.1111/jgs.13880.

Toots, A., Wiklund, R., Littbrand, H., Nordin, E., Nordstrom, P., Lundin-Olsson, L., … Rosendahl, E. (2018). The effects of exercise on falls in older people with dementia living in nursing homes: A randomized controlled trial. *Journal of the American Medical Directors Association*. https://doi.org/10.1016/j.jamda.2018.10.009.

van der Wardt, V., Hancox, J., Gondek, D., Logan, P., Nair, R. D., Pollock, K., & Harwood, R. (2017). Adherence support strategies for exercise interventions in people with mild cognitive impairment and dementia: A systematic review. *Preventive Medical Reports*, *7*, 38–45. https://doi.org/10.1016/j.pmedr.2017.05.007.

Verghese, J., Wang, C., Lipton, R. B., Holtzer, R., & Xue, X. (2007). Quantitative gait dysfunction and risk of cognitive decline and dementia. *Journal of Neurology, Neurosurgery, and Psychiatry*, *78*(9), 929–935. https://doi.org/10.1136/jnnp.2006.106914.

Vreugdenhil, A., Cannell, J., Davies, A., & Razay, G. (2012). A community-based exercise programme to improve functional ability in people with Alzheimer's disease: A randomized controlled trial. *Scandinavian Journal of Caring Sciences*, *26*(1), 12–19. https://doi.org/10.1111/j.1471-6712.2011.00895.x.

Wesson, J., Clemson, L., Brodaty, H., Lord, S., Taylor, M., Gitlin, L., & Close, J. (2013). A feasibility study and pilot randomised trial of a tailored prevention program to reduce falls in older people with mild dementia. *BMC Geriatrics*, *13*, 89. https://doi.org/10.1186/1471-2318-13-89.

Whitney, J., Close, J. C., Jackson, S. H., & Lord, S. R. (2012). Understanding risk of falls in people with cognitive impairment living in residential care. *Journal of the American Medical Directors Association*, *13*(6), 535–540. https://doi.org/10.1016/j.jamda.2012.03.009.

Whitney, J., Jackson, S. H. D., & Martin, F. C. (2017). Feasibility and efficacy of a multifactorial intervention to prevent falls in older adults with cognitive impairment living in residential care (ProF-Cog). A feasibility and pilot cluster randomised controlled trial. *BMC Geriatrics*, *17*(1), 115. https://doi.org/10.1186/s12877-017-0504-6.

Zeng, Z., Deng, H., Shuai, T., Zhang, H., Wang, Y., & Song, G. (2016). Effect of physical activity training on dementia patients: A systematic review with a meta-analysis. *Chinese Nursing Research, 3*, 168–175.

Zieschang, T., Schwenk, M., Becker, C., Uhlmann, L., Oster, P., & Hauer, K. (2017). Falls and physical activity in persons with mild to moderate dementia participating in an intensive motor training: Randomized controlled trial. *Alzheimer Disease and Associated Disorders, 31*(4), 307–314. https://doi.org/10.1097/WAD.0000000000000201.

CHAPTER 5

Optimizing independence in activities of daily living

Kate Laver[a], Catherine Verrier Piersol[b], and Rachel Wiley[c]
[a]Department of Rehabilitation, Aged and Extended Care, College of Medicine and Public Health, Flinders University, Adelaide, SA, Australia
[b]Department of Occupational Therapy, Thomas Jefferson University, Philadelphia, PA, United States
[c]Day By Day Home Therapy, Devon, PA, United States

Introduction

First symptoms of dementia often involve complaints about cognitive processes. Family members or friends usually notice these symptoms and observe the person to be having more difficulty than usual with their everyday activities (Speechly, Bridges-Webb, & Passmore, 2008). Overtime, people with dementia experience progressively more difficulty performing activities of daily living and require more assistance from others. Yet, this necessitates difficult familial, social, and ethical decisions about optimizing performance in daily activities while ensuring safety and proper care (Smebye, Kirkevold, & Engedal, 2015). On one hand, it is important to maintain dignity and autonomy as well as stay active and engaged to prevent further decline. Counterarguments involve the prevention of risk and societal views around caring for others and meeting needs. The balance between these factors and the person's care needs will change overtime. By the time the person has severe symptoms of dementia, they will require comprehensive help with all activities of daily living. Yet, there is good evidence that health interventions to promote activity engagement and environmental adaptation are beneficial (Gitlin et al., 2003). Such intervention can help people meet their functional goals and delay functional decline (Van't Leven et al., 2013). Even people in the later stages of dementia, such as those living in nursing homes, can be helped to maintain independence in self-care activities such as eating and grooming.

Activities of daily living

Activities of daily living include self-care tasks such as feeding, dressing, grooming, toileting, and bathing as well as domestic tasks such as shopping,

Dementia Rehabilitation
https://doi.org/10.1016/B978-0-12-818685-5.00005-2

meal preparation, cleaning, home maintenance, and managing finances and mail. The International Classification of Functioning developed by the World Health Organization provides a common language to describe body functions and structure as well as activities and participation (World Health Organization, 2017). Self-care and domestic life domains fall within the overall structure of activities and participation.

Common pattern of functional decline

Functional decline is a key feature of dementia arising due to changes in the person's physiological and cognitive function (Liu-Seifert et al., 2015). Changes in function may also arise due to changes in mood and behavior, which further impact on the person's capabilities (McKeith & Cummings, 2005).

One study conducted in the Netherlands (Verlinden et al., 2016) showed that people with dementia first reported (subjective) problems with memory an average of 16 years prior to diagnosis, which gradually progressed to a decline in global cognitive functioning (assessed by the mini-mental state examination) around 7 years before diagnosis, difficulty in household activities approximately 6 years before diagnosis and then self-care activities (Fig. 1).

Functional decline is, therefore, typically hierarchical with initial changes that affect complex activities such as driving, managing finances, following familiar routines, and current affairs. Overtime, changes occur in the performance of simpler tasks (bathing, dressing, and making a cup of tea) as physical and cognitive function worsens (Giebel, Sutcliffe, & Challis, 2017). As symptom severity progresses so does difficulty initiating and performing activities of daily living (Giebel et al., 2017).

There are a number of factors that may play a role in the speed of functional decline. These include the presence of apathy (associated with faster decline), age (with more rapid decline in people aged over 85 years), and level of educational attainment (faster decline in those with lower levels of education) (Delva et al., 2014). Trajectories may also differ across different types of dementia. For example, vascular dementia is typically associated with earlier decline in ADL and later decline in cognition than those with AD. People with the APOE gene have been observed to decline less in ADL functioning than in cognitive function (Verlinden et al., 2016).

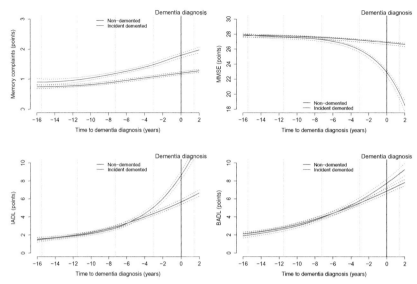

Fig. 1 Trajectories of decline in cognition and daily functioning before dementia diagnosis. (A) Trajectories for memory complaints. (B) Trajectories for MMSE. (C) Trajectories for IADL. (D) Trajectories for BADL. The trajectories are derived from the analyses and plotted for the mean age, sex, and education. The *vertical dark green (dark gray in print version) dotted lines* reflect the mean time to dementia at which the participants participated in the five separate study visits. The *red (gray in print version) lines* represent the incident dementia cases and the *blue (light gray in print version) lines* the controls. The *dotted lines* around the *red (gray in print version)* and *blue (light gray in print version) lines* reflect the 95% confidence intervals. Abbreviations: *MMSE*, mini-mental state examination; *IADL*, instrumental activities of daily living; *BADL*, basic activities of daily living (Verlinden et al., 2016).

Impact of functional decline on families and care partners

Most people with dementia are supported by family and friends who provide informal care and practical support (Prince, Ali, & Ali, 2015). People with dementia who are more dependent in activities of daily living require more time from care partners and consequently can make care more challenging for the care partner (Haro et al., 2014). A survey conducted in the United States revealed that informal care partners (family members) reported providing an average of 10 h per day of care for people with dementia living in the community (Nichols, Martindale-Adams, Burns, Graney, & Zuber, 2011). Much of this time is spent providing supervision and social and emotional support but practical assistance is commonly required for health-care management, mobility, self-care, and community transportation. Importantly, evidence is emerging that working with families to increase the amount of time that the person with dementia spends engaged in activities can reduce the amount of time that the family member spends providing supervision and assistance (Gitlin et al., 2008). Therefore, delaying functional decline can lead to the person with dementia remaining more independent (requiring less hands-on help) and more engaged in activities (therefore, requiring less of the caregivers time). Many family members are older themselves and have their own health concerns and the physical and emotional demands of caring can take their toll (Sörensen & Conwell, 2011).

Humans have an innate need to "do" and contribute

Traditional models of care have involved a dependency approach. When the person has difficulty, or is no longer able to complete a particular activity/role, the person's participation in that activity/role ends and others step in to take over the activity/role (Rogers et al., 2000). This approach reflected the care partner's good intentions as people do not like to see others struggle. However, it can lead to a cycle in which the person becomes more disengaged, less active, less confident, and loses their sense of purpose (Slaughter, Eliasziw, Morgan, & Drummond, 2011). More recent models of care involve approaches which may are described as "reabling," "restorative," or "habilitation" or "rehabilitating" (Sims-Gould, Tong, Wallis-Mayer, & Ashe, 2017) and the focus is on optimizing independence and maximizing activity and participation in spite of impairments.

Humans have an innate need to be active and productive, which is linked to increased well-being and quality of life (Chung, 2004). Studies in other populations show that depraving humans of having something to do or a sense of purpose has negative consequences for their health (Whiteford, 2000). Studies conducted with people with dementia support this concept, in terms of describing how activity engagement, purposefulness, and productivity are one of the key contributors to their autonomy and quality of life. People with dementia have described how participation in activities enhances connectedness to themselves, others, and the environment (Han, Radel, McDowd, & Sabata, 2016). This finding appears to hold regardless of the stage or severity of the condition. Milte and colleagues found that people with dementia and their care partners in nursing homes both reported that having access to activities was very important and contributed to dignity and autonomy (Milte et al., 2016).

Theoretical models underpin this need *to be, to do,* and *to contribute.* Dementia care literature frequently refers to Maslow's hierarchy of needs (Schölzel-Dorenbos, Meeuwsen, & Olde Rikkert, 2010). It is believed that unmet needs (and difficulty communicating needs) such as the need for food, water, emotional security, and social contact can be expressed by people with dementia as agitation and anxiety-type behaviors (e.g., pacing, repetitive vocalizations, and shadowing). As basic needs are met (physiological, safety, love, and belonging), there is the need for appreciation and respect (described as "esteem"). People have the need to accomplish, contribute, and be valued, which contributes to their self-esteem and quality of life (QOL). Research shows that people with dementia report self-esteem, being useful/giving meaning to life, enjoyment of activities to be vital to QOL (Schölzel-Dorenbos et al., 2010).

Assessment of self-care and domestic activities

A number of global assessment tools summarize performance, which includes ability to manage self-care and domestic activities (Table 1).

Activity analysis

Outcome assessment measures provide useful information and can be used to document and compare performance of activities of daily living. Many measures involve self-report completed by the person with dementia or a proxy (someone that knows the person well such as family or care staff). When applying a rehabilitation approach, observing the person perform the activity that they need to, want to, or are expected to do is advantageous (Fisher, 1998). Theories show actual task performance depend on the interaction between the person, environment, and occupation and underpin the process of activity analysis. Discussing the task with the care partner and person with dementia if appropriate, observing and noting each step of the task, and analyzing performance can help identify to what extent the person is capable of performing the activity and which factors affect their ability to perform the activity. Factors may include level of interest and familiarity with the activity, physical and cognitive ability, activity complexity, and nature of the environment (Polatajko, Mandich, & Martini, 2000). Analysis of strengths and capabilities helps to guide treatment as some factors may be amenable to change (such as the environment), whereas others many not (such as cognitive ability).

Table 1 An overview of assessment tools suitable for measuring activities of daily living in people with dementia.

Name	Description
WHODAS 2.0 (Üstün, Kostanjsek, Chatterji, & Rehm, 2010)	This assessment captures information about health and disability and can be used across different diagnostic conditions. The tool is directly linked to the International Classification of Functioning, Disability, and Health and is available in both 36 and 12 item versions. Can be administered by self, proxy, or interviewer
ADCS-MCI-ADL (Galasko et al., 1997)	This 23-item tool is a dementia specific tool which measures functional impairment in both Basic ADLs and Instrumental ADLs and therefore better suited to those with mild-to-moderate symptoms of dementia. It can be administered by any health professional with an informant and provides an overall score of function
Barthel Index (Mahoney & Barthel, 1965)	This Index is a very commonly used tool for older people with many diagnoses and is quite simple to administer by any health professional with an informant. The 10 items provide an indication of level of assistance required with Basic ADLs and therefore the tool is better suited to those with moderate-to-severe symptoms of dementia
Bayer Activities of Daily Living (Hindmarch, Lehfeld, de Jongh, & Erzigkeit, 1998)	The scale contains 25 items including Basic ADLs and Instrumental ADLs as well as items which reflect cognitive functioning (e.g., performing a task when under pressure). Each of the items is rated from 1 to 10 and therefore the tool can be useful with people with mild cognitive impairment and mild-to-moderate dementia
Disability Assessment for Dementia (Gélinas, Gauthier, McIntyre, & Gauthier, 1999)	This tool was designed specifically for use with people with dementia. With items pertaining to both Basic ADLs and Instrumental ADLs the tool is sensitive to change and can be used b health professionals based on interviews with an informant
Lawton (Lawton & Brody, 1969)	The scale has been used extensively to assess and describe performance in Instrumental ADLs. The tool is required to be completed either through direct observation or self-report of the person being assessed. It is short and only relevant to people who are living in the community due to the items assessed (such as food preparation and ability to use the telephone)
Katz Index of Independence in Activities of Daily Living (Katz, Ford, Moskowitz, Jackson, & Jaffe, 1963)	This short tool measures six items of Basic ADLs and the level of assistance required with each. As such, the tool is more appropriate for those with moderate-to-severe symptoms of dementia

Rehabilitation for dementia—An approach for optimizing participation of self-care and domestic tasks

Addressing self-care and domestic task performance should use a systematic and holistic approach. Rehabilitation for self-care and domestic tasks uses a systematic approach of identifying preserved capacities in the person with dementia and demands of the task, setting goals, and applying strategies designed to achieve those goals in order to *optimize participation and well-being*. This contrasts with traditional care models. See Box 1 for example:

BOX 1 Evelyn is a 78-year-old woman who lives alone and has mild dementia. As her cognitive and physical capabilities change, she is having more difficulty with preparing the nutritious and tasty meals that she is used to preparing.

One approach would be to arrange for someone else to perform the task by organizing ready meals for Evelyn either through a service such as Meals on Wheels or by purchasing frozen meals from the supermarket for Evelyn to reheat.

A rehabilitation approach would involve performance-based assessment to identify Evelyn's preserved cognitive and physical capacities and determining Evelyn's routines and interests related to meal preparation, with involvement of a care partner. Treatment might include steps such as:

1. Contacting and educating a family member about Evelyn's capacities and strategies to ensure safety, such as visiting regularly to check that all food items are being stored and used before their use-by dates.
2. Developing a plan for meals across the week (e.g., crumbed fish, salad, and a bread roll every Monday) to embed routine and familiarity.
3. Establishing a schedule that reflects a repeated routine of meals into the meal plan to simplify meal preparation.
4. Creating a shopping list so that Evelyn always has the ingredients on hand that she needs.
5. Assembling a booklet of recipes that complement the meal plan so that each step for each meal is presented in a written format to assist with cueing.
6. Placing labels across the kitchen so that items are easily found.
7. Ensuring safety mechanisms are present and functioning such as smoke alarms and that Evelyn has the cognitive capacity to respond appropriately.

The outcome is that Evelyn can be as independent and autonomous as possible. Overtime the setup and level of assistance will change. For example, a family member or professional care staff will need to help with meal preparation and eventually a meal service might be helpful.

Intervention to optimize participation in self-care and domestic activities may involve using a number of approaches including training, education, advising, counseling, performing the task on behalf of the person, and providing practical and emotional support (World Health Organization, 2015). These approaches should always include those involved in care such as family members or professional care staff.

Working with care partners

Family care partners have been described as the greatest therapeutic agent in dementia care (Gitlin & Hodgson, 2015). Family members often find it hard to adjust to becoming a care partner (rather than a spouse, child, other relative, or friend). Relationships, roles, knowledge and understanding about dementia, and the person's previous experiences in providing care for others will influence their ability to act as a care partners. It is important to understand the capabilities of both the person with dementia and their care partner when seeking to optimize activities of daily living performance.

How care partners appraise the capacity of the person with dementia influences the level of oversight and care they provide, which potentially can have an impact on safety and performance. Care partners who overestimate the functional capacity of the person with dementia may not provide the necessary supervision during activities of daily living, placing the person at risk for harm. For example, leaving someone home alone or not providing supervision in the bathtub or shower. In contract, care partners who underestimate the functional capacity of the person with dementia may help too much, limiting activity engagement of the person with dementia. When comparing care partner appraisal to standardized assessment, the majority of care partners, caring for someone in the home, overestimated the ability of the person with dementia (Piersol, Herge, Copolillo, Leiby, & Gitlin, 2016). Thus, health professionals should collaborate with care partners to understand how they are appraising the level of function and to prioritize rehabilitation goals accordingly, which can include care partner education. It is also important that health professionals understand which activities of daily living the care partner does and does not want to be involved in and these preferences should be respected.

Prioritizing rehabilitation goals in relation to activities of daily living

Identifying treatment goals should involve prioritizing the areas of need that are most important to the care partner and the person with dementia when appropriate. Determining the focus of intervention is best when a care partner is involved in identifying and prioritizing the areas of need and establishing realistic goals. This collaborative process offers the opportunity to provide education about the progressive nature of the disease and the potential treatment strategies that can optimize performance of activities of daily living.

The prioritization process starts by reviewing the daily challenges with the care partner and determining their preference for problem areas they wish to address in treatment sessions. Based on their preferences, rehabilitation goals can be prioritized that reflect the interests of the person with dementia and the concerns of the care partner. Through this structured approach, what may seem overwhelming can be transformed into a plan that promotes care partner confidence and skill.

Table 2 provides general intervention strategies for promoting optimal participation in self-care and domestic tasks to enhance activity participation. These strategies can also be taught to care partners.

Research evidence for interventions that maximize function and delay decline

An overview of reviews examined the most effective non-pharmacological approaches for delaying functional decline in people with dementia (Fig. 2) (Laver et al., 2016). The overview found for groups of people with dementia that the most effective approaches were exercise (so that the person is physically fit and capable of performing activities of daily living) and dyadic interventions. Dyadic interventions which involve working with the person with dementia and their caregiver to educate, train, and develop strategies to address goals and care challenges.

When we consider the dyadic interventions that were found to be most successful (Clare et al., 2019; Gitlin, Winter, Dennis, Hodgson, & Hauck, 2010; Graff et al., 2006; Laver, Clemson, Bennett, Lannin, & Brodaty, 2014), these included:

Focusing on strengths and capabilities: Intervention acknowledges and respects the person with dementia's life history, roles, and interests. There is a focus on strengths and capabilities (what the person can do) and how to ensure that they are able to utilize these capabilities in activities of daily living. Activities may need to be modified to match with the person's capabilities. Studies also show that when the person with dementia is engaged and supported to participate in activities of interest, they present with fewer symptoms of distress and are happier alone for longer (Gitlin et al., 2008).

Table 2 Intervention strategies for self-care and domestic tasks.

Type of intervention	Strategies
Task/activity adaptation	Allow significant amount of time to complete an activity
	Involve other family or friends to help provide care
	Only put out the items necessary for a given activity
	Break down task into its parts and give step-by-step directions
	Keep a consistent daily routine
	Adjust your expectations during a task/activity
	Provide breaks in between different self-care activities
	Limit choices involved in the task/activity
	Use contrasting solid colors so objects stand out
	Use assistive devices as appropriate
	Create a list of steps that helps the person participate
Environmental modification	Keep familiar objects that are recognized and are comforting in the environment
	Decrease environmental stimulation
	Remove unnecessary objects in the area in which an activity occurs
	Remove dangerous objects. Secure doors
	Secure drawers and cabinets where hazardous liquids (e.g., cleaning supplies) may be stored
	Provide adequate lighting
	Use adaptive equipment (e.g., tub bench) to promote a sense of security/safety
	Remove/hide objects that may trigger fear or anxiety
	Put out only the necessary items the table that are needed
	Keep space warm and comfortable
	Keep environment quiet and background noise to a minimum
	Reduce clutter or objects in the living area that may trigger a reaction
	Keep distractions to a minimum
Communication simplification	Provide specific, 1 or 2 step simple verbal instructions
	Give a simple, direct verbal or visual cue
	Use a calm and reassuring voice
	Be aware of your body language—Smile, position yourself at the same level, make eye contact, and use physical touch to reassure
	Use a light touch to reassure, calm, and redirect
	Use words of encouragement and positive statements; avoid rationalizing or arguing
	Give information about the activity as it takes place, rather than telling in advance
	Provide a visual demonstration and hand over hand assistance
	Talk about pleasant topics/memories to divert from anxious thoughts
	Allow extra time to perform tasks/activities
	Speak slowly and allow extra time for a response
	Provide simple choices for activities
	Use a picture or a sign to communicate location

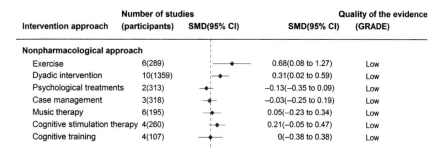

Intervention approach	Number of studies (participants)	SMD(95% CI)	SMD(95% CI)	Quality of the evidence (GRADE)
Nonpharmacological approach				
Exercise	6(289)		0.68(0.08 to 1.27)	Low
Dyadic intervention	10(1359)		0.31(0.02 to 0.59)	Low
Psychological treatments	2(313)		−0.13(−0.35 to 0.09)	Low
Case management	3(318)		−0.03(−0.25 to 0.19)	Low
Music therapy	6(195)		0.05(−0.23 to 0.34)	Low
Cognitive stimulation therapy	4(260)		0.21(−0.05 to 0.47)	Low
Cognitive training	4(107)		0(−0.38 to 0.38)	Low

Fig. 2 Effects of different non-pharmacological approaches on activities of daily living function in people with dementia (Laver, Dyer, Whitehead, Clemson, & Crotty, 2016).

Care partner education: Education about dementia is essential in order to assist the caregiver to understand common symptoms are attributed to the disease and that care challenges are often attributable to the environment or communication difficulties.

Care partner skills training: The health professional acts not as a care coordinator or as someone who solely provides advice or recommendations. The health professional works in collaboration with the person with dementia and the people involved in care (as appropriate in each situation) to jointly problem solve and identify possible solutions to challenges. Strategies are tested and refined as need in collaboration. The health professional seeks to build skills in the care partner using adult learning techniques.

Caregiver support and coping strategies: It is widely considered that care partners who look after their own health are better positioned to care for others. Programs that ensure that the care partner is receiving adequate support and has strategies in place to manage stress are beneficial.

Individualized problem solving: intervention addresses the goals and care challenges identified by the person with dementia and/or their care partner. The approaches used by the health professional are adapted based on knowledge, beliefs, and attitudes of the people involved in care. Care is culturally appropriate and respectful.

Environmental modification: There is consideration of how the person's environment may need to be altered in order to enhance their capability. Alteration may include changing the nature of the environment, modifying routine, changing communication styles, and prescription of assistive technology.

When should intervention to enhance performance in activities and participation occur?

People with dementia have reported that they value rehabilitation approaches, which focus on strengths and capabilities and maintaining independence and participation in life roles. It is often reported that there are gaps in care in the months following diagnosis. Therefore, offering rehabilitation services to address activities of daily living following diagnosis is a priority. However, it is inevitable that different challenges will occur over the course of the condition. For example, rehabilitation may focus early on more complex tasks such as driving and managing budgets and progress to simpler tasks such as meal preparation overtime.

The therapeutic approach required will change overtime too. As the condition progresses, there will be less capacity for the person with dementia to retrain functional and cognitive skills and there will be more focus on compensatory treatment approaches. Symptoms are progressive and so what works today will not work tomorrow or next week or next month. It is important that services are accessible at various time points post-diagnosis and are flexible enough to be able to cater for different needs and goals.

To date, most of the evidence for rehabilitation for dementia relates to people with mild-to-moderate symptoms (rather than those who have more severe symptoms) of those who live in nursing homes. This does not mean that intervention is not possible or worthwhile but that research is required to reveal more information about what should be offered and when.

Finally, while symptoms may vary depending on the subtype of dementia, the approach detailed within this chapter applies to people with all subtypes. Treatment and care should be individualized to the person's strengths, capabilities, and challenges and address individual needs and symptoms.

Gaps in clinical and research knowledge

There is now good evidence that non-pharmacological treatment approaches can delay functional decline in people with dementia enabling them to better manage activities of daily living. There is less detail which intervention approaches are superior to others as these have not been directly compared. Therefore, while effective interventions have common elements, it is not clear which intervention content is most useful (and for which outcome).

Furthermore, one of the biggest challenges has been in translating interventions, which have been shown to be effective in the research studies into practice. Common barriers include: lack of time and resources to offer programs involving multiple consultations, lack of opportunities to become trained in evidence-based interventions, and lack of confidence in offering programs to people with dementia and their care partners.

Clinical recommendations

Many of the studies in this field evaluate interventions that are described as "dyadic" or "occupational therapy" interventions. One of the key commonalities in successful approaches is that the intervention considers the person's strengths as well as meaningful tasks and the environment. Although not described as "rehabilitation" interventions, most of these interventions fit within the broader framework of rehabilitation programs in which function is optimized despite impairments.

Clinicians working in the field should adopt a systematic approach to care. This starts with assessment of the person, environment, and task and identified key priorities for managing activities of daily living of the person and their care partner. Intervention is holistic and may include adaptation of the task, modification of the environment, and training of care partners to optimize communication and the person's routines.

It is critical that the health professional is skilled in matching the person's abilities with tasks that are "just right" so that the person can experience mastery and satisfaction but is also performing at their optimal level. It is also important that the health professional takes a holistic approach and is able to appreciate how various activities impact on the person's quality of life. Intervention should focus on the priorities of the person with dementia and their care partner. While function will decline overtime and symptoms may worsen, there are approaches that will maintain or improve quality of life.

It has been our experience that assessment and intervention to maximize independence in activities of daily living takes time and often requires multiple consultations over weeks or months in order to implement the best approaches. Some strategies suggested by health professionals may not be successful or may not be acceptable. Trial and error is sometimes necessary.

Research recommendations

There are now multiple, high quality, randomized trials, which demonstrate that intervention can delay functional decline. A critical area for further research is how we can utilize approaches, which already exist and translate them into practice so that they are widely available for members of the general public. More research into knowledge translation in different settings is required.

Further research should also assist us to better understand the characteristics of effective intervention. Information is required regarding the optimal dose; the optimal duration of programs and which populations are most likely to benefit. To date, there has been less research that aims to delay functional decline taking place in longer-term (residential) care settings as most has been conducted in the community. There is also less research conducted in hospitals addressing rehabilitation of activities of daily living function.

As technologies become more sophisticated, the field will adapt. There will be new options to optimize environments and compensate for physical and cognitive impairment. It will also offer the ability to deliver programs remotely through telehealth models of service delivery; this will increase the accessibility of programs and reduce the time health professionals spend traveling to the person's home. These new technologies will require mixed methods evaluation, which considers efficacy, usefulness, and ease of use.

References

Chung, J. C. (2004). Activity participation and well-being of people with dementia in long-term—Care settings. *OTJR: Occupation, Participation and Health, 24*(1), 22–31.

Clare, L., Kudlicka, A., Oyebode, J. R., Jones, R. W., Bayer, A., Leroi, I., … Pool, J. (2019). Individual goal-oriented cognitive rehabilitation to improve everyday functioning for people with early-stage dementia: A multicentre randomised controlled trial (the GREAT trial). *International Journal of Geriatric Psychiatry, 34*(5), 709–721.

Delva, F., Auriacombe, S., Letenneur, L., Foubert-Samier, A., Bredin, A., Clementy, A., … Delabrousse-Mayoux, J.-P. (2014). Natural history of functional decline in Alzheimer's disease: A systematic review. *Journal of Alzheimer's Disease, 40*(1), 57–67.

Fisher, A. G. (1998). Uniting practice and theory in an occupational framework. *American Journal of Occupational Therapy, 52*(7), 509–521.

Galasko, D., Bennett, D., Sano, M., Ernesto, C., Thomas, R., Grundman, M., & Ferris, S. (1997). An inventory to assess activities of daily living for clinical trials in Alzheimer's disease. *Alzheimer Disease and Associated Disorders, 11*(Suppl 2), S33–S39.

Gélinas, I., Gauthier, L., McIntyre, M., & Gauthier, S. (1999). Development of a functional measure for persons with Alzheimer's disease: The disability assessment for dementia. *American Journal of Occupational Therapy, 53*(5), 471–481.

Giebel, C. M., Sutcliffe, C., & Challis, D. (2017). Hierarchical decline of the initiative and performance of complex activities of daily living in dementia. *Journal of Geriatric Psychiatry and Neurology, 30*(2), 96–103.

Gitlin, L. N., & Hodgson, N. (2015). Caregivers as therapeutic agents in dementia care: The context of caregiving and the evidence base for interventions. In *Family caregiving in the new normal* (pp. 305–353). Elsevier.

Gitlin, L. N., Winter, L., Burke, J., Chernett, N., Dennis, M. P., & Hauck, W. W. (2008). Tailored activities to manage neuropsychiatric behaviors in persons with dementia and reduce caregiver burden: A randomized pilot study. *The American Journal of Geriatric Psychiatry, 16*(3), 229–239.

Gitlin, L. N., Winter, L., Corcoran, M., Dennis, M. P., Schinfeld, S., & Hauck, W. W. (2003). Effects of the home environmental skill-building program on the caregiver–care recipient dyad: 6-month outcomes from the Philadelphia REACH initiative. *The Gerontologist, 43*(4), 532–546.

Gitlin, L. N., Winter, L., Dennis, M. P., Hodgson, N., & Hauck, W. W. (2010). A biobehavioral home-based intervention and the well-being of patients with dementia and their caregivers: The COPE randomized trial. *JAMA, 304*(9), 983–991.

Graff, M. J., Vernooij-Dassen, M. J., Thijssen, M., Dekker, J., Hoefnagels, W. H., & Rikkert, M. G. O. (2006). Community based occupational therapy for patients with dementia and their care givers: Randomised controlled trial. *BMJ, 333*(7580), 1196.

Han, A., Radel, J., McDowd, J. M., & Sabata, D. (2016). Perspectives of people with dementia about meaningful activities: A synthesis. *American Journal of Alzheimer's Disease & Other Dementias, 31*(2), 115–123.

Haro, J., Kahle-Wrobleski, K., Bruno, G., Belger, M., Dell'Agnello, G., Dodel, R., … Wimo, A. (2014). Analysis of burden in caregivers of people with Alzheimer's disease using self-report and supervision hours. *The Journal of Nutrition, Health & Aging, 18*(7), 677–684.

Hindmarch, I., Lehfeld, H., de Jongh, P., & Erzigkeit, H. (1998). The Bayer activities of daily living scale (B-ADL). *Dementia and Geriatric Cognitive Disorders, 9*(Suppl. 2), 20–26.

Katz, S., Ford, A. B., Moskowitz, R. W., Jackson, B. A., & Jaffe, M. W. (1963). Studies of illness in the aged: The index of ADL: A standardized measure of biological and psychosocial function. *JAMA, 185*(12), 914–919.

Laver, K., Clemson, L., Bennett, S., Lannin, N. A., & Brodaty, H. (2014). Unpacking the evidence: Interventions for reducing behavioral and psychological symptoms in people with dementia. *Physical & Occupational Therapy in Geriatrics, 32*(4), 294–309.

Laver, K., Dyer, S., Whitehead, C., Clemson, L., & Crotty, M. (2016). Interventions to delay functional decline in people with dementia: A systematic review of systematic reviews. *BMJ Open, 6*(4), e010767.

Lawton, M. P., & Brody, E. M. (1969). Assessment of older people: Self-maintaining and instrumental activities of daily living. *The Gerontologist, 9*(3_Part_1), 179–186.

Liu-Seifert, H., Siemers, E., Sundell, K., Price, K., Han, B., Selzler, K., … Mohs, R. (2015). Cognitive and functional decline and their relationship in patients with mild Alzheimer's dementia. *Journal of Alzheimer's Disease, 43*(3), 949–955.

Mahoney, F. I., & Barthel, D. W. (1965). Functional evaluation: The Barthel index: A simple index of independence useful in scoring improvement in the rehabilitation of the chronically ill. *Maryland State Medical Journal, 14*, 61–65.

McKeith, I., & Cummings, J. (2005). Behavioural changes and psychological symptoms in dementia disorders. *Lancet Neurology, 4*(11), 735–742.

Milte, R., Shulver, W., Killington, M., Bradley, C., Ratcliffe, J., & Crotty, M. (2016). Quality in residential care from the perspective of people living with dementia: The importance of personhood. *Archives of Gerontology and Geriatrics, 63*, 9–17.

Nichols, L. O., Martindale-Adams, J., Burns, R., Graney, M. J., & Zuber, J. (2011). Translation of a dementia caregiver support program in a health care system—REACH VA. *Archives of Internal Medicine, 171*(4), 353–359.

Piersol, C.V., Herge, E. A., Copolillo, A. E., Leiby, B. E., & Gitlin, L. N. (2016). Psychometric properties of the functional capacity card sort for caregivers of people with dementia. *OTJR: Occupation, Participation and Health, 36*(3), 126–133. https://doi.org/10.1177/1539449216666063.

Polatajko, H. J., Mandich, A., & Martini, R. (2000). Dynamic performance analysis: A framework for understanding occupational performance. *American Journal of Occupational Therapy*, *54*(1), 65–72.

Prince, M., Ali, G., & Ali, G. (2015). The global impact of dementia. In *World Alzheimer report* Alzheimer's Disease International.

Rogers, J. C., Holm, M. B., Burgio, L. D., Hsu, C., Hardin, J. M., & Mcdowell, B. J. (2000). Excess disability during morning care in nursing home residents with dementia. *International Psychogeriatrics*, *12*(2), 267–282.

Schölzel-Dorenbos, C. J., Meeuwsen, E. J., & Olde Rikkert, M. G. (2010). Integrating unmet needs into dementia health-related quality of life research and care: Introduction of the hierarchy model of needs in dementia. *Aging and Mental Health*, *14*(1), 113–119.

Sims-Gould, J., Tong, C. E., Wallis-Mayer, L., & Ashe, M. C. (2017). Reablement, reactivation, rehabilitation and restorative interventions with older adults in receipt of home care: A systematic review. *Journal of the American Medical Directors Association*, *18*(8), 653–663.

Slaughter, S. E., Eliasziw, M., Morgan, D., & Drummond, N. (2011). Incidence and predictors of excess disability in walking among nursing home residents with middle-stage dementia: A prospective cohort study. *International Psychogeriatrics*, *23*(1), 54–64.

Smebye, K. L., Kirkevold, M., & Engedal, K. (2015). Ethical dilemmas concerning autonomy when persons with dementia wish to live at home: A qualitative, hermeneutic study. *BMC Health Services Research*, *16*(1), 21.

Sörensen, S., & Conwell, Y. (2011). Issues in dementia caregiving: Effects on mental and physical health, intervention strategies, and research needs. *The American Journal of Geriatric Psychiatry*, *19*(6), 491–496.

Speechly, C. M., Bridges-Webb, C., & Passmore, E. (2008). The pathway to dementia diagnosis. *Medical Journal of Australia*, *189*(9), 487–489.

Üstün, T. B., Kostanjsek, N., Chatterji, S., & Rehm, J. (2010). *Measuring health and disability: Manual for WHO disability assessment schedule WHODAS 2.0.* World Health Organization.

Van't Leven, N., Prick, A.-E. J., Groenewoud, J. G., Roelofs, P. D., de Lange, J., & Pot, A. M. (2013). Dyadic interventions for community-dwelling people with dementia and their family caregivers: A systematic review. *International Psychogeriatrics*, *25*(10), 1581–1603.

Verlinden, V. J., van der Geest, J. N., de Bruijn, R. F., Hofman, A., Koudstaal, P. J., & Ikram, M. A. (2016). Trajectories of decline in cognition and daily functioning in preclinical dementia. *Alzheimer's & Dementia*, *12*(2), 144–153.

Whiteford, G. (2000). Occupational deprivation: Global challenge in the new millennium. *British Journal of Occupational Therapy*, *63*(5), 200–204.

World Health Organization. (2015). *International classification of health interventions*. Geneva: WHO.

World Health Organization. (2017). *Global action plan on the public health response to dementia 2017–2025*. Retrieved from https://www.who.int/classifications/ichi/en/.

CHAPTER 6

Active and engaged: Maintaining leisure activities in dementia

Claire M.C. O'Connor[a,b]**, Jacqueline B. Wesson**[c,d]**, and Lindy Clemson**[c]
[a]Centre for Positive Ageing, HammondCare, Sydney, NSW, Australia
[b]School of Population Health, University of New South Wales, Sydney, NSW, Australia
[c]Faculty of Medicine and Health, The University of Sydney, Sydney, NSW, Australia
[d]Montefiore Residential Care, Sydney, NSW, Australia

Introduction

What is leisure and why is it important?

For people living with dementia, engaging in regular leisure activities is an important part of life (Phinney, Chaudhury, & O'Connor, 2007) that helps maintain a sense of self (Wolverson, Clarke, & Moniz-Cook, 2016). It can increase feelings of self-efficacy and life purpose through a focus on remaining abilities and on positive engagement (DiLauro, Pereira, Carr, Chiu, & Wesson, 2017). Leisure also has an important role in minimizing social isolation, a known risk factor for dementia (Innes, Page, & Cutler, 2016), and leisure dysfunction predicts behavior changes (Chiu et al., 2013), which in turn, impacts on quality of life (Chiu, Shyu, Liang, & Huang, 2008).

Traditional definitions of leisure as activities undertaken during discretionary time or as a state of being relaxed or contented have found to be insufficient; leisure is more usefully defined in terms of how it is experienced (Bundy, du Toit, & Clemson, 2018). Form, purpose, meaning, achieving engagement, and matching challenges to skill are particularly important when disability impacts leisure participation (Bundy et al., 2018; Hammell, 2009).

The impact of not allowing people to perform what they are able to do has been referred to as "prescribed disengagement" (Swaffer, 2015). Throughout the course of dementia, it is common for the person with dementia and their family members to focus on the losses that occur, which may result in ill-being for both the person with dementia and their family members. Further, the majority of supportive intervention studies in dementia focus on the needs of the person with dementia or the family members separately (O'Connor et al., 2013), and often highlight the limitations associated with dementia, including cognitive decline, behavior changes,

Dementia Rehabilitation
https://doi.org/10.1016/B978-0-12-818685-5.00006-4

or the negative impact of supporting someone with dementia (Brodaty & Arasaratnam, 2012; Clare et al., 2019; Mioshi et al., 2013).

In contrast, emerging interventions that involve both the person with dementia and their family member (termed dyadic interventions) such as Gitlin et al. (2008) have demonstrated that tailoring activities to the interests and abilities of the person, along with teaching family members how to modify activities, environments, and hone their communication skills can both enable reengagement in enjoyable activities and provide positive outcomes for family members. These dyadic interventions often focus on leisure activities, providing a positive approach to occupational engagement and maintaining regular relationships (Cohen-Mansfield, Marx, Thein, & Dakheel-Ai, 2010).

Pleasant events are things we like doing, they keep us happy, contributing to our powerful drive to be active and thus contributing to our well-being (Perrin, 2000). Participating in pleasant events is an effective treatment for people living with dementia and depression (Teri & Logsdon, 1991). In addition to contributing to "happiness" and "enjoyment and pleasure" in general (Phinney et al., 2007; Schreiner, Yamamoto, & Shiotani, 2005), enabling participation and engagement in leisure can be restorative and therapeutic, improving well-being, quality of life and reducing the incidence of behavior changes, delaying decline in activities of daily living, or improving sleep (Cohen-Mansfield, Dakheel-Ali, & Marx, 2009; Connell, Sanford, & Lewis, 2007; Gitlin et al., 2008; Marshall & Hutchinson, 2001; O'Connor et al., 2019; Padilla, 2011; Schreiner et al., 2005; Teri & Logsdon, 1991; Volicer, Simard, Pupa, Medrek, & Riordan, 2006). Leisure participation is an essential part of everyday life for people with dementia, especially when access to many other everyday activities may be restricted.

Principles supporting engagement in leisure

There are many opportunities to support the person with dementia to engage in a leisure activity; once the reasons why they may have disengaged are understood, a detailed activity prescription can be devised. The following discussion outlines some of the common areas of difficulty for the person living with dementia.

- *Initiating* a leisure activity may be problematic, so the person may need help to start doing it. Participation may be more likely if family members set up the task requirements of the activity, then suggest the activity can start (Padilla, 2011; Volicer et al., 2006), as seeing the actual items may be more meaningful to the person with dementia than merely discussing the activity.

- *Remembering* or reading steps to an activity as they used to do, for example, during baking may cause task breakdown. When this is evident, they may benefit from a step-by-step pictorial recipe and standby verbal cueing from the family member. Once the person has moved on from that particular difficult step, assistance can be scaffolded away.
- *Continuing* to engage with complex activities, such as crosswords or memory-based language games may be too demanding. Simplifying the task would help engagement in a similar type of activity, such as find-a-words. Alternatively, relaxing the rules may also maintain interest and participation.

Family members and care partners may have difficulty working out how to support active engagement in leisure pursuits. For example, they may not understand the abilities of the person with dementia, inadvertently limiting the person's engagement by doing everything for them (Kovach & Magliocco, 1998). This can lead to disempowerment, whereby the person with dementia may begin to view themselves as less able than they actually are (Holthe, Thorsen, & Josephsson, 2007; Low, Swaffer, McGrath, & Brodaty, 2018). Dementia will invariably impact on a person's ability to participate, but assisting the person to engage in the way they are able, using intact abilities, is crucial to maintaining their self-efficacy (Carbonneau, Caron, & Desrosiers, 2011; DiLauro et al., 2017).

Finding activities that "fit" the person's current skills is a challenge faced by family members who may feel guilty at not being able to help their loved one engage in meaningful activities throughout the day (DiLauro et al., 2017). A functional cognition approach may help clarify abilities and strengths that can be drawn out to facilitate participation, and allows the amount and type of support to be estimated (Wesson & Giles, 2019).

Functional cognition has been defined as "the observable performance of everyday activities resulting from a dynamic interaction between motor abilities, activity demands, and the task environment, which is guided by cognitive abilities" (Wesson, Clemson, Brodaty, & Reppermund, 2016), and is a crucial consideration when planning activities for a person with dementia. What the person is able to do will impact on the length, complexity, and goals for an activity (Cohen-Mansfield et al., 2009).

In parallel with functional cognition, people have their own habits and routines that support them in getting through the day. Habits are deeply ingrained, and for people with dementia in particular, can be very difficult to change (Pollard, 2007). However, these can also represent strength, as this procedural memory enables performance of habits, which can be harnessed into activity engagement. For example, if Bob enjoys unpacking and sorting the groceries, offering other sorting activities may pique his interest and provide an opportunity for him to succeed in other enjoyable activities.

People with dementia may retain the ability to learn or relearn motor skills into the severe stages of disease (Buettner, Lundegren, Lago, Farrell, & Smith, 1996; Eslinger & Damsio, 1986; Zanetti et al., 2001). Family members and care partners can elicit these skills using a range of techniques, such as task/activity setup, activity simplification and graded verbal, and/or physical prompts and cues. As language skills and goal-directed behavior decline, it becomes more difficult for the person to imagine or conceptualize activities, therefore, using the actual activity or "task items" is essential to help prompt the memory and the actions associated with that task/item. For example, Peter used to really enjoy making omelets, but the severity of his cognitive impairment meant that he was no longer goal directed and did not understand how to complete activities. However, he was very much able to participate in actions, and using a hand-over-hand physical prompt, Peter could crack eggs into a bowl. With repetition, gradual fading of the physical cueing, and based on the familiarity of the actions, Peter was able to crack eggs without assistance after a few practices, indicating that the skilled action which related specifically to that object (the egg) was retained and could be elicited. Peter enjoyed his experience of participating in the activity and it provided a sense of meaning especially as he reminisced with his family about all the omelets he had made.

How to identify leisure activities for an individual with dementia

A person's existing hobbies, leisure interests, and abilities form an important part of developing appropriate and effective interventions (Buettner et al., 1996; Fitzsimmons & Buettner, 2002; Levy & Burns, 2005). Each person is different, so these must be satisfying to self but there is a broad range of possibilities: active, passive, individual or social, and completed both in and out of the home. The possibilities are endless, but examples might include creative therapies (music, dance), cafes, gardening, and jigsaws.

Identifying leisure pursuits starts with a conversation with the person living with dementia and usually their family member. People often can identify a few activities they enjoy, but challenges exist which may limit participation: activity restrictions imposed by cognitive impairment; family members with a poor understanding of the person's abilities; and accessibility and environmental barriers can be prohibitive (Innes et al., 2016). The process may also depend on family members' creativity and skills (Teri & Logsdon, 1991), and attending to the demands of caring often dominates, taking precedence over engagement in pleasant events (Amspoker et al., 2019).

The Pleasant Events Schedule-Alzheimer's Disease (PES-AD) (Teri & Logsdon, 1991—appendix) is the most widely used activities inventory for people living in the community with dementia. It identifies activities (to be modified or graded by the family member and/or therapist) so the person living with dementia can participate both successfully and regularly. While the content (items) is intended for people with mild Alzheimer's disease, the scale can be used with people with moderate to severe dementia in collaboration with family members, who like its ease of use: typically taking 30 min, in two sittings if required (Teri & Logsdon, 1991).

In all, 53 items or activities are rated three times: for frequency of participation (FREQ); for availability (AVAIL); and for enjoyability (NOW or PAST). A total score (NOW × FREQ) quantifies the frequency of participation in pleasant activities for the past month. A shorter 20-item version is available (PES-AD Short Form) (Logsdon & Teri, 1997) and a 30-item nursing home version has been published (Meeks, Shah, & Ramsey, 2009), though not yet validated for people living with dementia.

Measurement properties of the PES-AD and the PES-AD Short Form have been assessed in two studies (Amspoker et al., 2019; Logsdon & Teri, 1997). Reliability and construct validity are demonstrated (Table 1), though further work is required to replicate these findings in different populations and cultures, to refine understanding of subdimensions, and to explore responsiveness to change over time. However, these studies show that if using the scale as an outcome measure, there are sound foundations affording therapists some confidence that the scale is reliable, valid, and useful for clinical practice. When the scale is used more generally to stimulate identification of leisure interests, then it is useful regardless of the psychometrics.

Strategies to enable positive participation in leisure activities

Participating in any activity involves a confluence of factors, including performance skills (physical and cognitive ability), personal interest and value in the activity, activity demands (steps, objects, and skills involved in the

Table 1 Psychometric properties of the Pleasant Events Schedule—Alzheimer's Disease (PES-AD).

Study	Reliability	Validity	General findings
Logsdon and Teri (1997) 42 community-based older people with AD and/or depression—used PES-AD and PES-AD short form	Internal consistency: good to excellent for all subscales for both PES-AD and short form (alpha coefficients range 0.76–0.95 and split half reliabilities range 0.74–0.95)	Convergent validity: moderate relationships between measures of depression, cognition, and PES-AD	Scale measures various aspects of the same construct (internally consistent) for both long and short forms; less cognitive impairment and less depression were associated with increased participation in pleasant events
Amspoker et al. (2019) 220 (mostly male) older veterans with dementia (& pain) living in the community—used PES-AD short form	Internal consistency: borderline acceptable for active (0.70) and for social (0.67) factors and split half reliabilities 0.89 and 0.91, respectively	Structural validity: identified 2 factors (for 10 out of 20 items): enjoyment in *active events* (6 items; $\alpha = 0.70$) and *social events* (4 items; $\alpha = 0.67$). Items most frequently endorsed for active events: shopping/buying things, helping around the house, exercising and being outside; social events: being with family, laughing, and having meals with family or friends	Preliminary evidence of reliability and construct validity of two separate activity domains (active and social); frequency that people with dementia enjoy active vs social events is not uniform to either person or care partner characteristics, for example, people with lower cognitive impairment and mild depression could benefit from engaging in active events, whereas social events may be more appropriate for a person with dementia who has more education

activity), and the physical and social environment (Crepeau & Schell, 2009; Padilla, 2011). A person with dementia may experience challenges in some of these areas, which may limit their ability to participate in leisure activities. Anecdotally, this is often viewed by family members as the person no longer wanting to do their previously enjoyed activities, however, it may just be that the person can no longer initiate or engage with the activity in its original form. Modifying the demands of an activity can enable a person to continue to participate in valued leisure activities (Padilla, 2011).

Ultimately, the aim should be for the person to engage in an activity and achieve "flow" in doing (Reid, 2011); the outcome of the activity is not the objective. In fact, as little as 20 min engagement with a meaningful activity can make a difference: one study showed that after 4 months of participating in the Tailored Activity Program, people living with dementia showed greater activity engagement and ability to keep busy, while family members spent fewer hours doing things for their loved one and fewer hours "on duty" (Gitlin et al., 2008). Table 2 outlines a range of factors to consider when modifying an activity to match a person's abilities.

Many of these factors were used in Case 2 (see below). In this example, the care partner engaged in an occupational therapy activity-based intervention commented on how useful it was to learn how to break down an activity, and that as a care partner she tended to over- or underestimate her husband's abilities, which had impacted on his ability to successfully engage in activities.

Engagement in leisure activities allows the person with dementia to enhance their sense of belonging and identity, and provides an opportunity for their family members to perceive their supporting role more positively (Carbonneau, Caron, & Desrosiers, 2010; Dal Bello-Haas, O'Connell, Morgan, & Crossley, 2014; DiLauro et al., 2017). Improving the way family members view their role in engaging the person in leisure activities can ultimately improve the communication dynamics and the ongoing caregiving relationship (Barrado-Martin, Heward, Polman, & Nyman, 2019; DiLauro et al., 2017).

Conclusions and key recommendations

Engagement in leisure activities and pleasant events is a fundamental human right for people living with dementia. Interviewing the person with dementia and the family member, assessing functional cognition and using the Pleasant Events Schedule will identify interests and abilities to help

Table 2 Considerations to support participation in leisure activities.

Factor	Strategies to support engagement
Person with dementia	• Understand preferences, i.e., what does the person want to do, what did they used to enjoy doing, what do they enjoy doing now? (use the PES-AD) • Understand abilities, i.e., what is the person able to do? (Assess functional cognition; see Wesson & Giles, 2019)

Activity	• Break down an activity into separate steps, or "chunking" of actions; identify cognitive and physical components, and where task breakdown occurs. Replace or alter cognitively-difficult steps as necessary
	• Set up activity before introducing to person
	• Simplify the activity by (see Gitlin & Piersol, 2014 for further strategies):
	  • Reducing number of steps required, e.g., put the load of washing on and allow the person to unload and hang out the laundry
	  • Making the cues or objects clearer, or more visible/bigger, e.g., using color contrast to highlight relevant objects

Family members and support people	• Education on recognizing the current abilities of the person, including appropriate and inappropriate times to introduce an activity for their person on a day-to-day basis. Understanding the person's level of functioning means the family member can change their expectations around engagement, which can ultimately reduce frustration (O'Connor et al., 2016) • Training for family members in how to break an activity down into manageable steps and to provide appropriate cues can ultimately support quality of life for both the person with dementia and their family members (Padilla, 2011)
Communication	• Verbal cues and reinforcements to let the person know they should keep going, and/or are doing the activity correctly • Communicate face-to-face with the person • Simple instructions, one at a time, often with a demonstration at the same time • When asking the person a question, provide limited options e.g. "would you like to paint or go for a walk?" Too many choices and open-ended questions (what would you like to do?) can be overwhelming

Environment	• Reduce distractions by ensuring a clear space in activity area
	• Adequate lighting is crucial
	• Match to person's abilities and preferences, e.g.,
	  • go out to dinner earlier so there are fewer people and less noise in the restaurant
	  • if the person has "utilization behavior" (compulsion to interact with objects in view; Pandey & Sarma, 2015), provide one activity-related item at a time to support engagement

Table 2   Considerations to support participation in leisure activities.—cont'd

Factor	Strategies to support engagement
Technology	• Introduce technology as required to support activity engagement, e.g., • Timer to support cooking • iPad to facilitate playing sudoku, or Skyping family and friends • Computer-based cognitive recreation for enjoyment and stimulation

frame the activity and approach to implementation. This strengths-based approach is essential and activities should match a person's abilities as well as their preferences, routines, and habits. Emerging evidence of interventions supports the important role for the care partner in implementing relevant strategies to engage their family member in leisure activities (Laver, Dyer, Whitehead, Clemson, & Crotty, 2016).

Case studies

Case 1: Jack and Ursula: The just right challenge

Jack, who is aged 80 years, has vascular dementia and lives with his wife Ursula. Jack has been living with dementia for a few years and needs assistance with his basic activities of daily living like showering and dressing. When they engaged in the Tailored Activity Program (an occupational therapy activity-based intervention; O'Connor et al., 2019), Ursula was initially skeptical about being able to find any activities for Jack to do, and was aware she had taken over most tasks for him. She said it was "easier for him to sit on the couch, while I get on with things around the house." Indeed, much of Jack's time was spent sitting on the couch, looking out the window, or rummaging through drawers and closets.

The intervention goal was to introduce activities that Jack could do and enjoy, which matched his interests and abilities, and to help Ursula to recognize and support his retained abilities. Jack used to be an operator on the stock exchange, and enjoyed keeping things orderly, so sorting coins ($2 \times$ denominations) was established as his first activity. This was within his abilities (Jack scored 3.4 on the Allen's Cognitive Level Scale; Allen, Earhart, & Blue, 1992) as Jack was able to distinguish one coin from the other, meaning the coins were sorted, and he enjoyed repeating this process over and over.

Ursula collected coins for the task, but ended up collecting two denominations that are visually quite similar (AU $1 and 10c). Despite this, Jack

(Continued)

Case 1: Jack and Ursula: The just right challenge—cont'd

still really engaged with the activity, looking carefully at each coin individually, stating "well, this is a tough job." Rather than sorting the coins into the pots provided as originally intended, Jack sorted the coins into rows, which provided a good example to Ursula on relaxing the rules around an activity. Jack enjoyed sorting the coins; he talked about the coins and chuckled to himself a few times during the activity.

Ursula was excited about Jack's engagement with the activity, and between therapist visits introduced the activity using 3×denominations. Ursula reported that when Jack sat for the activity this time, he just looked at all of the coins and made comments such as "Why have we got these? Where did these come from?" Once Ursula understood Jack's abilities were better suited to sorting two denominations, she reestablished the activity using two distinct denominations (the larger AU 50c and small 10c) and Jack engaged happily for up to 60 min in one sitting, indicating his preference to focus on simple repetitive actions. Ursula observed that Jack seemed pleased when he'd finished sorting the coins into rows and that he'd stay sitting there and look at them all like "he's looking at his work." Following this activity, Jack enjoyed carrying some of the coins around in his pocket and jiggling them. Ursula commented that she finally realized what was meant by providing the "right fit" of challenge for Jack.

Case 2: Richard and Helen: Goals for both person with dementia and care partner

Richard, aged 66 years, had to stop work as a doctor and was diagnosed with frontotemporal dementia 6 months ago. Richard and his wife Helen were both struggling to come to terms with his diagnosis, and engaged in an activity-based occupational therapy intervention (the Tailored Activity Program) for support. Since diagnosis, Richard had reduced self-confidence as he felt that every appointment they attended brought more bad news. Richard was quiet and withdrawn but would engage if addressed directly. Helen was finding it difficult to adjust to Richard's changing abilities, once commenting she was finding his slowed pace of doing things a challenge.

During the assessment process, Helen commented on the child-like nature of an assessment task, which Richard later showed Helen with pride telling her he "did well!" At that point, Helen realized that her prior comments could have been more supportive, and it became clear to her that Richard enjoyed having an activity that was within his skillset, and that he was very responsive to being praised for doing something well.

Case 2: Richard and Helen: Goals for both person with dementia and care partner—cont'd

Helping Richard to successfully engage in enjoyable activities and supporting Helen to develop caring skills that would be complementary to her role as Richard's wife became the primary aims for intervention.

Helen and Richard had previously enjoyed archery together on a holiday in Indonesia, and they decided that this would be a good activity for them to take up together. Richard was enthusiastic about archery; he became very animated throughout the session, which was repeated when discussing their archery experience during the next therapy appointment. Helen also enjoyed this activity with Richard very much, reporting that they laughed together and it helped them to reconnect. Helen commented she was "so happy to see him… he's chatting, smiling, and happy in his face" (O'Connor et al., 2019), and that she felt Richard had been smiling more in general and seemed to have increased self-confidence.

References

Allen, C. K., Earhart, C. A., & Blue, T. (1992). *Occupational therapy treatment goals for the physically and cognitively disabled.* Bethesda, MD: American Occupational Therapy Association.

Amspoker, A. B., Hersch, G., Snow, A. L., Wilson, N., Morgan, R. O., Sansgiry, S., & Kunik, M. E. (2019). A psychometric evaluation of the pleasant events schedule–Alzheimer's disease (short version): Among a veteran population. *Journal of Applied Gerontology, 38*(5), 673–693. https://doi.org/10.1177/0733464817690675.

Barrado-Martin, Y., Heward, M., Polman, R., & Nyman, S. R. (2019). Acceptability of a dyadic tai chi intervention for older people living with dementia and their informal carers. *Journal of Aging and Physical Activity, 27*(2), 166–183. https://doi.org/10.1123/japa.2017-0267.

Brodaty, H., & Arasaratnam, C. (2012). Meta-analysis of nonpharmacological interventions for neuropsychiatric symptoms of dementia. *American Journal of Psychiatry, 169*(9), 946–953. https://doi.org/10.1176/appi.ajp.2012.11101529.

Buettner, L. L., Lundegren, H., Lago, D., Farrell, P., & Smith, R. (1996). Therapeutic recreation as an intervention for persons with dementia and agitation: An efficacy study. *American Journal of Alzheimer's Disease & Other Dementias, 11*(5), 4–12.

Bundy, A. C., du Toit, S., & Clemson, L. M. (2018). Leisure. In B. Bonder, & V. Bello-Haasanina (Eds.), *Functional performance in older adults* (4th ed.). PA: F.A. Davis (chapter 19).

Carbonneau, H., Caron, C., & Desrosiers, J. (2010). Development of a conceptual framework of positive aspects of caregiving in dementia. *Dementia, 9*(3), 327–353.

Carbonneau, H., Caron, C., & Desrosiers, J. (2011). Effects of an adapted leisure education program as a means of support for caregivers of people with dementia. *Archives of Gerontology and Geriatrics, 53*(1), 31–39.

Chiu, Y. C., Huang, C. Y., Kolanowski, A. M., Huang, H. L., Shyu, Y., Lee, S. H., … Hsu, W. C. (2013). The effects of participation in leisure activities on neuropsychiatric symptoms of persons with cognitive impairment: A cross-sectional study. *International Journal of Nursing Studies, 50*(10), 1314–1325. https://doi.org/10.1016/j.ijnurstu.2013.01.002.

Chiu, Y. C., Shyu, Y. I., Liang, J., & Huang, H. L. (2008). Measure of quality of life for Taiwanese persons with early to moderate dementia and related factors. *International Journal of Geriatric Psychiatry, 23*, 580–585.

Clare, L., Kudlicka, A., Oyebode, J. R., Jones, R. W., Bayer, A., Leroi, I., … Woods, B. (2019). Individual goal-oriented cognitive rehabilitation to improve everyday functioning for people with early-stage dementia: A multicentre randomised controlled trial (the GREAT trial). *International Journal of Geriatric Psychiatry*, *34*(5), 709–721. https://doi.org/10.1002/gps.5076.

Cohen-Mansfield, J., Dakheel-Ali, M., & Marx, M. S. (2009). Engagement in persons with dementia: The concept and its measurement. *American Journal of Geriatric Psychiatry*, *17*, 299–307.

Cohen-Mansfield, J., Marx, M. S., Thein, K., & Dakheel-Ai, M. (2010). The impact of past and present preferences on stimulus engagement in nursing home residents with dementia. *Aging & Mental Health*, *14*(1), 67–73. https://doi.org/10.1080/13607860902845574.

Connell, B. R., Sanford, J. A., & Lewis, D. (2007). Therapeutic effects of an outdoor activity program on nursing home residents with dementia. *Journal of Housing for the Elderly*, *21*, 194–209.

Crepeau, E. B., & Schell, B. A. B. (2009). Analyzing occupations and activity. In E. B. Crepeau, E. S. Cohn, & B. A. B. Schell (Eds.), *Willard & Spackman's occupational therapy* (11th ed.). Baltimore: Lippincott Williams & Wilkins.

Dal Bello-Haas, V. P. M., O'Connell, M. E., Morgan, D. G., & Crossley, M. (2014). Lessons learned: Feasibility and acceptability of a telehealth-delivered exercise intervention for rural-dwelling individuals with dementia and their caregivers. *Rural and Remote Health*, *14*(3), 2715.

DiLauro, M., Pereira, A., Carr, J., Chiu, M., & Wesson, V. (2017). Spousal caregivers and persons with dementia: Increasing participation in shared activities among hospital-based dementia support program participants. *Dementia*, *16*(1), 9–28.

Eslinger, P., & Damsio, A. (1986). Preserved motor learning in Alzheimer's disease: Implications for anatomy and behavior. *Journal of Neuroscience*, *6*(10), 3006–3009.

Fitzsimmons, S., & Buettner, L. L. (2002). Therapeutic recreation interventions for need-driven dementia-compromised behaviors in community-dwelling elders. *American Journal of Alzheimer's Disease & Other Dementias*, *17*(6), 367–381.

Gitlin, L. N., & Piersol, C. V. (2014). *A caregiver's guide to dementia: Using activities and other strategies to prevent, reduce and manage behavioral symptoms* (1st ed.). Philadelphia: Camino Books Inc.

Gitlin, L. N., Winter, L., Burke, J., Chernett, N., Dennis, M. P., & Huack, W. W. (2008). Tailored activities to manage neuropsychiatric behaviors in persons with dementia and reduce caregiver burden: A randomized pilot study. *American Journal of Geriatric Psychiatry*, *16*(3), 229–239. https://doi.org/10.1097/JGP.0b013e318160da72.

Hammell, K. W. (2009). Self-care, productivity, and leisure, or dimensions of occupational experience? Rethinking occupational "categories". *Canadian Journal of Occupational Therapy*, *76*(2), 107–114. https://doi.org/10.1177/000841740907600208.

Holthe, T., Thorsen, K., & Josephsson, S. (2007). Occupational patterns of people with dementia in residential care: An ethnographic study. *Scandinavian Journal of Occupational Therapy*, *14*, 96–107.

Innes, A., Page, S. J., & Cutler, C. (2016). Barriers to leisure participation for people with dementia and their carers: An exploratory analysis of carer and people with dementia's experiences. *Dementia*, *15*(6), 1643–1665.

Kovach, C. R., & Magliocco, J. S. (1998). Late-stage dementia and participation in therapeutic activities. *Applied Nursing Research*, *11*(4), 167–173.

Laver, K., Dyer, S., Whitehead, C., Clemson, L., & Crotty, M. (2016). Interventions to delay functional decline in people with dementia: A systematic review of systematic reviews. *British Medical Journal*, *6*(e010767). https://doi.org/10.1136/bmjopen-2015-010767.

Levy, L., & Burns, T. (2005). Cognitive disabilities reconsidered: Rehabilitation older adults with dementia. In *Cognition & occupation across the life span: Models for intervention in occupational therapy*. Bethesda, MD: AOTA.

Logsdon, R. G., & Teri, L. (1997). The pleasant events schedule-AD: Psychometric properties and relationship to depression and cognition in Alzheimer's disease patients. *Gerontologist*, *37*(1), 40–45. https://doi.org/10.1093/geront/37.1.40.

Low, L. F., Swaffer, K., McGrath, M., & Brodaty, H. (2018). Do people with early stage dementia experience prescribed disengagement? A systematic review of qualitative studies. *International Psychogeriatrics*, *30*(6), 807–831.

Marshall, M. J., & Hutchinson, S. A. (2001). A critique of research on the use of activities with persons with Alzheimer's disease: A systematic literature review. *Journal of Advanced Nursing*, *35*(4), 488–496.

Meeks, S., Shah, S. N., & Ramsey, S. K. (2009). The pleasant events schedule—Nursing home version: A useful tool for behavioral interventions in long-term care. *Aging & Mental Health*, *13*(3), 445–455. https://doi.org/10.1080/13607860802534617.

Mioshi, E., Foxe, D., Leslie, F., Savage, S., Hsieh, S., Miller, L., … Piguet, O. (2013). The impact of dementia severity on caregiver burden in frontotemporal dementia and Alzheimer disease. *Alzheimer Disease and Associated Disorders*, *27*(1), 68–73. https://doi.org/10.1097/WAD.0b013e318247a0bc.

O'Connor, C. M., Clemson, L., Brodaty, H., Low, L. F., Jeon, Y. H., Gitlin, L. N., … Mioshi, E. (2019). The tailored activity program (TAP) to address behavioral disturbances in frontotemporal dementia: A feasibility and pilot study. *Disability and Rehabilitation*, *41*(3), 299–310. https://doi.org/10.1080/09638288.2017.1387614.

O'Connor, C. M., Clemson, L., Brodaty, H., Gitlin, L. N., Piguet, O., & Mioshi, E. (2016). Enhancing caregivers' understanding of dementia and tailoring activities in frontotemporal dementia: Two case studies. *Disability and Rehabilitation*, *38*(7), 704–714. https://doi.org/10.3109/09638288.2015.1055375.

O'Connor, C. M., Clemson, L., da Silva, T. B. L., Piguet, O., Hodges, J. R., & Mioshi, E. (2013). Enhancement of carer skills and patient function in the non-pharmacological management of frontotemporal dementia (FTD): A call for randomised controlled studies. *Dementia & Neuropsychologia*, *7*(2), 143–150.

Padilla, R. (2011). Effectiveness of interventions designed to modify the activity demands of the occupations of self-care and leisure for people with Alzheimer's disease and related dementias. *American Journal of Occupational Therapy*, *65*, 523–532. https://doi.org/10.5014/ajot.2011.002618.

Pandey, S., & Sarma, N. (2015). Utilization behavior. *Annals of Indian Academy of Neurology*, *18*(2), 235–237.

Perrin, T. (2000). Doing and being in dementia: A return journey? *Alzheimer's Care Quarterly*, *1*(2), 29–37.

Phinney, A., Chaudhury, H., & O'Connor, D. L. (2007). Doing as much as I can do: The meaning of activity for people with dementia. *Aging and Mental Health*, *11*(4), 384–393.

Pollard, D. V. (2007). *Empowering caregivers: Relevant lifestyle profiles* (2nd ed.). Monona, WI: SelectOne Rehab.

Reid, D. (2011). Mindfulness and flow in occupational engagement: Presence in doing. *Canadian Journal of Occupational Therapy*, *78*(1), 50–56.

Schreiner, A. S., Yamamoto, E., & Shiotani, H. (2005). Positive affect among nursing home residents with Alzheimer's dementia: The effect of recreational activity. *Aging & Mental Health*, *9*(2), 129–134.

Swaffer, K. (2015). Dementia and prescribed disengagementTM. *Dementia*, *14*, 3–6.

Teri, L., & Logsdon, R. G. (1991). Identifying pleasant activities for Alzheimer's disease patients: The pleasant events schedule-AD. *Gerontologist*, *31*(1), 124–127.

Volicer, L., Simard, J., Pupa, J. H., Medrek, R., & Riordan, M. E. (2006). Effects of continuous activity programming on behavioral symptoms of dementia. *Journal of the American Medical Directors Association*, *7*, 426–431.

Wesson, J., Clemson, L., Brodaty, H., & Reppermund, S. (2016). Estimating functional cognition in older adults using observational assessments of task performance in complex everyday activities: A systematic review and evaluation of measurement properties. *Neuroscience and Biobehavioral Reviews, 68*, 335–360. https://doi.org/10.1016/j.neubiorev.2016.05.024.

Wesson, J. G., & Giles, G. M. (2019). Understanding functional cognition. In T. J. Wolf, D. F. Edwards, & G. M. Giles (Eds.), *Functional cognition and occupational therapy. A practical approach to treating individuals with cognitive loss* (pp. 7–20). Bethesda, MD: American Occupational Therapy Association, Inc.

Wolverson, E. L., Clarke, C., & Moniz-Cook, E. D. (2016). Living positively with dementia: A systematic review and synthesis of the qualitative literature. *Aging & Mental Health, 20*(7), 676–699.

Zanetti, O., Zanieri, G., Di Giovanni, G., DeVreese, L. P., Pezzini, A., Metitieri, T., & Trabucchi, M. (2001). Effectiveness of procedural memory stimulation in mild Alzheimer's disease patients: A controlled study. *Neuropsychological Rehabilitation, 11*(3–4), 263–272.

CHAPTER 7

Rehabilitation to improve psychological well-being in people with dementia

Lee-Fay Low[a], Monica Cations[b], Deborah Koder[c], and Annaliese Blair[d]

[a]Faculty of Medicine and Health, University of Sydney, Sydney, NSW, Australia
[b]College of Education, Psychology and Social Work, Flinders University, Adelaide, SA, Australia
[c]Department of Psychological Sciences, Swinburne University of Technology, Melbourne, VIC, Australia
[d]Aged Care Evaluation Unit, Southern NSW Local Health District, Queanbeyan, NSW, Australia

Introduction

What is psychological well-being?

Psychological well-being relates to functioning well within one's self and in relationships with others (Burns, 2017). Effective psychological functioning includes personal growth, having a sense of control or mastery, a sense of purpose, and meaningful social relationships (Huppert, 2009). However, psychological well-being is not the absence of ill-being, as the experience of painful emotions is a normal part of life (Huppert, 2009). Well-being is dependent on the balance between individuals' psychological, cognitive, social, and physical resource pool and the challenges they face (Dodge, Daly, Huyton, & Sanders, 2012). Dementia influences well-being via its impact on such resources.

Conceptualizing psychological well-being in dementia

Studies suggest that people living with dementia have psychological needs similar to the rest of the population. Studies involving people with dementia have found positive associations between higher levels of psychological well-being (e.g., self-esteem, optimism, self-efficacy, and the absence of depression and anxiety) and higher quality of life and life satisfaction, beyond the association with cognitive functioning (Clare et al., 2019; Lamont et al., 2019; Martyr et al., 2018). People with dementia want interventions that enhance their well-being, confidence, health, social participation, and human rights (Øksnebjerg et al., 2018).

Dementia Rehabilitation
https://doi.org/10.1016/B978-0-12-818685-5.00007-6
111

Levels of psychological well-being in dementia

There has been no comprehensive study of psychological well-being in dementia. However, available data suggest that many people with dementia experience suboptimal psychological well-being.

Depression and anxiety

Depression and anxiety present differently in older than younger people. Older people may not acknowledge mood and sleep changes, and concentration, memory, and loss of interest can be incorrectly attributed to old age (Fiske, Wetherell, & Gatz, 2009). There is some evidence that depression, anxiety, and other neuropsychiatric symptoms can be attributed to dementia-related neuropathology (Ehrenberg et al., 2018), and weaker evidence that depression is a reaction to the dementia diagnosis (Bennett & Thomas, 2014).

The prevalence of depression in people with any type of dementia was 25% pooled across 104 studies, significantly higher than the 13% prevalence in the general community from 23 studies (Kuring, Mathias, & Ward, 2018). The prevalence of anxiety was 14% in people with any dementia pooled across 30 studies, which did not differ significantly from the 3% rate for healthy controls from 5 studies (Kuring et al., 2018).

Behavior as an indicator of ill-being in dementia

Common behavioral changes in dementia such as aggression and agitation are often expressions of physical or psychological distress (Algase et al., 1996). Depending on the cause of the behaviors, psychological approaches may be appropriate in treating the underlying distress [e.g., calling out may be an expression of loneliness; aggression may be an expression of fear (Koder, 2018)].

Positive emotions

Dementia research has predominantly focused on negative emotions with little information on happiness or other positive emotions (Petty, Dening, Griffiths, & Coleston, 2016). A few studies suggest that there are low rates of expression of positive emotions in residential care settings. An observational study of 406 nursing home residents with dementia (10,339 min total during meal, free time, and structured activities) found that 6% of time residents appeared happy, 84% of time they had neutral affect, 7% of time they appeared anxious, and 2% of time they appeared sad (Casey, Low, Goodenough, Fletcher, & Brodaty, 2014). Another observational study reported that 44% of residents expressed happiness only during recreation (Schreiner, Yamamoto, & Shiotani, 2005).

Feelings about one's self, mastery, and personal growth

People who are aware of their diagnosis of dementia rate their psychological quality of life lower than those without dementia and those unaware of their diagnosis (Stites, Karlawish, Harkins, Rubright, & Wolk, 2017). After diagnosis, people with dementia struggle with self-identity, control and status, stigma, and hope for the future (Low, Swaffer, McGrath, & Brodaty, 2018). However, they continue to reshape their stories and find ongoing meaning in life (Holst & Hollberg, 2003). Qualitative studies have also highlighted that people living positively with dementia use personal strengths to face and "transcend the condition, and seek ways to maintain identity and achieve personal growth" (Wolverson, Clarke, & Moniz-Cook, 2016, p. 676).

Social relationships

A review of subjective social experiences of people with dementia highlighted that the perceived stigma or negative reactions of other people can diminish well-being (Patterson, Clarke, Wolverson, & Moniz-Cook, 2018). People with mild dementia say that friendship is important to them, and that while some friends fall away, their remaining friends can become closer (Harris, 2013). People with dementia report fewer friends (Balouch, Rifaat, Chen, & Tabet, 2019) and residents with dementia in nursing homes have few, if any, friends (Casey, Low, Jeon, & Brodaty, 2016).

Assessment

People with dementia differ in their ability to express their needs because of premorbid abilities, type, and stage of dementia. A personalized and collaborative approach to assessment of psychological well-being should be undertaken involving the person with dementia, family, and care staff. Specifically having therapeutic goals as the end point of the initial assessment process can be difficult for people with dementia (Anderson, Wickramariyaratne, & Blair, 2016; Blair & Bird, 2016). We suggest having organic conversations about goals throughout assessment and ongoing therapy. Small, concrete behavioral and activity-based goals might be more acceptable, at least initially (Chellingsworth, Kishita, & Laidlaw, 1998). Woods, Woods, and Clare (2008) urge therapists to consider outcomes that will be of value to people with dementia. Standardized reliable change indexes may not be suitable, given that cognition will decline over time. Stabilization of affective symptoms or well-being, maintenance of function, or improved coping may be more appropriate.

Assessment tools

Validated self-completed tools to assess mood include the Geriatric Depression Scale (Yesavage et al., 1982), Geriatric Anxiety Scale (Segal, June, Payne, Coolidge, & Yochim, 2010), and Geriatric Anxiety Inventory (Pachana et al., 2007). Nonverbal scales are also available to assess low mood (Lorish & Maisiak, 1986) and anxiety (Williams, Morlock, & Feltner, 2010). Clinician administered tools include the Cornell Scale for Depression in Dementia (CSDD, Alexopolous, Abrams, Young, & Shamoian, 1988).

Current approaches and evidence

Approaches to improving psychological well-being in people with dementia can be broadly classified into psychological approaches (a combination of talking therapies and behavioral approaches), activity-based interventions, and medication. We predominantly focus on talking therapies in this chapter. Interventions to improve psychological well-being in people with dementia might involve one-on-one therapy but often include care partners and family, paid staff, and volunteers.

Psychological approaches for dementia—Research evidence

The use of psychological approaches with people with dementia is a young science and few high-quality, adequately powered clinical trials have been published.

Manualized psychotherapy
Cognitive behavior therapy

Cognitive behavior therapy (CBT) is a structured, collaborative therapy that targets maladaptive thoughts and behaviors to improve mood and reduce distress. A recent systematic review concluded that CBT can be effective in reducing depression and anxiety symptoms among people with mild to moderate dementia (Tay, Subramaniam, & Oei, 2019). The only high-quality trial randomized 201 participants with mild dementia (MMSE ≥ 21) to usual care or 12 weekly, 60-min sessions of combined neurorehabilitation and CBT. Therapy focused on behavioral strategies such as day structuring, activity planning, establishing routines, and incorporating external memory aids into everyday life (Kurz et al., 2012). The intervention resulted in significantly improved self-reported quality of life across the whole sample and reduced depressive symptoms among female participants.

A pilot randomized-controlled trial of 50 older people with mild to moderate dementia (MMSE > 16) found a significant reduction in depression and anxiety after 10 sessions of adapted-CBT, which was sustained at 6-month follow-up (Spector et al., 2015). The authors noted that increasing severity of dementia necessitated increased therapist scaffolding, repetition, emphasis on behavioral rather than cognitive techniques, and involvement from family care partners. Several smaller feasibility or pilot studies, all including people with mild to moderate dementia, reported similar results (Burgener, Yang, Gilbert, & Marsh-Yant, 2008; Paukert et al., 2010; Stanley et al., 2013).

Other manualized psychological therapies

The efficacy of other manualized psychological therapies for this population is less clear. Two small studies have assessed the effectiveness of psychodynamic interpersonal therapy (PIT), which focuses on the identification and resolution of interpersonal conflicts that are causing or maintaining distress. One study ($n = 52$) identified a reduction in depression relapse with monthly PIT among older people with both cognitive impairment (MMSE > 17) and Major Depressive Disorder, compared to standard clinical management (Carreira et al., 2008). A second study suggested no effects of PIT for people with mild to moderate dementia who did not have clinical depression (Burns et al., 2005).

Validation therapy (VT) and its extension integrative validation therapy (IVT) were designed specifically for people with advanced dementia with a focus on validating and generalizing (rather than restructuring) the feelings and motivation of the person with dementia using elements from their biography (Erdmann & Schnepp, 2016). However, supportive evidence is limited to small studies linking VT to reductions in behaviors (Tondi, Ribani, Bottazzi, Viscomi, & Vulcano, 2007) and staff satisfaction with the program (Erdmann & Schnepp, 2016).

Three small randomized-controlled trials have demonstrated reduced depressive symptoms in people with dementia after nine to 12 sessions of "problem-focused" or "problem adaptation" therapy in comparison to supportive psychotherapy. Participants and their care partners in these studies were taught structured problem-solving skills to respond to situations of concern and to integrate accommodations for cognitive impairment into daily life (Alexopoulos, Raue, & Areán, 2003; Kiosses, Arean, Teri, & Alexopoulos, 2010; Teri, Logsdon, Uomoto, & McCurry, 1997). "Third wave" mindfulness-based approaches are of increasing interest for people with dementia because they rely less on new learning and recall. Mindfulness-based approaches promote focused attention without judgment of feelings and thoughts. Three small mindfulness-based interventions (all < 32 participants, 6–10 sessions), two of which were conducted in nursing homes, reported a nonsignificant trend toward improved quality of life (Churcher Clarke, Chan, Stott, Royan, & Spector, 2017; Paller et al., 2015; Wilson, Lantz, Buchalter, & McBee, 1997).

Nonmanualized psychotherapy

Generic group psychotherapy for people with mild dementia is supported by a small body of evidence (Cheston, Jones, & Gilliard, 2003; Cheston & Jones, 2009; Gaugler et al., 2011; Logsdon, McCurry, & Teri, 2007; Marshall et al., 2015). These interventions are typically delivered to people with dementia and care partners together and include psychoeducation, mutual support, and group problem-solving.

Some evidence also exists for non-manualized individual counseling techniques. The Danish Alzheimer Intervention Study (DAISY) reported significant improvements in depressive symptoms and quality of life after 12 months of counseling and support groups for people with mild to moderate dementia (MMSE $\geq$ 8) (Waldorff et al., 2012), although the effect was not sustained at 36 months (Phung et al., 2013). Tappen and Williams (2009) (n = 30, MMSE = 0–25) reported that Therapeutic Conversation counseling sessions three times a week for 16 weeks improved mood and decreased depressive symptoms of nursing home residents with Alzheimer's disease compared to usual care.

Peer support

Peer support by people with dementia for others with dementia has the potential to provide emotional and practical support and help with self and group advocacy. It was previously believed that people with dementia were unable to engage in peer support due to cognitive impairments (Kenny et al., 2016). However, observational and qualitative studies suggest that peer support is feasible and may have benefits on social connection, empowerment, and confidence (Femiola & Tilki, 2017; Keyes et al., 2016).

Activity-based therapies

Activity provision provides a sense of control, opportunities for creativity (Nyman & Szymczynska, 2016), and opportunities for positive emotions and social connectedness (Schneider, 2018). However, high-quality evidence that activities improve well-being is scant. A Cochrane review suggested no effect of physical exercise on psychological symptoms and depression (Forbes, Thiessen, Blake, Forbes, & Forbes, 2013). A Cochrane review of reminiscence therapy found no significant effect on depressed mood (10 studies with 973 participants) (O' Philbin, Woods, Farrell, Spector, & Orrell, 2018). A scoping review suggested that, based on small observational studies, intergenerational programs where older people engage with children or youth increase positive emotions, confidence, and sense of purpose for people with dementia (Galbraith, Larkin, Moorhouse, & Oomen, 2015). Qualitative studies indicate that life history books can improve depression for people with dementia and relationships with care partners (Elfrink, Zuidema, Kunz, & Westerhof, 2018).

Medications to promote well-being in people with dementia

A Cochrane review identified little or no effect of antidepressant medications for treating depression in people with dementia (Dudas, Malouf, McCleery, & Dening, 2018). Antidepressant medications with anticholinergic effects (such as tricyclic antidepressants) should be avoided because they can adversely affect cognition (Guideline Adaptation Committee, 2016). Benzodiazepines may be useful for short-term treatment of acute anxiety and sleep problems (Tampi, Tampi, & Balachandran, 2017) but are associated with falls, worsening cognition, respiratory depression, and paradoxical disinhibition when used long term (Defrancesco, Marksteiner, Fleischhacker, & Blasko, 2015).

Summary of evidence

Most intervention studies have focused on low mood or depression, and with few studies measuring other aspects of psychological well-being, interpersonal functioning has been particularly neglected. Randomized controlled trials suggest that manualized psychological treatments (e.g., CBT, PIT) and nonmanualized supportive counseling individually and in groups can promote psychological well-being in people with dementia. Peer support is feasible but there is no evidence of efficacy. There is limited evidence that activity-based programs or psychotropic medications improve psychological well-being.

See Fig. 1 for an overview of components of psychological well-being and demonstrated and hypothesized effects of different therapies.

Case study 1—Mr G

Mr. G, 78 years, was referred to the psychologist for anxiety. He had been diagnosed with mixed Alzheimer's and vascular dementia 6 months ago

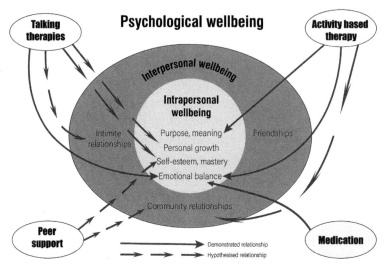

Fig. 1 Components of psychological well-being and demonstrated and hypothesized impact of therapies for people with dementia.

following 5 years of short-term memory and word-finding difficulties. He lived with his wife in their own home. He had worked as a barrister and was finding his naming difficulties challenging. Physical comorbidities included poor mobility because of osteoarthritis in both knees, congestive cardiac failure, and diabetes.

Case conceptualization: Mr. G had low self-confidence because of difficulty adjusting to reduction of independence and decline in verbal skills. There was evidence of a sharp decline in engagement in previously enjoyable activities and subsequent low mood. He tended to avoid activities that might expose the extent of his decline: for example, previously a daily tennis player, he spent his days housebound saying that he was unable to play tennis "as good as I used to." Mr. G was becoming increasingly isolated, avoiding socializing ("I can't remember his name, it's embarrassing!"). His wife was encouraging but felt frustrated.

Intervention: Multimodal therapy

Mr. G was able to identify the first signs of feeling anxious when confronted by cognitive difficulties, calling them "the Wobblies." Psychoeducation on the impact of his anxiety on memory and recall, and brief slow breathing helped lower anxiety. Mrs. G prompted use of slow breathing with illustrated instruction cards. Each session began with relaxation practice and used Mr. G's words to describe his sensations.

Mr. G was encouraged to discuss his frustration. His change in self-identity ("I'm no good"), negative self-view, and dichotomous thinking style (incompetence means not able to exercise) was addressed through validation, by giving examples of "competence" and focusing on intact skills. Once he was able to recognize that he was able to do some parts of exercise safely, activity scheduling was introduced. Mr. G was willing to see an occupational therapist and attend group fitness classes. This allowed him to socialize regularly and provided respite for Mrs. G.

His anxiety secondary to expressive language problems was partly addressed via a diary where he wrote new events, meetings, and names. He was prompted to carry this diary and refer to it in social situations. Cognitive restructuring helped challenge his belief that he was incompetent when he used memory aids, comparing them to his four-wheel walker for mobility.

Outcomes: After 4 months of therapy, Mr. G's self-rated anxiety was significantly lower, scores on the CSDD significantly improved.

Case study 2—Ms J

Ms. J was a 70-year-old divorced woman referred to the psychologist at a residential aged care facility. Her behavior would vacillate between overactive, intrusive, and loud interactions with others to lying on her bed in the dark for hours, refusing to speak. She repeatedly asked which staff were taking care of her that day and hoarded tissues and continence pads. Unmet requests resulted in yelling, pushing others with her walker, and blocking staff from leaving rooms.

Case conceptualization: Assessment was multimodal including rapport building with Ms. J, cognitive testing, behavioral monitoring with staff, behavioral observations, history taking from family, and review of medical records. Ms. J was premorbidly an intelligent, lively, well-traveled woman who worked in academic research. In her mid-60s, after a significant period of stress caring for her dying partner and parents and her own health difficulties, Ms. J developed significant obsessive, anxious thoughts and was eventually hospitalized with psychotic depression. She was given various diagnoses over several years including obsessive compulsive disorder, psychotic depression, schizophrenia, and dementia. Cognitive testing and a review of her history and current behavior suggested frontotemporal dementia.

Intervention

Ms. J's treatment involved multiple approaches:
1. Individual counseling: Initially, Ms. J refused to engage with the therapist, lying on her bed with eyes closed, restricted affect, and minimal

verbal responses. Having short but frequent rapport building sessions enabled assessment, as well as developing and implementing Ms. J's behavioral goals. Ms. J was eventually able to articulate her wish (mostly via her behavior and knowledge of her premorbid preferences/strengths, rather than her words) for positive social interactions and she and facility staff were supported to gradually increase her behavioral activation. She began leaving her room for short periods, then accompanying staff to take her washing to the laundry and later on bus trips. She gradually transitioned from being supported by the psychologist to a weekly volunteer visitor for social conversation and outings.

2. Working with staff:
   a. Behavior support: Staff assisted in developing a detailed plan for responding to Ms. J's behaviors with cue cards prompting how to respond if asked for supplies or confronted with aggression.
   b. Supportive counseling: Staff stress was reflected and validated. Staff were provided with information about stress reduction and managers rotated staff to give them breaks.
   c. Education and empathy building: Once staff understood the unique difficulties caused by frontal lobe impairment, they could see how Mrs. J's behavior was expressing her needs rather than a personal attack or "intentionally manipulative." Staff skillfully managed Ms. J's anxiety about increasing activities, firstly finding meaningful tasks for her (e.g., taking washing to the laundry, setting the table) and gradually increasing social activities. Staff were regularly observed laughing with Ms. J post-intervention.

3. Medication review—Ms J had been on an antidepressant and antipsychotic for over 3 years. After medication review by the mental health team, her antipsychotic was stopped, resulting in a marked increase in her reactivity.

Outcomes: Ms. J's repetitive questioning and physical aggression reduced from 189 incidents in the 2 weeks pre-intervention to 24 incidents in the 2 weeks after intervention. Her observer rated CSDD improved from 16 to 9. Her sister described her transformation as a miracle.

Conducting psychological therapy with people with dementia

Box 1 provides a summary of adaptations to psychotherapy to improve applicability for people with dementia. Repetition, modeling, and written instruction are needed where memory impairment is a key feature. Encouraging clients to develop their own memory aids can improve motivation.

Box 1 Adaptations when conducting psychological therapies for people with dementia

Contextual considerations

(i) Ensure understanding of dementia and gerontology, e.g., aging process, common physical, functional, and sensory morbidities

(ii) Understand major historical events for each cohort

(iii) Obtain consent or, as appropriate, verbal or nonverbal assent

(iv) Ideally, therapy occurs within a multidisciplinary team (e.g., pain is managed by a general practitioner, physiotherapist is improving mobility)

(v) Take a systems approach—involve family and/or staff to reinforce and support use of strategies and/or to alter their responses

(vi) Scheduling: Consider transport and mobility, better times of day for the person with dementia, e.g., more frequent, shorter sessions

(vii) Consider self-stigma around age, dementia, and mental health

(viii) Terminology and language should be congruent with recovery principles, be enabling and strength focused, avoid use of terms such as "dementia sufferer"

(ix) Include health promotion incorporating relapse prevention

During sessions

(i) Older people may have lower mental health literacy (Wuthrich & Frei, 2015)—spend time on psychoeducation and building trust

(ii) Consider personal history, trauma history, cultural backgrounds, sexual preferences

(iii) Tailor according to cognitive abilities

(iv) Use the person's priorities, personal biography, personal values, and existing strengths

(v) Stage therapy appropriately

(vi) Address grief and loss

(vii) Take a flexible approach

(viii) Consider scaffolding, a slower pace, repetition of instructions, modeling of behavior

(ix) Behavioral techniques may be more appropriate than cognitive strategies

(x) Simplify materials as required

(xi) Provide written and pictorial summaries of key points in the person's own words or imagery

People with dementia may benefit from a family care partner attending sessions with them to help reinforce the strategies they learn, but this should only occur with their express consent and where it does not undermine individual agency (Boyle, 2014). Therapists should recognize that relationships between people with dementia and their care partners vary in closeness (Fauth et al., 2012) and that shared sessions may not allow the person with dementia to address issues important to them. Case series published by Bird and Blair (2007) and Blair and Bird (2010) provide a range of case conceptualizations and adapted psychological therapies for people with dementia.

System and clinical recommendations

- Poor mental health literacy including treatment efficacy is a barrier to help-seeking and acceptance.
- Health practitioners, including psychologists, can have ageist attitudes and therapeutic nihilism about dementia. Practitioner training should address this.
- Psychology training should include approaches to work with older people and placements with older people. Specialist training should be developed for old age psychologists.
- Funding for psychological services for older people is usually inadequate.
- Rehabilitation programs should consider psychological well-being, including social participation, rather than focusing exclusively on physical health.

Research recommendations

Research should be undertaken in the following areas:
- Assessment and measurement of psychological well-being in dementia beyond depression, including anxiety and interpersonal functioning
- Selecting the most appropriate approach for each person
- Understanding the interrelationships between different aspects of psychological well-being in dementia
- Higher quality evidence for current therapies, including by stage of dementia, and understanding active ingredients
- Understanding the impact of premorbid personality, psychological resilience, and earlier-life trauma on psychological well-being in dementia and how to adapt therapy
- Models of care to support psychological well-being in hospital, community, and residential settings
- Telehealth is promising in assessment of dementia (Kim, Jhoo, & Jang, 2017; Lindauer et al., 2017), and should be investigated as a mode for provision of psychological support for people with dementia

References

Alexopolous, G., Abrams, R., Young, R., & Shamoian, C. (1988). Scale for depression in dementia. *Biological Psychiatry, 23*(3), 271–284.

Alexopoulos, G. S., Raue, P., & Areán, P. (2003). Problem-solving therapy versus supportive therapy in geriatric major depression with executive dysfunction. *American Journal of Geriatric Psychiatry, 11*(1), 46–52.

Algase, D. L., Beck, C., Kolanowski, A., Whall, A., Berent, S., Richards, K., & Beattie, E. (1996). Need-driven dementia-compromised behavior: An alternative view of disruptive behavior. *American Journal of Alzheimer's Disease and Other Dementias, 11*(6), 10–19.

Anderson, K., Wickramariyaratne, T., & Blair, A. (2016). *A feasibility study of group-based cognitive behaviour therapy for older adults in residential care.* https://doi.org/10.1111/cp.12109.

Balouch, S., Rifaat, E., Chen, H. L., & Tabet, N. (2019). Social networks and loneliness in people with Alzheimer's dementia. *International Journal of Geriatric Psychiatry, 34*(5), 666–673. https://doi.org/10.1002/gps.5065.

Bennett, S., & Thomas, A. J. (2014). Depression and dementia: Cause, consequence or co-incidence? *Maturitas, 79*(2), 184–190. https://doi.org/10.1016/j.maturitas.2014.05.009.

Bird, M. J., & Blair, A. C. (2007). Clinical psychology with complex presentations in old age. *Nordic Psychology, 59*(1), 59–74. https://doi.org/10.1027/1901-2276.59.1.59.

Blair, A. C., & Bird, M. J. (2010). Clinical psychology and anxiety and depression in dementia. *Nordic Psychology, 62*(2), 44–54. https://doi.org/10.1027/1901-2276/a000010.

Blair, A. C., & Bird, M. J. (2016). A pilot trial of psychological therapy groups for the very old in residential care: Clinical and logistical issues. *Clinical Psychologist, 20*(2), 68–79. https://doi.org/10.1111/cp.12031.

Boyle, G. (2014). Recognising the agency of people with dementia. *Disability & Society, 29*(7), 1130–1144. https://doi.org/10.1080/09687599.2014.910108.

Burgener, S. C., Yang, Y., Gilbert, R., & Marsh-Yant, S. (2008). The effects of a multi-modal intervention on outcomes of persons with early-stage dementia. *American Journal of Alzheimer's Disease and Other Dementias, 23*(4), 382–394. https://doi.org/10.1177/1533317508317527.

Burns, R. A. (2017). Psychosocial well-being. In N. A. Pachana (Ed.), *Encyclopedia of geropsychology* (pp. 1977–1984). Singapore: Springer Singapore.

Burns, A., Guthrie, E., Marino-Francis, F., Busby, C., Morris, J., Russell, E., ... Byrne, J. (2005). Brief psychotherapy in Alzheimer's disease: Randomised controlled trial. *British Journal of Psychiatry, 187*, 143–147. https://doi.org/10.1192/bjp.187.2.143.

Carreira, K., Miller, M. D., Frank, E., Houck, P. R., Morse, J. Q., Dew, M. A., ... Reynolds, C. F., 3rd. (2008). A controlled evaluation of monthly maintenance interpersonal psychotherapy in late-life depression with varying levels of cognitive function. *International Journal of Geriatric Psychiatry, 23*(11), 1110–1113. https://doi.org/10.1002/gps.2031.

Casey, A. N., Low, L. F., Goodenough, B., Fletcher, J., & Brodaty, H. (2014). Computer-assisted direct observation of behavioral agitation, engagement, and affect in long-term care residents. *Journal of the American Medical Directors Association, 15*(7), 514–520.

Casey, A.-N. S., Low, L.-F., Jeon, Y.-H., & Brodaty, H. (2016). Residents perceptions of friendship and positive social networks within a nursing home. *The Gerontologist, 56*(5), 855–867. https://doi.org/10.1093/geront/gnv146.

Chellingsworth, M., Kishita, N., & Laidlaw, K. (1998). *A Clinician's guide to: Low intensity CBT with older people.* Retrieved from Norwich, UK: https://www.uea.ac.uk/documents/246046/8314842/LICBT_BOOKLET_FINAL_JAN16.pdf/48f28e80-dc02-45b6-91cd-c628d36e8bca.

Cheston, R., & Jones, R. (2009). A small-scale study comparing the impact of psycho-education and exploratory psychotherapy groups on newcomers to a group for people with dementia. *Aging & Mental Health, 13*(3), 420–425. https://doi.org/10.1080/13607860902879409.

Cheston, R., Jones, K., & Gilliard, J. (2003). Group psychotherapy and people with dementia. *Aging & Mental Health*, 7(6), 452–461. https://doi.org/10.1080/136078603100015947.

Churcher Clarke, A., Chan, J. M.Y., Stott, J., Royan, L., & Spector, A. (2017). An adapted mindfulness intervention for people with dementia in care homes: Feasibility pilot study. *International Journal of Geriatric Psychiatry*, 32(12), e123–e131. https://doi.org/10.1002/gps.4669.

Clare, L., Wu, Y. T., Jones, I. R., Victor, C. R., Nelis, S. M., Martyr, A., … Matthews, F. E. (2019). A comprehensive model of factors associated with subjective perceptions of "living well" with dementia: Findings from the IDEAL study. *Alzheimer Disease and Associated Disorders*, 33(1), 36–41. https://doi.org/10.1097/wad.0000000000000286.

Defrancesco, M., Marksteiner, J., Fleischhacker, W.W., & Blasko, I. (2015). Use of benzodiazepines in Alzheimer's disease: A systematic review of literature. *The International Journal of Neuropsychopharmacology*, 18(10). https://doi.org/10.1093/ijnp/pyv055. pyv055.

Dodge, R., Daly, A. P., Huyton, J., & Sanders, L. D. (2012). The challenge of defining wellbeing. 2(3), 222–235. https://doi.org/10.5502/ijw.v2.i3.4.

Dudas, R., Malouf, R., McCleery, J., & Dening, T. (2018). Antidepressants for treating depression in dementia. *Cochrane Database of Systematic Reviews*, 8. https://doi.org/10.1002/14651858.CD003944.pub2.

Ehrenberg, A. J., Suemoto, C. K., Franca Resende, E. P., Petersen, C., Leite, R. E. P., Rodriguez, R. D., … Grinberg, L. T. (2018). Neuropathologic correlates of psychiatric symptoms in Alzheimer's disease. *Journal of Alzheimer's Disease*, 66(1), 115–126. https://doi.org/10.3233/jad-180688.

Elfrink, T. R., Zuidema, S. U., Kunz, M., & Westerhof, G. J. (2018). Life story books for people with dementia: A systematic review. *International Psychogeriatrics*, 30(12), 1797–1811. https://doi.org/10.1017/S1041610218000376.

Erdmann, A., & Schnepp, W. (2016). Conditions, components and outcomes of Integrative Validation Therapy in a long-term care facility for people with dementia. A qualitative evaluation study. *Dementia (London)*, 15(5), 1184–1204. https://doi.org/10.1177/1471301214556489.

Fauth, E., Hess, K., Piercy, K., Norton, M., Corcoran, C., Rabins, P., … Tschanz, J. (2012). Caregivers' relationship closeness with the person with dementia predicts both positive and negative outcomes for caregivers' physical health and psychological well-being. *Aging & Mental Health*, 16(6), 699–711. https://doi.org/10.1080/13607863.2012.678482.

Femiola, C., & Tilki, M. (2017). Dementia peer support: Service delivery for the people, by the people. *Working with Older People*, 21(4), 243–250. https://doi.org/10.1108/WWOP-08-2017-0020.

Fiske, A., Wetherell, J. L., & Gatz, M. (2009). *Depression in Older Adults.*, 5(1), 363–389. https://doi.org/10.1146/annurev.clinpsy.032408.153621.

Forbes, D., Thiessen, E. J., Blake, C. M., Forbes, S. C., & Forbes, S. (2013). Exercise programs for people with dementia. *Cochrane Database of Systematic Reviews*, 4, Cd006489. https://doi.org/10.1002/14651858.CD006489.pub3 (12).

Galbraith, B., Larkin, H., Moorhouse, A., & Oomen, T. (2015). Intergenerational programs for persons with dementia: A scoping review. *Journal of Gerontological Social Work*, 58(4), 357–378. https://doi.org/10.1080/01634372.2015.1008166.

Gaugler, J. E., Gallagher-Winker, K., Kehrberg, K., Lunde, A. M., Marsolek, C. M., Ringham, K., … Barclay, M. (2011). The memory club: Providing support to persons with early-stage dementia and their care partners. *American Journal of Alzheimer's Disease and Other Dementias*, 26(3), 218–226. https://doi.org/10.1177/1533317511399570.

Guideline Adaptation Committee. (2016). *Clinical practice guidelines and principles of care for people with dementia.* Retrieved from Sydney: http://sydney.edu.au/medicine/cdpc/documents/resources/CDPC-Dementia-Recommendations_WEB.pdf.

Harris, P. B. (2013). Dementia and friendship: The quality and nature of the relationships that remain. *International Journal of Aging and Human Development*, 76(2), 141–164. https://doi.org/10.2190/ag.76.2.c.

Holst, G. (2003). Exploring the meaning of everyday life, for those suffering from dementia. *American Journal of Alzheimer's Disease and Other Dementias, 18*(6), 359–365. https://doi.org/10.1177/153331750301800605.

Huppert, F. A. (2009). Psychological well-being: Evidence regarding its causes and consequences. *Applied Psychology: Health and Well-Being, 1*(2), 137–164. https://doi.org/10.1111/j.1758-0854.2009.01008.x.

Kenny, J., Asquith, I., Guss, R., Field, E., Slade, L., Bone, A., ... Norris, C. (2016). Facilitating an evolving service user involvement group for people with dementia: What can we learn? *The Journal of Mental Health Training, Education and Practice, 11*(2), 81–90. https://doi.org/10.1108/jmhtep-09-2015-0046.

Keyes, S. E., Clarke, C. L., Wilkinson, H., Alexjuk, E. J., Wilcockson, J., Robinson, L., ... Cattan, M. (2016). "We're all thrown in the same boat ... ": A qualitative analysis of peer support in dementia care. *Dementia, 15*(4), 560–577. https://doi.org/10.1177/1471301214529575.

Kim, H., Jhoo, J. H., & Jang, J.-W. (2017). The effect of telemedicine on cognitive decline in patients with dementia. *Journal of Telemedicine and Telecare, 23*(1), 149–154. https://doi.org/10.1177/1357633x15615049.

Kiosses, D. N., Arean, P. A., Teri, L., & Alexopoulos, G. S. (2010). Home-delivered problem adaptation therapy (PATH) for depressed, cognitively impaired, disabled elders: A preliminary study. *American Journal of Geriatric Psychiatry, 18*(11), 988–998. https://doi.org/10.1097/JGP.0b013e3181d6947d.

Koder, D. (2018). The use of cognitive behaviour therapy in the management of BPSD in dementia (innovative practice). *Dementia, 17*(2), 227–233. https://doi.org/10.1177/1471301216636261.

Kuring, J. K., Mathias, J. L., & Ward, L. (2018). Prevalence of depression, anxiety and PTSD in people with dementia: A systematic review and meta-analysis. *Neuropsychology Review, 28*(4), 393–416. https://doi.org/10.1007/s11065-018-9396-2.

Kurz, A., Thone-Otto, A., Cramer, B., Egert, S., Frolich, L., Gertz, H. J., ... Werheid, K. (2012). CORDIAL: Cognitive rehabilitation and cognitive-behavioral treatment for early dementia in Alzheimer disease: A multicenter, randomized, controlled trial. *Alzheimer Disease and Associated Disorders, 26*(3), 246–253. https://doi.org/10.1097/WAD.0b013e318231e46e.

Lamont, R. A., Nelis, S. M., Quinn, C., Martyr, A., Rippon, I., Kopelman, M. D., ... Clare, L. (2019). Psychological predictors of 'living well' with dementia: findings from the IDEAL study. *Aging & Mental Health*, 1–9. https://doi.org/10.1080/13607863.2019.1566811.

Lindauer, A., Seelye, A., Lyons, B., Dodge, H. H., Mattek, N., Mincks, K., ... Erten-Lyons, D. (2017). *Dementia care comes home: Patient and caregiver assessment via telemedicine.* https://doi.org/10.1093/geront/gnw206.

Logsdon, R. G., McCurry, S. M., & Teri, L. (2007). Evidence-based interventions to improve quality of life for individuals with dementia. *Alzheimer's Care Today, 8*(4), 309–318.

Lorish, C. D., & Maisiak, R. (1986). The face scale: A brief, nonverbal method for assessing patient mood. *Arthritis and Rheumatism, 29*(7), 906–909.

Low, L.-F., Swaffer, K., McGrath, M., & Brodaty, H. (2018). Do people with early stage dementia experience prescribed disengagement®? A systematic review of qualitative studies. *International Psychogeriatrics, 30*(6), 807–831. https://doi.org/10.1017/S1041610217001545.

Marshall, A., Spreadbury, J., Cheston, R., Coleman, P., Ballinger, C., Mullee, M., ... Bartlett, E. (2015). A pilot randomised controlled trial to compare changes in quality of life for participants with early diagnosis dementia who attend a Living Well with Dementia group compared to waiting-list control. *Aging and Mental Health, 19*(6), 526–535. https://doi.org/10.1080/13607863.2014.954527.

Martyr, A., Nelis, S. M., Quinn, C., Wu, Y. T., Lamont, R. A., Henderson, C., ... Clare, L. (2018). Living well with dementia: A systematic review and correlational meta-analysis of factors associated with quality of life, well-being and life satisfaction in people with dementia. *Psychological Medicine, 48*(13), 2130–2139. https://doi.org/10.1017/s0033291718000405.

Nyman, S. R., & Szymczynska, P. (2016). Meaningful activities for improving the well-being of people with dementia: Beyond mere pleasure to meeting fundamental psychological needs. *Perspectives in Public Health, 136*(2), 99–107. https://doi.org/10.1177/1757913915626193.

O'Philbin, L., Woods, B., Farrell, E. M., Spector, A. E., & Orrell, M. (2018). Reminiscence therapy for dementia: An abridged Cochrane systematic review of the evidence from randomized controlled trials. *Expert Review of Neurotherapeutics, 18*(9), 715–727. https://doi.org/10.1080/14737175.2018.1509709.

Øksnebjerg, L., Diaz-Ponce, A., Gove, D., Moniz-Cook, E., Mountain, G., Chattat, R., & Woods, B. (2018). Towards capturing meaningful outcomes for people with dementia in psychosocial intervention research: A pan-European consultation. *Health expectations: An International Journal of Public Participation in Health Care and Health Policy, 21*(6), 1056–1065. https://doi.org/10.1111/hex.12799.

Pachana, N. A., Byrne, G. J., Siddle, H., Koloski, N., Harley, E., & Arnold, E. (2007). Development and validation of the geriatric anxiety inventory. *International Psychogeriatrics, 19*(01), 103. https://doi.org/10.1017/s1041610206003504.

Paller, K. A., Creery, J. D., Florczak, S. M., Weintraub, S., Mesulam, M. M., Reber, P. J., … Maslar, M. (2015). Benefits of mindfulness training for patients with progressive cognitive decline and their caregivers. *American Journal of Alzheimer's Disease and Other Dementias, 30*(3), 257–267. https://doi.org/10.1177/1533317514545377.

Patterson, K. M., Clarke, C., Wolverson, E. L., & Moniz-Cook, E. D. (2018). Through the eyes of others—The social experiences of people with dementia: A systematic literature review and synthesis. *International Psychogeriatrics, 30*(6), 791–805. https://doi.org/10.1017/S1041610216002374.

Paukert, A. L., Calleo, J., Kraus-Schuman, C., Snow, L., Wilson, N., Petersen, N. J., … Stanley, M. A. (2010). Peaceful Mind: an open trial of cognitive-behavioral therapy for anxiety in persons with dementia. *International Psychogeriatrics, 22*(6), 1012–1021. https://doi.org/10.1017/s1041610210000694.

Petty, S., Dening, T., Griffiths, A., & Coleston, D. M. (2016). Where is the happiness in dementia? *International Psychogeriatrics, 28*(10), 1752–1753. https://doi.org/10.1017/S1041610216000879.

Phung, K. T. T., Waldorff, F. B., Buss, D. V., Eckermann, A., Keiding, N., Rishøj, S., … Waldemar, G. (2013). A three-year follow-up on the efficacy of psychosocial interventions for patients with mild dementia and their caregivers: The multicentre, rater-blinded, randomised Danish Alzheimer Intervention Study (DAISY). *BMJ Open, 3*(11). https://doi.org/10.1136/bmjopen-2013-003584.

Schneider, J. (2018). The arts as a medium for care and self-care in dementia: Arguments and evidence. *International Journal of Environmental Research and Public Health, 15*(6), 1151. https://doi.org/10.3390/ijerph15061151.

Schreiner, A. S., Yamamoto, E., & Shiotani, H. (2005). Positive affect among nursing home residents with Alzheimer's dementia: The effect of recreational activity. *Aging & Mental Health, 9*(2), 129–134. https://doi.org/10.1080/13607860412331336841.

Segal, D. L., June, A., Payne, M., Coolidge, F. L., & Yochim, B. (2010). Development and initial validation of a self-report assessment tool for anxiety among older adults. *The Geriatric Anxiety Scale, 24*(7), 709–714. https://doi.org/10.1016/j.janxdis.2010.05.002.

Spector, A., Charlesworth, G., King, M., Lattimer, M., Sadek, S., Marston, L., … Orrell, M. (2015). Cognitive-behavioural therapy for anxiety in dementia: pilot randomised controlled trial. *British Journal of Psychiatry, 206*(6), 509–516. https://doi.org/10.1192/bjp.bp.113.140087.

Stanley, M. A., Calleo, J., Bush, A. L., Wilson, N., Snow, A. L., Kraus-Schuman, C., … Kunik, M. E. (2013). The peaceful mind program: A pilot test of a cognitive-behavioral therapy-based intervention for anxious patients with dementia. *American Journal of Geriatric Psychiatry, 21*(7), 696–708. https://doi.org/10.1016/j.jagp.2013.01.007.

Stites, S. D., Karlawish, J., Harkins, K., Rubright, J. D., & Wolk, D. (2017). Awareness of mild cognitive impairment and mild Alzheimer's disease dementia diagnoses associated with lower self-ratings of quality of life in older adults. *The Journals of Gerontology: Series B, 72*(6), 974–985. https://doi.org/10.1093/geronb/gbx100.

Tampi, R. R., Tampi, D. J., & Balachandran, S. (2017). Antipsychotics, antidepressants, anticonvulsants, melatonin, and benzodiazepines for behavioral and psychological symptoms of dementia: A systematic review of meta-analyses. *Current Treatment Options in Psychiatry, 4*, 55–79. https://doi.org/10.1007/s40501-017-0104-2.

Tappen, R. M., & Williams, C. L. (2009). Therapeutic conversation to improve mood in nursing home residents with Alzheimer's disease. *Research in Gerontological Nursing, 2*(4), 267–275. https://doi.org/10.3928/19404921-20090428-02.

Tay, K. W., Subramaniam, P., & Oei, T. P. (2019). Cognitive behavioural therapy can be effective in treating anxiety and depression in persons with dementia: A systematic review. *Psychogeriatrics, 19*(3), 264–275. https://doi.org/10.1111/psyg.12391.

Teri, L., Logsdon, R. G., Uomoto, J., & McCurry, S. M. (1997). Behavioral treatment of depression in dementia patients: A controlled clinical trial. *Journals of Gerontology Series B-Psychological Sciences & Social Sciences, 52*(4), 159–P166.

Tondi, L., Ribani, L., Bottazzi, M., Viscomi, G., & Vulcano, V. (2007). Validation therapy (VT) in nursing home: a case-control study. *Archives of Gerontology and Geriatrics, 44*(Suppl 1), 407–411. https://doi.org/10.1016/j.archger.2007.01.057.

Waldorff, F. B., Buss, D. V., Eckermann, A., Rasmussen, M. L. H., Keiding, N., Rishoj, S., … Waldemar, G. (2012). Efficacy of psychosocial intervention in patients with mild Alzheimer's disease: The multicentre, rater blinded, randomised Danish Alzheimer Intervention Study (DAISY). *British Medical Journal, 345*(1). https://doi.org/10.1136/bmj.e4693. e4693–e4693.

Williams, V. S., Morlock, R. J., & Feltner, D. (2010). Psychometric evaluation of a visual analog scale for the assessment of anxiety. *8*(1), 57. https://doi.org/10.1186/1477-7525-8-57.

Wilson, N. L., Lantz, M. S., Buchalter, E. N., & McBee, L. (1997). The wellness group: A novel intervention for coping with disruptive behavior in elderly nursing home residents. *The Gerontologist, 37*(4), 551–557. https://doi.org/10.1093/geront/37.4.551.

Wolverson, E. L., Clarke, C., & Moniz-Cook, E. D. (2016). Living positively with dementia: A systematic review and synthesis of the qualitative literature. *Aging & Mental Health, 20*(7), 676–699. https://doi.org/10.1080/13607863.2015.1052777.

Woods, R. T., Woods, R. T., & Clare, L. (Eds.). (2008). Assessing mood, wellbeing and quality of life. In *Handbook of the clinical psychology of ageing* (2nd ed., pp. 415–427). Wiley. 2008 ed.

Wuthrich, V. M., & Frei, J. (2015). Barriers to treatment for older adults seeking psychological therapy. *International Psychogeriatrics, 27*(07), 1227–1236. https://doi.org/10.1017/s1041610215000241.

Yesavage, J. A., Brink, T. L., Rose, T. L., Lum, O., Huang, V., Adey, M., & Leirer, V. O. (1982). Development and validation of a geriatric depression screening scale: A preliminary report. *Journal of Psychiatric Research, 17*(1), 37–49.

CHAPTER 8

Driving and community mobility for people living with dementia

Theresa L. Scott[a], Jacki Liddle[b], and Nancy A. Pachana[a]
[a]School of Psychology, The University of Queensland, St Lucia, QLD, Australia
[b]School of Information Technology & Electrical Engineering, The University of Queensland, St Lucia, QLD, Australia

Introduction

Mobility and community participation

Community mobility is an important and often overlooked social determinant of health and well-being (WHO, 2007). The ability to get out and about, to participate in social activities and to have some degree of independence, despite a medical condition, is essential to maintaining well-being and to live an autonomous life in the community for as long as possible. Maintaining social participation and social relationships is vital to well-being across the lifespan, and for preserving cognitive and emotional health. Conversely, loss of mobility and decline in community connectivity and social participation has been shown to have a significant negative impact on the quality of life and mortality for people living with dementia. The transition to non–driving comes at significant personal cost, including increased risk of depression, anxiety, loneliness, isolation, grief, and loss (Chihuri et al., 2016).

Driving is the primary form of transportation for many older adults

We live in a hypermobile society and the private motor vehicle remains the principal form of transport in many countries where travel distance between work, family, and services is more dispersed and requires a longer travel time (Musselwhite, 2011). The pattern of car use has been growing steadily over the past several decades and seems set to continue alongside population aging. Driving has become the most common method of transport for Australians, with 17.5 million Australians (approximately 71%) holding a current driver's license (BITRE, 2017) and over 19.2 million vehicles registered for use (Australian Bureau of Statistics, 2019). A recent

Dementia Rehabilitation
https://doi.org/10.1016/B978-0-12-818685-5.00008-8

analysis of licensed drivers showed that in 2015, 80% of those aged over 65 years held licenses, compared to 96% of those aged 49–64, suggesting the older driving population may grow in coming decades (BITRE, 2017).

Needs and motivations for travel in later life

Recent research examining mobility has considered the subjective meaning and motivations for engaging in travel behaviors in later life. Mobility needs have been conceptualized as a hierarchical model, in which each of three levels is said to be of equal importance, particularly to older people (Musselwhite & Haddad, 2010). That is, driving provides a convenient and accessible means of meeting (i) utilitarian needs (getting from A to B); (ii) affective needs of freedom, autonomy, and independence, and (iii) aesthetic needs, travel for its own sake. However, these needs are not equally prioritized in terms of provisions of services for those that have ceased driving (Musselwhite & Haddad, 2010; Musselwhite & Scott, 2019). For example, fundamental to promoting well-being and quality of life is meeting these higher order needs which relate to travel for its own sake. This is especially important for people living with dementia as driving may be a pleasurable activity and a way to access and engage with the natural environment.

Stopping driving may diminish life space

Driving cessation can diminish "life space"—defined as the extent of movement through the environment that reflects an individual's coping ability and community mobility (Baker, Bodner, & Allman, 2003). Research highlights the negative consequences of giving up driving on an individual's life space mobility, emotional and social well-being, and life expectancy. Driving cessation is related to life space constriction, and difficulty in recovering from life space constriction (Shah et al., 2012). Changes to executive functioning, learning, memory, and processing speed appear to be particularly related to lower life space. A diminished life space may lead to a more rapid cognitive decline for those with preexisting cognitive impairment (De Silva, Gregory, Venkateshan, Verschoor, & Kuspinar, 2019), and premature nursing home placement (Taylor, Buchan, & van der Veer, 2018).

Meaning of driving to identity

Driving may mean more to people than simply getting from A to B, and loss of driving may represent more than loss of transportation. Stopping driving can have symbolic meaning for individuals, embodying loss of independence, control, freedom, and pleasurable activity. Emerging research highlights the importance of driving to an individual's continued sense of self and identity (Pachana, Jetten, Gustafsson, & Liddle, 2017; Rudman, Friedland, Chipman, & Sciortino, 2006). Driving is an important form of independence and autonomy, linked with perceptions about aging and "staying young" (Eisenhandler, 1990; Jetten & Pachana, 2011). One reason why driving cessation may be experienced so negatively is that it may be threatening to an individual's self-perceptions of their own aging and capacity, indicating an unalterable identity shift into such stigmatized categories as "old" (Jetten & Pachana, 2011) and living with a "dementia" (Cahill, Pierce, Werner, Darley, & Bobersky, 2015; Scott, Kugelman, & Tulloch, 2019).

The effects of dementia on driving safety

Driving is a complex task requiring cognitive, sensory and physical functions that can be compromised by dementia, such as visuospatial skills, situational awareness, judgment and decision-making, psychomotor functioning, reaction time, and way-finding. Drivers with dementia have significantly increased risk of accidents, injury, and loss of life compared with age-matched drivers without cognitive decline (Vaa, 2003). While a diagnosis of dementia does not mean that a person needs to immediately retire from driving, due to the progressive nature of the disease all persons with dementia will eventually have to give up driving.

Optimal outcomes

Giving up driving may be a significant challenge. Research suggests that the best outcomes are to plan early, to try out and become comfortable with, alternative modes of transport while still driving. For example, older people may modify their driving behavior, to avoid difficult driving situations and minimize their risk of accident. They may avoid driving at night, or during peak periods, or take a low traffic route—to "self-regulate" their driving in order to continue to drive safely before they eventually stop. Insight and awareness of one's functional abilities and deficits in safe driving ability is necessary to self-moderate. People living with dementia may continue to drive for emotional, logistical, and mobility reasons, or due to a lack of insight and awareness into their safe driving capabilities (Choi, Mezuk, & Rebok, 2012; Scott, Liddle, Pachana, Beattie, & Mitchell, 2019). Furthermore, while preparation is key to managing driving cessation, it may not always be possible because of the difficulties of early identification of dementia and difficult formal processes (Scott, Liddle, Pachana, et al., 2019). However, striving to prepare leads to better outcomes (Scott, Liddle, Pachana, et al., 2019).

Theoretical underpinnings

Numerous theoretically based models of driving competence have been proposed to provide a framework that may inform the clinical assessment of driving competence, and designing and assessing interventions. Measures of overall mental status, insight and awareness, which have been associated with driving performance are implicated in several models of safe driving behavior. For example, Michon's (1985) hierarchical model considers the driver as an "active problem solver," whose performance is structured at three levels of skills and control: strategical, tactical, and operational. According to this model, drivers must be aware of their functional capabilities and adjust their driving behaviors accordingly (Michon, 1985). For people living with dementia, adjustment may be complicated, however, if insight and awareness of one's level of safe driving capability are compromised.

The multifactorial model for enabling driving safety

The multifactorial model of driving safety describes a framework for clinical assessment of driving competence, and it can be used as a research tool (Anstey, Wood, Lord, & Walker, 2005). According to the model, the capacity to drive safely depends on three factors: cognition, and sensory and physical functioning. Where self-monitoring of these factors, in addition to driving capacity and beliefs about capacity, enable (safe) driving behavior. One example is avoiding driving at night due to poor vision (Anstey et al., 2005). Once more, insight into one's cognitive and physical abilities and deficits is necessary for effective self-monitoring.

Driving as an everyday competence model

Driving as an everyday competence model incorporates global, individual, and environmental factors. Global factors refer to those that may impact the driver's life but are not necessarily specific to the driving task, for example, disease diagnosis, and social policies. Individual factors include overall physical and mental health and cognitive functioning which impact driving, such as chronic medical conditions that have been implicated in crash risk, e.g., stroke, heart disease, and depression. Environmental factors refer to physical factors in the environment, such as darkness, wet roads, and in-vehicle features that may reduce visibility, vehicle age, and maintenance. Social factors include such things that may increase cognitive load, e.g., the difficulty of the driving environment, the behaviors of other road users and passengers. Cognitive factors refer to attention, reaction time, perception, visuospatial abilities, and memory. Level of driving "competence" is said to be a fit be-tween the individual and their environment, modified by their beliefs and awareness, that is, an individual's beliefs, self-monitoring, self-awareness, and self-restriction moderates their actual driving performance. According to this model, the presence of dementia is not sufficient to determine driving abilities; however, increased severity is related to poorer overall driving abilities and increased risk of crashes (Lindstrom-Forneri, Tuokko, Garrett, & Molnar, 2010).

Selection optimization and compensation model (SOC)

The SOC model applied to driving reduction and cessation suggests that age-related declines can be effectively managed through three interactive components: Selection, Optimization, and Compensation (Baltes & Baltes, 1990). Selection refers to goal selection and the prioritization of engagement in activities that are of high importance to the individual. Optimization can be understood as skill refinement in line with the individual's desired goals. Compensation describes a process of using alternative and compensatory methods or technological support, to achieve goals when there is limited capacity to maintain existing behaviors (Baltes & Baltes, 1990). In terms of the driving cessation process, to accommodate for health-related losses, the SOC model would suggest that selection occurs when age-related declines impact ability and the individual chooses to self-regulate their driving to avoid difficult situations, such as driving in rain, or at night, to maintain mobility, independence, and autonomy. Optimization occurs when the individual completes daily tasks, such as grocery shopping, in a travel pattern that meets their newfound travel needs (e.g., in daylight hours and close proximity to home). Compensation occurs when the individual sources alternative modes of transport, such as asking for a lift from family or using public transportation, to complement self-regulatory practices or if they have ceased driving altogether.

Mobility capitals: A model of coping after driving cessation

A model of coping after driving cessation has been proposed by Musselwhite and Scott (2019). The model describes the strategies that people might employ to mitigate the negative effects of giving up driving, as per capitals: infrastructure, cultural, individual, and social (Musselwhite & Scott, 2019). Infrastructure capital relates to drawing on the provision of services, finances, and economics. Cultural capital describes the norms and expectations, rules and laws around driving, and alternatives to driving. Individual capital relates to personal skills, abilities, and resilience. Social capital includes the family, friends, and social supports available to the retired driver. These four capitals provide a way of categorizing the different barriers and enablers to managing without a car and maintaining well-being.

Person-environment-occupation models

Driving, community mobility, and use of transportation are considered instrumental activities of daily living (IADL)—regular, more complex essential activities within daily life. Driving in particular also is recognized as an occupation, a role linked to individual identity. The driving role has symbolic individual and societal meaning and value. It is linked to the milestones of independence and acts as a symbolic distancer from negative perceptions of age and disability (Eisenhandler, 1990; Jetten & Pachana, 2011). In addition to participation and identification with the role itself, driving is also recognized as an enabling occupation, that is, a role that supports participation in other roles and activities. Being able to drive enables familiar and meaningful participation in community and life roles and activities. This means that a threat to continued driving can have an impact of multiple areas of life participation, which can be unanticipated, not accounted for within standard clinical support, and challenging to manage (Adler, Rottunda, & Kuskowski, 2012; Silverstein, Dickerson, & Schold Davis, 2016; Stav, 2014).

When shaping clinical approaches, occupational therapists use models of practice that consider, the person, their occupations, and the environment in which the participation occurs, and how they overlap to shape performance and participation. The Person-Environment-Occupation (PEO) Model (Law et al., 1996) has been used to frame driving and alternative transportation use (e.g., Broome, McKenna, Fleming, & Worrall, 2009). It considers the person's abilities, values, and changes and needs related to their condition; the occupation of driving in terms of its meaning, components and demands; and the environment in which it occurs which includes vehicular characteristics, other drivers and road and weather conditions. This helps to recognize and frame with the complexity of considerations in assessing and supporting driving or its alternatives. An evaluation of bus use for older people, for example, Broome et al. (2009) illustrated a range of barriers and facilitators to use, ranging from the text being too small on timetables, friendliness of bus drivers, and ability to learn new processes. It looked particularly on the overlapping areas of person–occupation fit (individuals' functional capacity or ability to manage the demands); occupation-environment fit (design and policy considerations or how the system and the component meet the needs of users) and person-environment fit (accessibility or how well the environment supports a person's abilities). Any clinical approach to support driving and community mobility will need to consider the individual, their participation, and the environmental factors (Silverstein et al., 2016). Rehabilitative approaches can consider building the capacity of the person and enacting their strengths, adapting the tasks within the occupation to enable safe participation and modifying the environmental components or systems to facilitate performance.

Current approaches: Primary care

In Australia, general practitioners are often the first medical professionals consulted about memory problems. They are, therefore, often best placed to diagnose particular medical conditions that may impact driving safety (Anstey et al., 2016). As the first point of contact with the health system, GPs are tasked with evaluating the capacity to continue driving in their patients with dementia.

Medical assessment of fitness to drive

Assessment of an individual's driving performance is a complex area of primary care practice, negatively impacted by a lack of objective in-office tests. When making decisions about an individual's driving safety, health professionals must find a balance between [supporting] an individual's independence [mobility] and safety (O'Neill, Walshe, Romer, & Winston, 2019).

General practitioners are encouraged to proactively raise medical fitness-to-drive issues with their patients with dementia. However, system-level constraints such as limited time in consultation and competing priorities, and concerns about the negative effects on the therapeutic relationship, makes them reluctant to do so (Scott, Liddle, Pachana, et al., 2019). Furthermore, they worry that patients who fear losing their license, may not disclose memory problems or will withhold important clinical information from their GP (Scott, Liddle, Pachana, et al., 2019). The Australian Medical Association's position paper regards the treating doctor's position—as the decision-maker in licensing decisions—as an unacceptable ethical conflict. Nevertheless, the demands on GPs to deal with the issues are growing along with increasing numbers of older drivers. With limited information and prior training about how to evaluate fitness-to-drive in primary care, it is an under-resourced and complicated area of clinical dementia care.

Limited guidelines and supports for clinicians in assessing medical fitness to drive is an international concern (Rapoport et al., 2018). Moreover, the regulations regarding medical standards for fitness to drive and requirements for mandatory reporting [of drivers who are medically unfit] vary across the Australian States and Territories. Not surprisingly, studies identify that clinicians' lack of knowledge and confidence in managing driving cessation issues which leads to reluctance to do so (Carr & O'Neill, 2015). Further complicating the process is that some drivers avoid their responsibility to stop driving even when their license is terminated or they may "doctor shop" to seek permission to drive from another doctor, who is potentially unaware of their diagnosis (Scott, Liddle, Pachana, et al., 2019).

There currently exists a lack of suitable off-road tests for identifying potential at-risk drivers without falsely identifying a large proportion of drivers as unsafe, when in fact they are safe to continue to drive.

Unfortunately, in the absence of valid, objective, in-office tests of medical fitness to drive, clinicians must resort to using what tests are available to them, often memory tests, such as the Mini Mental State Examination, The Montreal Cognitive Assessment, and the Trail Making Task (Scott, Liddle, Pachana, et al., 2019). The issue with these types of tests is that they impart the wrong message to drivers with dementia—that being medically fit to drive is all about memory. Without standardized guidelines, education and such medical resources, practitioners may feel underconfident in their ability to assess patients' medical fitness to drive (Sims, Rouse-Watson, Schattner, Beveridge, & Jones, 2012).

The so-called "gold standard" of assessment of driver medical fitness is regarded as an off and on-road assessment carried out by an occupational therapist with additional training in driver evaluation. These tests often come with long waiting periods (up to 24 months in some areas of Australia) if subsidized, or unviable out of pocket expenses for people living with dementia. Further, these tests may not be available in some regional parts of Australia.

While some people living with dementia may voluntarily stop driving before they are advised to by a medical professional, many others find the decision to cease difficult to accept (Scott, Liddle, Pachana, et al., 2019). GPs report that unprepared patients react with the most anger and grief at being told they should no longer be driving. Acceptance of the decision to stop driving is fundamental to successfully managing the transition to no longer driving, and to individuals finding and trying out and becoming comfortable with alternative modes of transport. Restricting or removing driving licenses without just cause and valid and reliable tests can result in drivers not accepting the medical decision to do so. It is important to understanding and acceptance of any recommendations that the individual perceives the relevance of a particular test to driving competence and to perceive their own performance accurately.

Cross-disciplinary approaches

Currently, there are calls to consider dementia a social disability (Clare, 2017), requiring a rehabilitation approach rather than focusing entirely on the currently intractable neurological components. This requires a broad conceptualization of the broader issues requiring consideration, beyond organ, and function level changes (Clare, 2017; Maki, Sakurai, Okochi, Yamaguchi, & Toba, 2018). The World Health Organization's International Classification of Functioning ("ICF"; WHO, 2001) identifies that participation, or the conduct of activities and roles within the community, as the area requiring focus. It frames issues with participation as arising from the social and physical environment's lack of fit for the person's support requirements, rather than arising solely from an individual's health status. Driving and community mobility are represented within the ICF under a subsection of activities, participation, and mobility. The model also includes the broader access and support considerations within a person's environment as contributing to either their functioning or experience of disability. This includes the inclusive design (or lack of inclusive design) of built environments, community set up, and transportation systems (Silverstein et al., 2016). In addition, supportive technologies, community members, and government policies may also reduce the experience of disability for people living with changes at the health or organ level. It also identifies access to usable transportation as a social determinant of health (Levasseur et al., 2015), with limited access to transport leading to poorer health outcomes given the same condition.

In applying these broader conceptualizations, it becomes clear that dementia and mobility-related concerns require comprehensive multidisciplinary approaches that extend beyond the person living with dementia. A rehabilitation approach would enable people to continue functioning as well as to maintain involvement in meaningful roles and to sustain a coherent sense of identity (Clare, 2017). Changes to skills and abilities may need goal-led approaches to support skill maintenance, external and environmental supports and supports for the emotional impact of the changes (Adler et al., 2012).

Relevant outcome measures

Given the understanding of driving and community mobility as multifaceted and complex, assessment tools and outcome measures to guide and evaluate the impact of practice need to reflect this. Tools that help to identify the range of issues under consideration may be used, with a more detailed assessment of key components (e.g., specific identified areas of performance components or environmental issues). The WHO suggests the ICF checklist and the WHO Disability Assessment Schedule (WHODAS 2.0) to indicate areas of focus and to enable comparison between groups and environments. These provide brief capture of key issues across six functional domains including cognition, mobility, and participation in community activities (WHODAS), as well as environments (including technology) and services (ICF checklist).

An alternative approach is to measure a relevant broad global outcome that considers the combined impact of these components (Taylor et al., 2018). Life space is a potential outcome that may serve this purpose for considering driving and community mobility. Life space is a gerontological construct that captures the geographical area in which a person conducts their life activities. It measures lived mobility over a specified period of time and in doing so reflects a person's capacity to be mobile within their community and considering their participation needs and available supports. It can be measured using self-report (interviews and questionnaires; Baker et al., 2003; Peel et al., 2005), observational techniques, or passively measured using technology (geolocation data from wearables and smartphones; Liddle, Haynes, et al., 2014; Liddle, Ireland, et al., 2014; Taylor et al., 2018). It can, therefore, be reported as schools or various metrics including distances travelled, amount of time spent away from home and trips away from home in the week (Liddle, Haynes, et al., 2014; Liddle, Ireland, et al., 2014).

Intervention approaches

Driving rehabilitation

Consideration of driving issues always involves a consideration of mobility and safety (Carr & O'Neill, 2015). Driving rehabilitation is a role that is undertaken across several settings, involving multidisciplinary teams and professionals with specialist qualifications. In fitting with rehabilitation approaches for people with dementia, the focus is on maintaining and optimizing functioning, through applying strengths and resources as well as external supports. In contrast to other IADLs, licensing to drive is regulated by the government, and requires formal assessment for attaining and maintaining licenses. Varying across states and countries, there are additional requirements based on age and medical conditions. While these vary, analyses of crash data indicate that these have not made differences in safety outcomes (Stav, 2014; Wilson & Pinner, 2013). Regardless, health professionals working with clients on driving issues, need to be up to date with their local requirements and the requirements for assessments and reporting their local jurisdiction (Wheatley, Carr, & Marottoli, 2014; Wilson & Pinner, 2013).

In recognizing that diagnosis of dementia alone is not a sufficient requirement for an immediate cessation of driving (O'Neill, 2015), an important aspect of the driving rehabilitation role focuses on monitoring and providing appropriate services at the appropriate time. It is important to note that because driving is a highly emotive subject, the issue may be avoided by the person living with dementia, their families, and by health professionals (Liddle et al., 2016; Meuser, Carr, Berg-Wege, Niewoehner, & Morris, 2006; Scott, Liddle, Pachana, et al., 2019). They may also not be involved with services during the time when their driving abilities are starting to change. It is therefore important for all members of healthcare teams to consider driving and raise the issues even while people are safe to drive. In the early stages of dementia, general healthcare teams have a role in monitoring potential symptoms and functional difficulties that would indicate difficulties with driving, as well as reported changes to driving performance. Discussion and the beginning of planning for future transportation changes are required at this stage as well (Carr & O'Neill, 2015; Dickerson, 2014; Dickerson et al., 2017).

While there is a consensus that people with moderate to severe dementia no longer have the capacity to drive, people with mild dementia may or may not be medically fit to drive, depending on many factors. Once there is concern about driving, a formal driving assessment may be required. Self-report of risks or driving performance can be an inaccurate indicator of issues faced due to changes to awareness or a strong desire to maintain the driving role (Wheatley et al., 2014). This is conducted, often involving on and off-road assessment of performance components and performance in context. This aims to evaluate performance across operational, tactical, and strategic domains but does require a specialist driving assessor (a health professional with specialized postgraduate qualifications) for understanding the safety and performance implications. A formal assessment of driving which involves on-road evaluation may also have better face validity for drivers, who can have difficulty accepting recommendations to stop driving that are based on the assessment that does not appear related to their driving performance (Scott, Liddle, Pachana, et al., 2019).

If the assessment of driving indicates issues in a performance that could be remedied, driving rehabilitation may support performance through modification of vehicles, building performance components or making recommendations about driving contexts to reduce risk. Some approaches used include programs like CarFit to help set up the vehicle to support performance, educational programs about driving skills and road rules, and physical activity programs to improve range of motion and strength (Golisz, 2014b). There is mixed evidence for the impact of programs to improve visual perception and hazard perception (Golisz, 2014b). There is also support for education, conversations, and future planning at this stage, including encouraging people to make advanced directives about their driving plans and to begin to become familiar with alternative transport. While it is possible that vehicle modifications and education may assist in the short term, the effort of driving with unfamiliar setups and effort of learning needs to be considered. Ongoing monitoring of driving performance is required (Silverstein et al., 2016; Wheatley et al., 2014).

An important component of driving rehabilitation is framing the driving role as transitional for the person living with dementia and their family members. Support and education around the readiness for mobility transition is required (Meuser, Berg-Weger, Chibnall, Harmon, & Stowe, 2013). Individualized planning as well as support for future transportation is required. Ideally, supporting the transition to cessation will enable it to be chosen rather than forced, and gradual, enabling maintenance of meaningful participation (Dickerson, 2014; Silverstein et al., 2016). Intensive support for the emotional and practical transitions at cessation may be required. The educational and support needs of families need consideration within rehabilitation (Liddle et al., 2016).

Driving cessation support

While planning may ease the nature of the change at cessation, it is likely that additional support for driving cessation will be required. There have been education and support approaches. A metanalysis indicated that this is a growing area and suggests a promising approach used with older people, may have value with people living with dementia (Rapoport, Cameron, Sanford, & Naglie, 2017).

The CarFreeMe program, an education and support program to promote continued safe participation when driving stops, indicated that it was able to support community mobility and related self-efficacy and retired and retiring older drivers without cognitive decline (Liddle, Haynes, et al., 2014; Liddle, McKenna, & Bartlett, 2007). It is a community-based group program encompassing discussion, adjustment to loss, skills acquisition, transit training, future planning, and advocacy for further development, involving health professionals and peer leaders. Consideration of the range of related life transitions that may be linked to driving cessation including relocation and role surrender means that practical and emotional/identity support is required (Pachana et al., 2017). This program has been adapted based on the reported needs and recommendations of people living with dementia and their family members (Liddle et al., 2016; Scott, Liddle, Mitchell, Beattie, & Pachana, 2019). Adjustments for people living with dementia include a more flexible, responsive approach, inclusion of family members and simplification of content. Table 1 shows the content of the adapted program for older people living with dementia.

Community mobility rehabilitation

Rehabilitation for community mobility can require multidisciplinary intervention and targeting a range of performance components and contextual factors (Dickerson, 2014; Silverstein et al., 2016). With the cessation

Table 1 Structure and content of the CarFreeMe for people with dementia program.

Modules	CarFreeMe for people with dementia
1	Living with dementia: focuses on the changes that may occur with dementia, and strategies to live positively
2	Balancing independence and safety: information about driving safety in later life and things for consideration as you retire from driving
3	Adjusting to losses and changes: covers changes that may occur to lifestyle, feelings of loss and grief from retiring from driving, and strategies to help with adjustment
4	Experiences of retiring from driving: covers stories of other retired drivers and family members and the ways that people adjusted
5	Alternative transport: covers the range of alternatives to driving and ideas of where to find out more
6	Lifestyle planning: covers things to consider in planning for achieving a balanced lifestyle
7	Advocacy and support: focuses on services that are available (in a particular area) and steps to take to improve a service, or make service providers aware of needs
8	Family care partner's needs and adjustment (when care partners are involved in the process)

of driving, most people transition to a range of different transportation options. This can require learning about the use of a new system, building skills and strengths to support the use, and prioritizing the decisions and use based on personal goals and values. This often requires health professional evaluation, planning, and support. It should be noted that while driving requires a complex interaction of performance in a changing environment, many alternative transportation options also require a high level of planning and adjustment, especially if they are unfamiliar. Their use may also pose risks to the person living with dementia (Golisz, 2014a, 2014b).

For this reason, eliciting the community mobility needs, locations related to valued occupations, and abilities can help with developing an individualized plan. Finding the most acceptable and accessible transportation to access those locations and providing support for learning and integrating into the routine is a focus of rehabilitation (Golisz, 2014a). Support to build the strength, endurance, and safety for community walking, for example, maybe a focus. Introducing assistance technology to support way-finding and safety may be indicated (Jarvis, Clemson, & Mackenzie, 2017). Maintaining a focus on the valued occupations and locations and finding ways of maintaining access to these where possible is required. This is likely to need ongoing involvement over time with changes to the person's abilities and prioritized needs. Importantly community mobility programs must consider involvement and intervention within the environment including in the development of new transportation services, policies, and supports (Stav, 2014). Effective programs consider both practical and emotional adjustment related to transportation and status changes and support change at the individual and systems levels (Silverstein et al., 2016).

Involvement of care partners and family members

Research shows that care partners, family members, and friends can influence the decision to stop driving. Family members play a central role in supporting driving self-regulation and planning for eventual cessation. For example, in one study transportation provided by both family and friends was associated with decisions to not resume driving after voluntary driving cessation (Johnson, 2008). The dynamics between families in managing driving and driving cessation issues can be very complex (Liddle et al., 2016). It is recommended that involved health professionals consider these dynamics in individualizing their approaches to support. For those supporting someone transitioning from driver to retired driver, sensitivity in all aspects of communication around driving cessation is paramount. However, it is an extremely difficult topic for family members to raise and they need information about how to have informed discussions around driving with dementia, and education about the effects of the disease on safe driving, legalities, insurance, managing conflict, and unsafe and unlicensed driving. Without the necessary training and education support to family members to facilitate the difficult and personal conversation, it is often avoided until a crisis situation.

Future directions

Driving, community mobility, and transportation are experiencing rapid changes for a variety of reasons. Technology-mediated change has introduced widespread ridesharing services (e.g., DiDi, Lyft, Uber) which has had an effect on people living with transport limitations (Dickerson et al., 2017). It has been suggested that in the future, there will be a move away from mass transit type transportation services, and toward technology-driven, individually responsive services, known as Mobility as a Service (MaaS; Mulley, 2017). MaaS has been cited as a potential game changer in the way that people travel. MaaS is seen to solve, in part, problems such as congestion, carbon emissions, air pollution, and alternative transportation for people with limited mobility. A move away from individual driving is also predicted with the development of autonomous vehicles. While it has been assumed that this will be more supportive of people with dementia and other disabilities, if their accessibility and acceptability needs are not considered within the development of the services and technologies, it is possible that this group will not be accommodated. This could lead to further exclusion as it is likely that specialized transport support services will not continue to be provided once MaaS fills that role (Shergold, Wilson, & Parkhurst, 2016). Regardless of the success of these developments, support for the transition to unfamiliar technology is likely to be needed for people living with dementia and their family members. It is therefore essential that people living with dementia, their families, and health professionals become involved in the development of communities, mobility services, and transport technology to ensure their continued access and participation.

Clinical recommendations

For people living with dementia, the timing of the decision to stop driving is critically important. If the decision to cease driving is delayed, then a loss of insight into declining driving abilities complicates the challenges of stopping for everyone involved.

GPs and health professionals must work together with family members to support driving cessation adjustment and continued community mobility if the person with dementia is no longer safe to drive. People with dementia and their families need accessible built environments, equitable alternative transportations to access shops and services but importantly to participate in social and cultural events.

There is an urgent need to reduce stigma around a dementia diagnosis and following on from that the potential loss of driving license. Stigma is a noticeable barrier to disclosing driving difficulties and acceptance of decisions to restrict or cease driving. Community education and awareness-raising about the effects of dementia on safe driving, normalizing retiring from driving, and the need to have a plan for alternative transport is particularly important to ensure that driving cessation decisions are accepted.

References

Adler, G., Rottunda, S. J., & Kuskowski, M. A. (2012). Occupational therapy practice as it relates to drivers with dementia. *Physical & Occupational Therapy in Geriatrics, 30*(4), 361–367. https://doi.org/10.3109/02703181.2012.730120.

Anstey, K. J., Eramudugolla, R., Ross, L. A., Lautenschlager, N. T., & Wood, J. (2016). Road safety in an aging population: Risk factors, assessment, interventions, and future directions. *International Psychogeriatrics, 28*(3), 349–356.

Anstey, K. J., Wood, J., Lord, S., & Walker, J. G. (2005). Cognitive, sensory and physical factors enabling driving safety in older adults. *Clinical Psychology Review, 25*(1), 45–65.

Australian Bureau of Statistics. (2019). *Causes of Death, Australia, 2018.* Australian Bureau of Statistics. Cat. 3303.0.

Baker, P. S., Bodner, E. V., & Allman, R. M. (2003). Measuring life-space mobility in community-dwelling older adults. *Journal of the American Geriatrics Society, 51*(11), 1610–1614. https://doi.org/10.1046/j.1532-5415.2003.51512.x.

Baltes, P. B., & Baltes, M. M. (1990). Psychological perspectives on successful aging: The model of selective optimization with compensation. In P. B. Baltes, & M. M. Baltes (Eds.), *Successful aging: Perspectives from the behavioral sciences* (pp. 1–34). New York: Cambridge University Press.

BITRE. (2017). *Drivers Licences in Australia.* Canberra: BITRE.

Broome, K., McKenna, K., Fleming, J., & Worrall, L. (2009). Bus use and older people: A literature review applying the person–environment–occupation model in macro practice. *Scandinavian Journal of Occupational Therapy, 16*(1), 3–12. https://doi.org/10.1080/11038120802326222.

Cahill, S., Pierce, M., Werner, P., Darley, A., & Bobersky, A. (2015). A systematic review of the public's knowledge and understanding of Alzheimer's disease and dementia. *Alzheimer Disease & Associated Disorders, 29*, 255–275.

Carr, D. B., & O'Neill, D. (2015). Mobility and safety issues in drivers with dementia. *International Psychogeriatrics, 27*(10), 1613–1622. https://doi.org/10.1017/S104161021500085X.

Chihuri, S., Mielenz, T. J., DiMaggio, C. J., Betz, M. E., DiGuiseppi, C., Jones, V. C., & Li, G. (2016). Driving cessation and health outcomes in older adults. *Journal of the American Geriatrics Society, 64*, 332–341.

Choi, M., Mezuk, B., & Rebok, G. W. (2012). Voluntary and involuntary driving cessation in later life. *Journal of Gerontological Social Work, 55*(4), 367–376.

Clare, L. (2017). Rehabilitation for people living with dementia: A practical framework of positive support. *PLoS Medicine, 14*(3). https://doi.org/10.1371/journal.pmed.1002245.

De Silva, N. A., Gregory, M. A., Venkateshan, S. S., Verschoor, C. P., & Kuspinar, A. (2019). Examining the association between life-space mobility and cognitive function in older adults: A systematic review. *Journal of Aging Research.* https://doi.org/10.1155/2019/3923574.

Dickerson, A. E. (2014). Driving with dementia: Evaluation, referral, and resources. *Occupational Therapy in Health Care, 28*(1), 62–76. https://doi.org/10.3109/07380577.2013.867091.

Dickerson, A. E., Molnar, L., Bedard, M., Eby, D. W., Classen, S., & Polgar, J. (2017). Transportation and aging: An updated research agenda for advancing safe mobility. *Journal of Applied Gerontology.* https://doi.org/10.1177/0733464817739154.

Eisenhandler, S. A. (1990). The asphalt identikit: Old age and the driver's license. *The International Journal of Aging and Human Development, 30*(1), 1–14. https://doi.org/10.2190/0MF5-HQ1L-7EBY-XNXV.

Golisz, K. (2014a). Occupational therapy and driving and community mobility for older adults. *American Journal of Occupational Therapy, 68*(6), 654–656. https://doi.org/10.5014/ajot.2014.013144.

Golisz, K. (2014b). Occupational therapy interventions to improve driving performance in older adults: A systematic review. *American Journal of Occupational Therapy, 68*(6), 662–669. https://doi.org/10.5014/ajot.2014.011247.

Jarvis, F., Clemson, L. M., & Mackenzie, L. (2017). Technology for dementia: Attitudes and practices of occupational therapists in providing assistive technology for way finding. *Disability and Rehabilitation. Assistive Technology, 12*(4), 373–377. https://doi.org/10.3109/17483107.2016.1173729.

Jetten, J., & Pachana, N. A. (2011). Not wanting to grow old: A social identity model of identity change (SIMIC) analysis of driving cessation among older adults. In J. Jetten, C. Haslam, & S. A. Haslam (Eds.), *The social cure: Identity, health and well-being* (pp. 97–114). Hove: Psychology Press.

Johnson, J. E. (2008). Informal social support networks and the maintenance of voluntary driving cessation by older rural women. *Journal of Community Health Nursing, 25,* 65–72.

Law, M., Cooper, B., Strong, S., Stewart, D., Rigby, P., & Letts, L. (1996). The person-environment-occupation model: A transactive approach to occupational performance. *Canadian Journal of Occupational Therapy, 63*(1), 9–23.

Levasseur, M., Généreux, M., Bruneau, J.-F., Vanasse, A., Chabot, É., Beaulac, C., & Bédard, M.-M. (2015). Importance of proximity to resources, social support, transportation and neighborhood security for mobility and social participation in older adults: Results from a scoping study. *BMC Public Health, 15*(1), 503. https://doi.org/10.1186/s12889-015-1824-0.

Liddle, J., Haynes, M., Pachana, N. A., Mitchell, G., McKenna, K., & Gustafsson, L. (2014). Effect of a group intervention to promote older adults' adjustment to driving cessation on community mobility: A randomized controlled trial. *The Gerontologist, 54*(3), 409–422. https://doi.org/10.1093/geront/gnt019.

Liddle, J., Ireland, D., McBride, S. J., Brauer, S. G., Hall, L. M., Ding, H., … Chenery, H. J. (2014). Measuring the lifespace of people with Parkinson's disease using smartphones: Proof of principle. *JMIR mHealth and uHealth, 2*(1). https://doi.org/10.2196/mhealth.2799.

Liddle, J., McKenna, K., & Bartlett, H. (2007). Improving outcomes for older retired drivers: The UQDRIVE program. *Australian Occupational Therapy Journal, 54*(4), 303–306.

Liddle, J., Tan, A., Liang, P., Bennett, S., Allen, S., Lie, D. C., & Pachana, N. A. (2016). "The biggest problem we've ever had to face": How families manage driving cessation with people with dementia. *International Psychogeriatrics, 28*(1), 109–122. https://doi.org/10.1017/S1041610215001441.

Lindstrom-Forneri, W., Tuokko, H. A., Garrett, D., & Molnar, F. (2010). Driving as an everyday competence: A model of driving competence and behavior. *Clinical Gerontologist*, *33*(4), 283–297.

Maki, Y., Sakurai, T., Okochi, J., Yamaguchi, H., & Toba, K. (2018). Rehabilitation to live better with dementia. *Geriatrics & Gerontology International*, *18*(11), 1529–1536. https://doi.org/10.1111/ggi.13517.

Meuser, T. M., Berg-Weger, M., Chibnall, J. T., Harmon, A. C., & Stowe, J. D. (2013). Assessment of readiness for mobility transition (ARMT): A tool for mobility transition counseling with older adults. *Journal of Applied Gerontology*, *32*(4), 484–507. https://doi.org/10.1177/0733464811425914.

Meuser, T. M., Carr, D. B., Berg-Wege, M., Niewoehner, P., & Morris, J. C. (2006). Driving and dementia in older adults: Implementation and evaluation of a continuing education project. *The Gerontologist*, *46*(5), 680–687.

Michon, J. A. (1985). A critical view of driver behavior models: What do we know, what should we do? In *Human behavior and traffic safety* (pp. 485–524). Boston, MA: Springer.

Mulley, C. (2017). Mobility as a services (MaaS)—Does it have critical mass? *Transport Reviews*, *37*(3), 247–251. https://doi.org/10.1080/01441647.2017.1280932.

Musselwhite, C. (2011). The importance of driving for older people and how the pain of driving cessation can be reduced. *Signpost: Journal of Dementia and Mental Health Care of Older People*, *15*(3), 22–26.

Musselwhite, C., & Haddad, H. (2010). Mobility, accessibility and quality of later life. *Quality in Ageing*, *11*(1), 25–37.

Musselwhite, C. B. A., & Scott, T. L. (2019). Developing a model of mobility capital for an ageing population. *International Journal of Environmental Research and Public Health*, *16*(18), 1–13.

O'Neill, D. (2015). Transport, driving and ageing. *Reviews in Clinical Gerontology*, *25*(2), 147.

O'Neill, D., Walshe, E., Romer, D., & Winston, F. (2019). *Transportation equity, health, and aging: A novel approach to healthy longevity with benefits across the life span*. Washington, DC: NAM Perspectives. Commentary, National Academy of Medicine. https://doi.org/10.31478/201912a.

Pachana, N. A., Jetten, J., Gustafsson, L., & Liddle, J. (2017). To be or not to be (an older driver): Social identity theory and driving cessation in later life. *Ageing and Society*, *37*(8), 1597–1608.

Peel, C., Baker, P. S., Roth, D. L., Brown, C. J., Bodner, E. V., & Allman, R. M. (2005). Assessing mobility in older adults: The UAB study of aging life-space assessment. *Physical Therapy*, *85*(10), 1008–1019. https://doi.org/10.1093/ptj/85.10.1008.

Rapoport, M. J., Cameron, D. H., Sanford, S., & Naglie, G. (2017). A systematic review of intervention approaches for driving cessation in older adults. *International Journal of Geriatric Psychiatry*, *32*(5), 484–491. https://doi.org/10.1002/gps.4681.

Rapoport, M. J., Chee, J. N., Carr, D. B., Molnar, F., Naglie, G., Dow, J., … O'Neill, D. (2018). An international approach to enhancing a national guideline on driving and dementia. *Current Psychiatry Reports*, *20*(3), 16.

Rudman, D. L., Friedland, J., Chipman, M., & Sciortino, P. (2006). Holding on and letting go: The perspectives of pre-seniors and seniors on driving self-regulation in later life. *Canadian Journal on Aging*, *25*(1), 65–76.

Scott, T. L., Kugelman, M., & Tulloch, K. (2019). How medical professional students view older people with dementia: Implications for education and practice. *PLoS One*, *14*(11). https://doi.org/10.1371/journal.pone.0225329.

Scott, T. L., Liddle, J., Mitchell, G., Beattie, E., & Pachana, N. (2019). Implementation and evaluation of a driving cessation intervention to improve community mobility and well-being outcomes for people living with dementia: Study protocol of the 'CarFreeMe' for people with dementia program. *BMC Geriatrics*, *19*(1), 66. https://doi.org/10.1186/s12877-019-1074-6.

Scott, T. L., Liddle, J., Pachana, N. A., Beattie, E., & Mitchell, G. K. (2019). Managing the transition to non-driving in patients with dementia in primary care settings: Facilitators and barriers reported by primary care physicians. *International Psychogeriatrics*, 1–10.

Shah, R. C., Maitra, K., Barnes, L. L., James, B. D., Leurgans, S., & Bennett, D. A. (2012). Relation of driving status to incident life space constriction in community-dwelling older persons: A prospective cohort study. *The Journals of Gerontology Series A: Biological Sciences and Medical Sciences*, *67*(9), 984–989. https://doi.org/10.1093/gerona/gls133.

Shergold, I., Wilson, M., & Parkhurst, G. (2016). *The mobility of older people, and the future role of connected autonomous vehicles*. Retrieved from University of the West of England. website http://www1.uwe.ac.uk/et/research/cts.

Silverstein, N. M., Dickerson, A. E., & Schold Davis, E. (2016). Community mobility and dementia: The role for health care professionals. In M. Boltz, & J. E. Galvin (Eds.), *Dementia care: An evidence-based approach* (pp. 123–148). https://doi.org/10.1007/978-3-319-18377-0_9.

Sims, J., Rouse-Watson, S., Schattner, P., Beveridge, A., & Jones, K. (2012). To drive or not to drive: Assessment dilemmas for GPs. *International Journal of Family Medicine*. https://doi.org/10.1155/2012/417512.

Stav, W. B. (2014). Updated systematic review on older adult community mobility and driver licensing policies. *American Journal of Occupational Therapy*, *68*(6), 681–689. https://doi.org/10.5014/ajot.2014.011510.

Taylor, J. K., Buchan, I. E., & van der Veer, S. N. (2018). Assessing life-space mobility for a more holistic view on wellbeing in geriatric research and clinical practice. *Aging Clinical and Experimental Research*. https://doi.org/10.1007/s40520-018-0999-5.

Vaa, T. (2003). *Impairment, diseases, age and their relative risks of accident involvement: results from meta-analysis*. Oslo, Norway: Report 690 for Institute of Transport Economics.

Wheatley, C. J., Carr, D. B., & Marottoli, R. A. (2014). Consensus statements on driving for persons with dementia. *Occupational Therapy in Health Care*, *28*(2), 132–139. https://doi.org/10.3109/07380577.2014.903583.

Wilson, S., & Pinner, G. (2013). Driving and dementia: A clinician's guide. *Advances in Psychiatric Treatment*, *19*(2), 89–96. https://doi.org/10.1192/apt.bp.111.009555.

World Health Organization. (2001). *International classification of functioning, Disability and Health: ICF*. World Health Organization.

World Health Organization. (2007). *Global age-friendly cities: A guide*. World Health Organization.

CHAPTER 9

Supporting people with dementia in employment

David Evans[a], Carolyn Murray[a], Angela Berndt[a], and Jacinta Robertson[b]
[a]University of South Australia, Adelaide, SA, Australia
[b]Anglicare South Australia, Adelaide, SA, Australia

Introduction

People are living longer and wish to be active, so some remain in the workforce beyond the traditional retirement age of 65 years (Commonwealth of Australia, 2015). A retirement age of 67 years has become more common in some countries (Organisation for Economic Co-operation and Development, 2013) and a greater number of older people are remaining in the workforce (United Nations, 2013). There is a lot of variability internationally, but in countries such as Japan, Korea, Mexico, New Zealand, and Israel more than 20% of people aged 65 years and older are still engaged in the workforce (Organisation for Economic Co-operation and Development, 2019). Participation rates are greater for men, and in some countries, more than 40% of men aged 65 years and older are still working (Organisation for Economic Co-operation and Development, 2019). Workplaces have traditionally been oriented around adults under 65 years, so an ageing workforce is a significant change, and means health conditions that would have previously developed after retirement, such as dementia, may occur while people are still employed.

There is only a small body of research addressing dementia developing in workers, so little is known about the phenomenon. The concept of rehabilitation for people with dementia in the context of employment is still very new. This chapter explores vocational rehabilitation for workers with dementia. Firstly, we explore existing definitions and frameworks on rehabilitation and disability. Secondly, we discuss existing literature about challenges for workers with dementia and then explore suggestions provided for workplaces about how to support a worker with dementia. We conclude by linking the suggestions from the literature with the frameworks on rehabilitation and disability to offer a practical guide for workplace rehabilitation.

Dementia Rehabilitation
https://doi.org/10.1016/B978-0-12-818685-5.00009-X

Workplace rehabilitation and dementia

The World Health Organization (WHO) definition of rehabilitation enables us to situate the discussion within a universally accessible and shared understanding about workplace rehabilitation and dementia. Rehabilitation is defined as "a set of measures that assist individuals who experience, or are likely to experience, disability to achieve and maintain optimal functioning in interaction with their environments" (World Health Organization, 2011, p. 96). Core features of rehabilitation include methods that target body functions and structures, activities and participation, environmental factors, and personal factors (World Health Organization, 2011). The rehabilitation process is deemed to occur in a cycle that:

- Identifies problems and needs
- Relates problems to modifiable and limiting factors
- Defines the target problems, target mediators, and selects appropriate methods
- Plans, implements, and coordinates interventions
- Assesses effects (World Health Organization, 2011)

Rehabilitation outcomes are achieved through prevention of loss or slowing the rate of loss of function, improvement or restoration of function, compensation for lost function or maintenance of current function (World Health Organization, 2011). Stucki, Ewert, and Cieza (2002) state that rehabilitation options are threefold: (1) treatment of impaired body structures and functions, (2) overcoming activity limitations and participation restrictions, and (3) prevention of further symptoms and disability. This chapter focuses on option two, as this is a good fit for vocational rehabilitation for people with dementia. Given this focus, we will discuss vocational rehabilitation in the context of the compensatory and maintenance elements including potential for training or retraining, compensatory strategies, education, support and counseling, modifications to the physical, cultural, social or institutional environments, and provision of resources or assistive technologies (World Health Organization, 2011, p. 100).

In the absence of any framework for vocational rehabilitation for people with dementia, we turned to the WHO International Classification of Disability, Functioning, and Health (ICF). The ICF is a unifying framework to advance systematic methods of rehabilitation in work domains. There is a global model of vocational rehabilitation based on the ICF, where vocational rehabilitation is matched against the core elements of a rehabilitation approach. These core elements include the provision of rehabilitation in different settings and services, focus on work engagement or reengagement along a continuum (time and phase), involving multi-professional interventions that are person-centered and evidence-based to optimize work participation of people with disability and to promote full integration and participation in society (Escorpio et al., 2011). The ICF is a biopsychosocial model; disability and functioning are viewed as outcomes of the interaction between health conditions (such as dementia) and contextual factors including external environmental factors (e.g., social attitudes, architectural characteristics, legal, and structures) and internal person factors (e.g., age, coping styles, education and profession, past and current experiences, behavior patterns) that influence how disability is experienced by an individual (World Health Organization, 2003).

Dementia in the workplace

To investigate the evidence for this chapter a broad search was undertaken of databases, gray literature, and reference lists of relevant papers. However, the current evidence about dementia and employment is very limited. A small number of studies have investigated the difficulties faced by workers with dementia. But there is little evidence on how workplaces should manage or support a worker diagnosed with dementia. We describe the challenges for workers with dementia before and after their diagnosis, explore the perspective of coworkers and managers, and discuss workplace support and reasonable adjustment of work.

Research on dementia in the workplace

The search uncovered four reviews, which were used as the basis for the following description of challenges faced by workers with dementia, looked at before and after diagnosis, and from the perspective of coworkers and managers. See Table 1 for a summary of the reviews that investigated issues related to dementia and employment.

Andrew et al. (2019) undertook a scoping review to explore the impact of dementia on occupational competence, participation, and identity and uncovered six articles reporting qualitative data and no quantitative studies. McCulloch et al. (2016) undertook a systematic review of qualitative evidence to explore the needs, experiences, and perspectives of dementia in employment and identified eight studies. Ritchie et al. (2015) explored support strategies for employees with dementia or mild cognitive impairment to remain employed and drew on six studies (two of which used questionnaires

Table 1 Overview of the reviews that have investigated dementia and employment.

Review aim	Type of review	Discipline of authors	Date range of search/inclusions	included studies	Types and number of participants	Study designs
Andrew, Phillipson, and Sheridan (2019) To report experiences of workers with dementia	Scoping	Occupational therapy and management	2000–17	6 journal articles	90 workers with dementia (either undiagnosed or diagnosed) across a variety of occupations. 15 care partners	All qualitative
McCulloch, Robertson, and Kirkpatrick (2016) Needs experiences and perspectives of people with dementia or MCI in or looking for employment	Systematic	Occupational therapy and business	2001–15	8 journal articles	97 workers with dementia 26 care partners	All qualitative
Ritchie, Banks, Danson, Tolson, and Borrowman (2015) Explore the nature of support for people with dementia or MCI to continue working after diagnosis	Integrative	Nursing and management	2001–14	6 journal articles	45 people with dementia 15 care partners 6 coworkers 25 human resource/ employment specialists	4 qualitative 1 mixed methods 1 quantitative (descriptive)
Thomson, Stanyon, Dening, Heron, and Griffiths (2019) the management of employees who develop dementia while in employment	Systematic	Occupational medicine	1985–2016	22 journal articles	Studies on employer perspectives unavailable therefore relied on data from employees with dementia or MCI— number of participants not given	All qualitative

Abbreviation: MCI, mild cognitive impairment.

with employers). Thomson et al. (2019) undertook a broad systematic review of the peer-reviewed literature to explore management of employees who develop dementia while employed and included 22 journal articles. Thomson et al. (2019) also used gray literature to look at the support available for workers with dementia. The four reviews included mostly qualitative studies which relied heavily on interviews as their method of data collection. The three systematic reviews undertook critical appraisals of their included studies (McCulloch et al., 2016; Ritchie et al., 2015; Thomson et al., 2019) with consistent problems identified with low-quality studies and the position of the researcher not being clearly stated. This meant that there were possibilities of researcher and interpretation bias within the process of data collection and analysis across the included studies. There was minimal overlap of included studies in the systematic reviews and only two studies (Chaplin & Davidson, 2016; Harris & Keady, 2009) were included in all four reviews. The synthesis below draws on the findings from the four reviews.

Challenges for workers with dementia before diagnosis

Some workers reported they noticed that their abilities were changing and began to question and second-guess themselves (Andrew et al., 2019). In contrast, McCulloch et al. (2016) reported some workers lacking insight into the changes occurring with the development of awareness is dependent on the nature of the work and the extent or type of symptoms being experienced. Table 2 gives an overview of some of the ways cognitive challenges presented in the workplace. Generally, workers slowed down in their completion of work tasks, had issues with organization and started to make errors (Andrew et al., 2019). McCulloch et al. (2016) found that decision making of participants and retention of information became impaired as fatigue levels increased toward the end of the day.

In response to their declining performance, some participants experienced a period of denial (Andrew et al., 2019; Ritchie et al., 2015; Thomson et al., 2019). This manifested in trying to hide and dismiss their difficulties (Ritchie et al., 2015; Thomson et al., 2019) through covertly managing errors (Andrew et al., 2019; Ritchie et al., 2015), and using compensatory strategies such as investing time in planning and organization (i.e., using diaries) (McCulloch et al., 2016). During this phase, participants were undergoing significant emotional upheaval, extreme stress, worry about workplace bullying, and being under scrutiny (McCulloch et al., 2016; Thomson et al., 2019). Oftentimes these factors worsened their dementia symptoms (McCulloch et al., 2016; Ritchie et al., 2015).

Table 2 Overview of challenges experienced by workers with undiagnosed dementia.

Presentation of challenges	Andrew et al. (2019)	McCulloch et al. (2016)	Ritchie et al. (2015)	Thomson et al. (2019)
Absence from work	✓			✓
Adjusting to new tasks				✓
Anxiety, hallucinations, and delusions	✓		✓	✓
Becoming increasingly slow	✓	✓	✓	
Boredom	✓		✓	✓
Change in work standards/diminished quality	✓		✓	
Coping with work stressors	✓	✓		
Decision-making impaired		✓	✓	
Decreased information processing ability	✓	✓		
Decreased participation in work activities		✓		✓
Disturbance in language	✓	✓	✓	
Easily distracted		✓		
Errors in writing and spelling	✓	✓	✓	
Feeling overwhelmed	✓		✓	
Forgetfulness			✓	✓
Intense fatigue			✓	
Irritability and apathy	✓		✓	
Lack of initiative			✓	
Lack of insight			✓	
Learning new material			✓	

Symptom / Ability	Column 1	Column 2	Column 3	Column 4
Maintaining concentration	✓	✓		
Making mistakes	✓			
Managing abstract ideas	✓	✓		✓
Memory loss	✓	✓		✓
Missing appointments			✓	✓
Multitasking			✓	✓
Numerical ability such as managing money		✓		✓
Planning	✓			
Problem solving	✓			
Processing information	✓		✓	
Reluctance to engage with others	✓			✓
Remembering names	✓			
Remembering work routine	✓	✓		
Repeating same information in conversations	✓			✓
Rigid thinking	✓			
Using logic		✓		
Using technology		✓		✓
Verbal and physical aggression	✓	✓	✓	
Visual scanning and visual-spatial ability	✓	✓		
Word finding	✓	✓		✓

Challenges for workers with dementia following diagnosis

Following a diagnosis of dementia, the workers began to mistrust their abilities (Andrew et al., 2019). Some participants were keen to continue upholding their right to keep working (McCulloch et al., 2016) and made plans for how this might be possible and for how long (Thomson et al., 2019). Following their diagnosis, some participants were relieved (McCulloch et al., 2016) as it explained their diminishing performance, but this feeling was short-lived as they started to come to terms with the implications of having dementia.

Following the cessation of work, there was a considerable gap left in participants' lives. They felt isolated (Thomson et al., 2019) with increasing financial and personal strain placed on families (McCulloch et al., 2016; Ritchie et al., 2015). Some experienced a loss of identity (McCulloch et al., 2016; Thomson et al., 2019), and some were challenged by negative feelings of self-worth (Andrew et al., 2019) with depression being quite common (McCulloch et al., 2016; Thomson et al., 2019). There was a need to feel they could contribute (McCulloch et al., 2016; Thomson et al., 2019) and fill the void left in their lives with the loss of work.

Behavior and reactions of coworkers and managers

Many employees newly diagnosed with dementia were fearful about how their colleagues would react (Thomson et al., 2019). Little attention was given in the reviews to the perspectives of coworkers and managers as their colleagues began to present with some of the challenges outlined in Table 2. Ritchie et al. (2015) was the only review that included data about the perspectives of employers and managers. They described variable reactions from colleagues, ranging from judgmental to supportive.

From the employee's perspective, prior to the diagnosis they believed some coworkers and managers engaged in heightened surveillance of their performance, which was often covert due to the sensitivities surrounding work performance (McCulloch et al., 2016). This lack of transparency in the process meant that the observations made by coworkers and managers were not discussed with the worker. Sometimes performance management processes were initiated but as these occurred prior to diagnosis, the process became difficult for all parties once it was discovered that the underperformance was an effect of their developing condition (Ritchie et al., 2015).

There were also reports of coworkers being deeply concerned about witnessing the decline in their colleague's abilities (McCulloch et al., 2016;

Ritchie et al., 2015) and trying to cover up for them (Ritchie et al., 2015). Conflicts sometimes arose in workplace relationships as the person with dementia inadvertently said inappropriate things and upset coworkers (Thomson et al., 2019).

Workplace support and reasonable adjustment

There is minimal information in the literature about supporting the worker with dementia. The idea that the person with dementia may wish to continue their employment seems to be a relatively recent concept, so has not been widely considered. The next section will explore some recommendations and suggestions drawn from the literature reviews, journal articles, and gray literature about the options and support for working individuals with dementia.

When considering how dementia in the workplace is managed, Andrew et al. (2019) recommended that attention be given to processes of consultation, reasonable adjustment, and how the cessation of work occurs. Similarly, Thomson et al. (2019) identified the themes of reasonable adjustment and provision of information. Dementia support organizations internationally have also offered suggestions for workers with a diagnosis of dementia and for their employers. However, these suggestions are based on expert opinion rather than research, so have not been evaluated for effectiveness and appropriateness. But they do offer a framework to consider how people with dementia can be supported to remain at work for as long as possible. The suggestions have focused on five areas

1. Assessing the situation and seeking advice
2. Telling people about the dementia
3. Workplace support
4. Reasonable adjustment of work duties
5. Leaving work

Assessing the situation and seeking advice

Problems with establishing a diagnosis and making sense of why the worker was experiencing difficulties arose consistently in the literature. Colleagues struggled to understand why their coworker was not performing well and perceived them as lazy and lacking motivation (Evans, 2019). Employers sometimes attributed the cognitive decline to mental illness and stress (Cox & Pardasani, 2013) and in some cases, medical professionals took the same stance thus not exploring the symptoms further (Ritchie et al., 2015). This dismissive attitude along with the time it takes for investigations and eventual diagnosis can result in some workers staying in the workforce to the detriment of their well-being (Cox & Pardasani, 2013). Andrew et al. (2019) found a mismatch between workplace processes for managing declining worker performance due to cognitive issues and the protection of the rights of the worker. This mismatch took the form of a lack of tolerance and support, or little attempt to modify work duties to help the person with dementia remain at work. This added to the person's stress and anxiety in the workplace and contributed to a poorer transition to retirement. The issue of declining work performance due to cognitive issues needs more consideration from the perspective of worker rights (Cox & Pardasani, 2013) and disability legislation.

A diagnosis of dementia will be a shock for most people, so there is a risk that workers may make a hasty decision about their employment. As a result, some may leave work earlier than needed or miss out on employee entitlements. The literature is silent on the role of health professionals offering advice about employment decisions at the time of diagnosis. But the gray literature cautions workers with dementia not to make hasty decisions (Alzheimer's Society, 2016) and to allow time to absorb the diagnosis before making any decisions about employment (Dementia Australia, 2017). It has been recommended that workers seek advice before resigning, from health professionals, dementia experts, trade union representatives, workplace counseling, or family (Dementia Australia, 2017). Employers may also need to seek legal and human resource advice about how best to uphold and respect the rights of a worker with dementia (Alzheimer's Society, 2015; Thomson et al., 2019).

Telling people about the dementia

The literature recommends that workers with dementia should consider if they wish to remain at work before they share their diagnosis with others and talk to their employer. When work responsibilities include such things as driving, working on a plane or ship, operating machinery, armed forces or being responsible for financial matters, it may be necessary for the newly diagnosed person to notify their employer immediately (Dementia Australia, 2017). Workers may worry that they will be pushed out if they disclose their diagnosis (Roach & Drummond, 2014), but on the other hand, it may be difficult to carry on and be sufficiently supported if coworkers are not aware of the diagnosis (Egan, 2006). Before any discussions with employers, it is recommended, the person with dementia think what they will say and how much they will tell (Dementia Australia, 2015) and it may be helpful for them to be accompanied by a support person to meetings with their workplace manager (Dementia Australia, 2015). It is recommended they seek advice from disability, advocacy or legal organizations about how to handle the negotiation process (Dementia Australia, 2017). The person must also decide who else they trust and try to find a coworker who will provide support for them in the workplace (Dementia Australia, 2015).

Workplace support

Cox and Pardasani (2013) undertook a survey which was completed by 103 employers recruited through human resource organizations in the United States. They found that just under half (approximately 44%) of respondents had experience with employees developing dementia, with symptoms most commonly manifesting through problems with punctuality or missing work (Cox & Pardasani, 2013). For those choosing to stay in the workplace following diagnosis and disclosure, the literature gives strong recommendations about the need for coworkers to receive education about dementia (so they can adequately support their colleague) and for the employee with dementia to have a clear understanding of their own limits (Cox & Pardasani, 2013). Unfortunately, there were some accounts of employees with a known diagnosis of dementia being subject to emotional abuse, bullying and financial exploitation in the workplace due to their vulnerable state (Evans, 2019; Thomson et al., 2019). There were also reports of the person with dementia being "laid off without empathy" following confirmation of the diagnosis (Roach & Drummond, 2014, p. 892).

There have been many suggestions about workplace support strategies for workers with dementia in gray literature. Some of the suggestions are linked to broader discussions about dementia-friendly workplaces. These suggestions focus on having appropriate policies in place that support the needs and rights of people with dementia (Alzheimer's Society, 2015). Dementia-friendly also means creating an environment where other workers feel comfortable talking about dementia (Alzheimer's Society, 2015), are aware of the symptoms of dementia and understand how the symptoms may impact on work (Dementia Engagement and Empowerment Project, 2013). It has been suggested that those workplaces that implement strategies that support occupational choices help support a respectful transition from paid employment to retirement for the worker with dementia (Andrew et al., 2019; Cox & Pardasani, 2013; McCulloch et al., 2016).

Reasonable adjustment of work duties

One of the key recommendations emerging from the literature is about modification and reasonable adjustment of work duties to help support the person with dementia to continue to do their work for as long as reasonably possible (Dementia Australia, 2017). Reasonable adjustment (or accommodation) is a concept from the disability discrimination act (Office of Parliamentary Counsel, 1992) which recognizes that some individuals with physical, sensory, intellectual, or psychosocial impairments may be disadvantaged if conventional requirements are applied to them (Lawson, 2008); this means they may be disadvantaged if treated the same way as other people. Reasonable adjustment is about taking steps to remove that disadvantage by treating the person with a disability differently from the way others are treated (Lawson, 2008). However, there is only limited information about what reasonable adjustment means in the context of dementia and employment.

There are some examples in the literature of how workers modified their habits and routines to maintain their longevity in the workforce. A person described by Ritchie et al. (2015) had a plan that involved checking his timetable on the computer at the start of every workday, but this solution was not effective as he forgot to check the computer. Similar stories were reported by Evans (2019) whereby a person started arriving at work early and finishing late to try and cope with his work duties, but this was not sustainable due to lost sleep and fatigue. Suggestions in the gray literature included simplifying routines (Alzheimer's Society, 2016), regular breaks to minimize fatigue (Dementia Australia, 2017; Dementia UK, 2019), and support through strategies such as a buddy scheme (Dementia UK, 2019). Other recommendations include technology such as computerized diaries and reminders (Alzheimer's Society, 2016; Dementia Australia, 2015), or moving the person to a quieter workspace to minimize distractions and reduce noise (Alzheimer's Society, 2016; Dementia Australia, 2015; Dementia UK, 2019). It has also been suggested that it may be necessary to consider a job change, a reduction in the number of hours worked or a move to a less demanding role within the organization (Dementia UK, 2019).

However, research has found that making modifications to work duties was difficult due to time pressures and sometimes required new learning which was a high expectation for someone with dementia (Egan, 2006). A survey of employment specialists with clients with cognitive impairment in supported employment programs (not limited to dementia) found many rated the support strategies as not effective (McGurk & Mueser, 2006). Accommodations for differing abilities were easier within specifically designed and supported work programs such as the 'Side-by-Side' program organized by Robertson and Evans (2015); but these are rare and do not always include remuneration. Despite a growing interest in the literature in the adjustment of work duties for people with dementia, there has been little attempt to evaluate the impact of this adjustment, so it is unclear if any of the suggestions help people with dementia continue to work.

Leaving work

The final area highlighted in the literature is about the person with dementia leaving work. As noted above, there are recommendations in the gray literature that the person with dementia should not make hasty decisions, should seek advice, and consider their options. However, the literature suggests many people leave their jobs as soon as they received a diagnosis of dementia, or in some cases before a diagnosis was confirmed (Evans, 2019; Ritchie et al., 2015). Some people had the potential to keep working but chose to leave work because their modified work duties were a reminder of their lost abilities (Egan, 2006), and they felt they were a bother to others and embarrassed by their situation (Andrew et al., 2019; Egan, 2006). Some workers with dementia reported having little control over work participation decisions and some employers advocated for early retirement for workers with dementia (Chaplin & Davidson, 2016). Leaving work often happened quickly and was a very difficult and traumatic transition with little support offered (Evans, 2019; McCulloch et al., 2016; Roach & Drummond, 2014).

However, the information in the literature about assisting the transition out of paid employment to early retirement is limited. The void created by leaving work could potentially be filled by alternative programs, but these need to be carefully designed and implemented to ensure dignity, respect, and monitoring for those people engaged in programs (Egan, 2006; Robertson & Evans, 2015). There has been some interest in volunteer programs as a strategy to assist in the transition from work to retirement. Stansell (2001) described a program for people in the early stages of dementia that included volunteer services at community agencies. To ensure the success of this type of program, Stansell (2001) recommends clear admission and discharge criteria, consideration of the safety challenges and having a strategy to help people transition out of the program when their dementia progresses. Other volunteer programs have been established in a hardware store (Robertson & Evans, 2015) and the zoo

(Kinney, Kart, & Reddecliff, 2011). Despite documentation about some programs, the literature about volunteer and workplace programs for people with dementia remains limited.

A framework for supporting workers with dementia

Given the lack of research and available literature, we propose that the WHO definitions of rehabilitation combined with the ICF definitions of activity and participation provides a process and framework by which the vocational rehabilitation needs of people living with dementia could be assessed and addressed. The use of this framework is consistent with rehabilitation for other complex disability interventions. Although core sets for dementia and vocational rehabilitation processes and outcomes do not yet exist in the ICF Checklist (World Health Organization, 2003), it provides a practical tool by which integrated, multisectoral assessment and interventions could be implemented for vocational rehabilitation for people with dementia. Based on our review of the evidence, we have concluded that there is a vocational rehabilitation continuum consisting of three phases for people with dementia:

- assessing the situation and telling people following diagnosis;
- reasonable adjustment and workplace support; and
- planning transition to new participatory roles or leaving work.

In the absence of a core set in the ICF checklist, we created a framework for considering vocational rehabilitation and dementia (see Table 3). In Table 3, we have used the language from the ICF Checklist (World Health Organization, 2003) (impairments of body function and structures; activity limitations and participation restrictions; environmental factors and personal factors) to describe these three phases on the vocational rehabilitation continuum and line them up with the challenges and the compensatory vocational rehabilitation strategies identified from the literature. We have further organized these findings from our review against the five-step rehabilitation process from the World Health Organization (2011). The temporal aspects of the three phases are impossible to standardize due to the person-centered variability of experience of each person with dementia and the fit between their work roles and their capacities. Our proposed framework caters for both individual plans and institutional and systems changes to be advocated for and designed with and for people with dementia. We have proposed three possible outcomes of the vocational rehabilitation process for an employee with dementia which is outlined at the bottom of Table 3 and are consistent with the three phases on the vocational rehabilitation continuum.

Table 3 The rehabilitation continuum: assessing the situation and telling people following diagnosis; reasonable adjustment and workplace support; transition to new participatory roles or leaving work.

Rehabilitation process	Strategy and actions
Step 1 Identify problems and needs Processes continue via regular review	*Impairments of body function and structures* Assess: • Fatigue • Mental functions, e.g., memory, attention, and concentration • Emotional resilience, e.g., feeling overwhelmed, irritability, apathy • Visual scanning and other perceptual functions or symptoms, e.g., hallucinations • Higher level cognitive functions, e.g., flexibility, information processing, planning and organization, judgment, insight, and awareness • Language *Activity limitations and participation restrictions* Assess: • Writing and spelling, numerical ability, managing money, or accounts • Problem-solving abilities • Multitasking, task completion, and planning • Communication
Step 2 Relate problems to modifiable and limiting factors	*Modifiable environmental factors and personal factors* • Support for people to understand strengths and limits • Workplace adjustments • Safety risks • Coworker understanding • Advise Identification of changed activity limitations and participation restrictions is ongoing throughout rehabilitation continuum

Continued

Table 3 The rehabilitation continuum: assessing the situation and telling people following diagnosis; reasonable adjustment and workplace support; transition to new participatory roles or leaving work—cont'd

Rehabilitation process	Strategy and actions
Step 3 Define the target problems, target mediators, select appropriate methods	**Target problems** *Impairments of body function and structures* • Changing body functions *Activity limitations* • Mismatch with work roles *Environmental factors and personal factors* • Mismatch with work environmental demands (social, physical, institutional), • Coworker understanding and knowledge of dementia **Appropriate methods** *Environmental factors and personal factors* • Compensation, environmental modification, and assistive technology • Education • Support and counseling • Policy and procedures As move toward transition, the focus on educating others in external environment is essential. Advocacy for and with person is central to implementation through the continuum of compensatory rehabilitation methods.

Step 4 Plan, implement, and coordinate intervention	**Interventions**
	Compensation, modification, and assistive technology
	• Arrive at work early to setup for day
	• Regular rest breaks during the day
	• Plan high demand roles for when person at their best
	• Allow more time for planning, processing, and completing complex tasks
	• More note taking during formal and informal work processes
	• Provide emotional support and notice positive roles and contributions, use a strength–based approach
	• Modify and simplify work duties
	• Allocate individual tasks and reduce team work
	• Simplify routines
	• Change aspects of a job role
	• Computerized diaries, alerts, reminders, planners
	• Minimize environmental stimulation, quieter spaces, improved lighting, and signage
	Education
	• Strengths based well facilitated coworker education
	Support and counseling
	• Side-by-side work
	• Seek professional support for in work counseling
	Policy and procedures
	• Develop policies to support needs and rights of people with dementia with Human Resources departments or consultants
	Volunteer programs or supports employment schemes are identified early, ready for the transition stage.
	Systems level advocacy for access to funding and policy changes is important.
	Support for transition to new roles occurs with counseling and ongoing education of newly formed support networks and community staff or coparticipants (e.g., in supported participation programs)

Continued

Table 3 The rehabilitation continuum: assessing the situation and telling people following diagnosis; reasonable adjustment and workplace support; transition to new participatory roles or leaving work—cont'd

Rehabilitation process	Strategy and actions	
Step 5 Assess effects and outcomes	• Review situation regularly • Strategies are updated • Person is involved in decisions Begin Step 1 again if required	
Outcome 1 of rehabilitation continuum • Adjustments are evident • Roles are being modified but work is maintained • Economic self-sufficiency • Forward planning is documented and agreed • Quality of life and well-being	*Outcome 2 of rehabilitation continuum* • No further workplace modifications are possible • New plans are actioned • Financial and emotional security is addressed • Activity and participation restrictions are addressed in new environmental context	*Outcome 3 of rehabilitation continuum* • Person with dementia transitions from paid employment to other participatory roles or tasks of meaning • Quality of Life and well-being

Gaps in clinical and research knowledge

Our analysis of dementia and employment literature highlights the limitations in current evidence is very limited. A small number of studies have investigated the difficulties faced by workers with dementia, but there is little evidence on how workplaces should manage or support workers who are diagnosed with dementia. Studies highlight that workers with dementia encounter problems at work and are exposed to a range of different risk in the workplace. Studies also report poor treatment, intolerance, and a lack of support in the workplace for workers with dementia.

The literature offers suggestions about reasonable adjustment and workplace support, but these have not been evaluated and are not based on research evidence. We, therefore, propose that the notion of supporting people with dementia at work is an innovative and relatively under-considered concept in vocational rehabilitation. The reasons for the gap in knowledge about vocational rehabilitation for people with dementia are unknown but may be related to stigma and negative prejudices about the capacity of people with dementia. Furthermore, clear processes and systems are not available to enable people with dementia to continue to work. Our review highlights that we do not know enough about what happens when a worker is diagnosed with dementia or how best to support them at work. This chapter focused on workers, but given that older people make up a significant proportion of the volunteer workforce (Australian Institute of Health and Welfare, 2019), it is likely that volunteers engaged in unpaid work in the community may face similar challenges.

Clinical and research recommendations

There is an urgent need for greater policy support for workplaces, to provide a clearer direction for the management and support of people with dementia who are still working. Policy needs to be informed by different forms of data to triangulate recommendations from different perspectives. To achieve this, it is recommended that research and policy development occur in multi-disciplinary ways; involving health professionals, human resource professionals, legal experts, and employee groups. Existing data is largely qualitative and there is now a need for bigger quantitative data sets that give an accurate picture of the incidence, prevalence, implications, and practices occurring when people develop dementia in the workplace. The rehabilitation framework presented in Table 3 could be implemented as a tool for use by employers in collaboration with health, human resource, and legal professionals to guide strategies and actions when symptoms are noticed. Trial sites for use of such a framework would ideally be large enough to be sufficiently resourced to keep evaluation data.

Much of the published literature presents a negative picture of employer/employee experiences when symptoms of dementia are noticed in workplaces. There is a common theme about intolerance and a lack of support for workers who develop dementia, and there is scope for some positive stories to be shared. There are suggestions in the gray literature for employers and workers, but it is a confusing territory that lacks clear direction. This ambiguity highlights the urgent need for research to investigate workplace support strategies that have been used effectively for workers diagnosed with dementia. Information about effective support strategies would guide both employers and health professionals.

There is most likely a role for health professionals offering employment to offer advice at the time of diagnosis, but little is known about how this could occur. Based on our review of the literature, this advice at diagnosis could include the importance of pausing before making critical decisions, getting advice about employment and sickness benefits, and discussing with family and employers about when is the time to stop working.

While there is disability legislation in many countries to support the rights of workers who have a disability, the place of people with dementia within this legal framework seems to be a little ambiguous. The literature suggests that some workers with dementia are not offered the support and adjustment of work duties that are offered to workers with other types of disability. This is an area in need of urgent consideration, to better define the rights of workers who are diagnosed with dementia and to provide better guidance for workplaces about the rights of workers with dementia.

Conclusion

We have highlighted that some people will develop dementia while they are employed in the workforce. The evidence about dementia in the workplace offers some practical strategies to help workplaces manage and support the worker with dementia, but these are under-evaluated. Our proposed framework for thinking about vocational rehabilitation for people living with dementia in the workforce, using the WHO definitions of rehabilitation combined with the ICF definitions of activity and participation, provides one possible way for thinking about multifaceted assessment and intervention.

This framework moves society one step closer to overcoming some of the current stigma and assumption-laden responses to a person developing dementia while still in the workforce and also provide a means for conceptualizing research in this area.

References

Alzheimer's Society. (2015). *Creating a dementia-friendly workplace.* Retrieved January 28, 2020, from https://www.alzheimers.org.uk/sites/default/files/migrate/downloads/creating_a_dementia-friendly_workplace.pdf.

Alzheimer's Society. (2016). *Living with dementia: Employment.* Retrieved January 28, 2020, from https://www.alzheimers.org.uk/sites/default/files/2018-10/Employment.pdf.

Andrew, C., Phillipson, L., & Sheridan, L. (2019). What is the impact of dementia on occupational competence, occupational participation and occupational identity for people who experience onset of symptoms while in paid employment? A scoping review. *Australian Occupational Therapy Journal, 66*(2), 130–144. https://doi.org/10.1111/1440-1630.12535.

Australian Institute of Health and Welfare. (2019). Retrieved viewed February 24, 2020, from. In *Volunteers.* https://www.aihw.gov.au/reports/australias-welfare/volunteers.

Chaplin, R., & Davidson, I. (2016). What are the experiences of people with dementia in employment? *Dementia, 15*(2), 147–161. https://doi.org/10.1177/1471301213519252.

Commonwealth of Australia. (2015). *2015 Intergenerational report: Australia in 2055.* Retrieved January 28, 2020, from https://treasury.gov.au/sites/default/files/2019-03/2015_IGR.pdf.

Cox, C. B., & Pardasani, M. (2013). Alzheimer's in the workplace: A challenge for social work. *Journal of Gerontological Social Work, 56*(8), 643–656. https://doi.org/10.1080/01634372.2013.821693.

Dementia Australia. (2015). *About you: Making employment decisions.* Retrieved January 28, 2020, from https://www.dementia.org.au/files/helpsheets/Helpsheet-InformationForPeopleWithDementia10-MakingEmploymentDecisions_english.pdf.

Dementia Australia. (2017). *Younger onset dementia: Employment.* January 28, 2020, from https://www.dementia.org.au/files/helpsheets/Helpsheet-YoungerOnsetDementia06-Employment_english.pdf.

Dementia Engagement and Empowerment Project. (2013). *Tips for employers who want to be more dementia friendly.* Retrieved August 18, 2019, from http://dementiavoices.org.uk/wp-content/uploads/2013/11/DEEP-Guide-Tips-for-employers.pdf.

Dementia UK. (2019). *Employment and younger onset Dementia.* Retrieved January 28, 2020, from https://www.dementiauk.org/wp-content/uploads/2019/03/Employment-and-Young-Onset-Dementia-Web-1.pdf.

Egan, M. (2006). Dementia and occupation: A review of the literature. *The Canadian Journal of Occupational Therapy, 73*(3), 132–140. https://doi.org/10.2182/cjot.05.0015.

Escorpio, R., Renemen, D. F., Ekholm, J., Fritz, J., Krupa, T., Marneroft, S., et al. (2011). A conceptual definition of vocational rehabilitation based on the ICF: Building a shared global model. *Journal of Occupational Rehabilitation, 21*(2), 126–133. https://doi.org/10.1007/s10926-011-9292-6.

Evans, D. (2019). An exploration of the impact of younger-onset dementia on employment. *Dementia, 18*(1), 262–281. https://doi.org/10.1177/1471301216668661.

Harris, P., & Keady, J. (2009). Selfhood in younger onset dementia: Transitions and testimonies. *Aging and Mental Health, 13*(3), 437–444. https://doi.org/10.1080/13607860802534609.

Kinney, J., Kart, C., & Reddecliff, L. (2011). That's me, the Goother': Evaluation of a program for individuals with early-onset dementia. *Dementia, 10*, 361–377.

Lawson, A. (2008). *Disability and equality law in Britain*. Oxford: Hart Publishing.

McCulloch, S., Robertson, D., & Kirkpatrick, P. (2016). Sustaining people with dementia or mild cognitive impairment in employment: A systematic review of qualitative evidence. *British Journal of Occupational Therapy*, *79*(11), 682–692. https://doi.org/10.1177/0308022616665402.

McGurk, S., & Mueser, K. (2006). Strategies for coping with cognitive impairments of clients in supported employment. *Psychiatric Services : A Journal of the American Psychiatric Association.*, *57*(10), 1421–1429. https://doi.org/10.1176/ps.2006.57.10.1421.

Office of Parliamentary Counsel. (1992). *Disability Discrimination Act*. Retrieved from https://www.legislation.gov.au/Details/C2018C00125.

Organisation for Economic Co-operation and Development. (2013). Retrieved January 28, 2020, from. In *Pensions at a glance 2019: OECD and G20 indicators*. https://doi.org/10.1787/b6d3dcfc-en.

Organisation for Economic Co-operation and Development. (2019). *OECD labour force statistics 2019*. Paris: OECD Publishing.

Ritchie, L., Banks, P., Danson, M., Tolson, D., & Borrowman, F. (2015). Dementia in the workplace: A review. *Journal of Public Health*, *14*(1), 24–34. https://doi.org/10.1108/JPMH-04-2014-0015.

Roach, P., & Drummond, N. (2014). It's nice to have something to do: Early-onset dementia and maintaining purposeful activity. *Journal of Psychiatric and Mental Health Nursing*, *21*, 889–895. https://doi.org/10.1111/jpm.12154.

Robertson, J., & Evans, D. (2015). Evaluation of a workplace engagement project for people with younger onset dementia. *Journal of Clinical Nursing*, *24*(15–16), 2331–2339. https://doi.org/10.1111/jocn.12852.

Stansell, J. (2001). A volunteer program for people with dementia. *Alzheimer's Care Quarterly*, *2*(2), 4–7.

Stucki, G., Ewert, T., & Cieza, A. (2002). Value and application of the ICF in rehabilitation medicine. *Disability and Rehabilitation*, *24*(7), 932–938. https://doi.org/10.1080/0963828021014859 4.

Thomson, L., Stanyon, M., Dening, T., Heron, R., & Griffiths, A. (2019). Managing employees with dementia: A systematic review. *Occupational Medicine*, *69*(2), 89–98. https://doi.org/10.1093/occmed/kqy161.

United Nations. (2013). *World population ageing 2013*. Retrieved January 28, 2020, from https://www.un.org/en/development/desa/population/publications/pdf/ageing/WorldPopulationAgeing2013.pdf.

World Health Organization. (2003). *ICF checklist version 2.1a, clinician form*. Retrieved January 28, 2020, from https://www.who.int/classifications/icf/icfchecklist.pdf?ua=1.

World Health Organization. (2011). *World report on disability*. Retrieved January 28, 2020, from https://www.who.int/disabilities/world_report/2011/en/.

CHAPTER 10

Can buildings contribute to the rehabilitation of people living with dementia?

Richard Fleming
Faculty of Science, Medicine and Health, University of Wollongong, Wollongong, NSW, Australia

Introduction

Worldwide, there is a growing interest in ensuring that the United Nations Convention on the Rights of Persons with Disabilities (CRPD) (United Nations, 2006) is applied to people living with dementia (Byrnes, 2019; Clare, 2017; Steele, Swaffer, Phillipson, & Fleming, 2019).

This chapter draws on a description of rehabilitation that provides a framework for understanding how the built environment can contribute to the rehabilitation of people with dementia. Mountain (2005) reviewed the literature on rehabilitation and dementia and proposed the following framework:

1. Assessment of function
2. Psychosocial activities
3. Psychotherapeutic modalities, e.g., reminiscence therapy
4. Sensory stimulation, e.g., music and Snoezelen
5. Interventions for improving functional abilities and abilities to undertake activities of daily living
6. Interventions to improve memory and cognition
7. Self-management
8. Technologies to compensate for failing mental and physical capacities
9. Interventions to assist both formal (paid) and informal (relatives, friends, and neighbors) carers

This chapter utilizes these domains, with the exception of assessment of function, to structure a sampling of the literature on environmental design and modifications for people with dementia that will illustrate the role a building can play in rehabilitation. The chapter follows Clare's lead in considering rehabilitation as being synonymous with tertiary prevention (Clare, 2017), i.e., the activity of trying to improve quality of life by reducing

Dementia Rehabilitation
https://doi.org/10.1016/B978-0-12-818685-5.00010-6

171

disability, limiting or delaying complications, and restoring function. The environment is taken to be the combination of the architectural aspects (permanent features), interior/exterior design features (furnishings, objects, décor, and garden layout), and the ambient environment (e.g., lighting and noise).

Readers are referred to existing systematic reviews for a comprehensive analysis of the state of the art (Chaudhury, Cooke, Cowie, & Razaghi, 2017; Fleming & Purandare, 2010; Marquardt, Bueter, & Motzek, 2014). These reviews have come to the conclusion that the work on designing environments for people with dementia has progressed relatively well over the past 30 years to the point that there is now an established body of evidence. This evidence should be drawn on when considering size, layout, homelike design, sensory environment, and the characteristics of spaces intended for socializing (Chaudhury et al., 2017). However, experts are also cautious not to overstate the level of evidence available because of the cross-sectional nature of the much of the research and the small sample sizes involved in the studies.

Current approaches and evidence

Psychosocial activities

One of the most debilitating conditions that often accompanies dementia is lowered mood and depression resulting in withdrawal from psychosocial activities. If mood can be improved and depression can be alleviated, then the likelihood that a person with dementia will engage in psychosocial activities increases.

One of the most insidious contributors to low mood in people living with dementia, particularly those in nursing homes, is feeling "locked up." A building that clearly appears to be designed to lock people with dementia away may contribute to low mood and depression. A building that provides an unobtrusively safe environment for people with dementia provides a context in which they feel more able to engage with life. Zeisel et al. (2003) found that levels of depression were negatively correlated with exit design. People with dementia living in facilities which had well-camouflaged exits and silent electronic locks (instead of alarms) were less likely to be depressed. This may reduce the attempts of people with dementia trying to leave the facility and staff within the setting considering the environment to be safer and, therefore, more likely to allow independence within the residents. Residents who perceived that they had more freedom then may have felt a greater sense of control and higher mood (Zeisel et al., 2003). In a cross-sectional study of 11 nursing homes, Low and colleagues found that harmful behaviors, particularly risk taking and passive self-harm were associated with greater security features (Low, Draper, & Brodaty, 2004). This further supports the hypothesis that an overemphasis on safety can have unwanted side effects. This finding was further validated in a study carried out in the United Kingdom (Torrington, 2006). The researcher found that safety and health (assessed using the DICE) was negatively associated with reported quality of life. Where scores were high for safety and health, they were lower for enjoyment of activities and ability to control the environment.

Greater recognition of the human rights of people with dementia, particularly the right to liberty enshrined in Article 14 of the CRPD (Steele et al., 2019), should lead to greater awareness of the detrimental effects of locking up people with dementia and result in the provision of buildings that do not, by their very nature, depress people and instead foster a context for psychosocial interactions.

It is not only the nature of the perimeter of the building that establishes the context for social interaction. The nature of the internal spaces is also important. The beneficial effects on psychosocial activities of providing a variety of places, ranging from places where the person can be by themselves, through spaces where they can interact with a small number of people to spaces for large social gatherings, have been well documented. Zeisel et al. (2003) found that where there was variability in social spaces within a facility there was less social withdrawal amongst residents (Zeisel et al., 2003). Common areas that varied in ambience were seen to reduce depression, misidentification, and the amount of hallucinations (Zeisel et al., 2003). Similarly, Barnes found that residents in homes with more gradation between private, semiprivate, and public spaces were likely to experience higher levels of well-being as well as more environmental control than residents living in homes with less privacy gradation (Barnes, 2006). In a paper which provides several hints on creating environments thought to be helpful to people with dementia, Hoglund, Dimotta, Ledewitz, and Saxton (1994) stated that.

"…one thing that works well is having a variety of rooms and allowing them to have a definite purpose, rather than being a multipurpose space" (p. 76).

An investigation of the relationships between quality of life and the subscale scores of the Environmental Audit Tool (Fleming, 2011), which measures the quality of the environment against a set of 10 principles, revealed a significant, positive correlation between quality of life, and the provision of a range of spaces. This study involved 275 residents in 35 aged care homes in Australia and controlled for a number of potentially confounding factors (Fleming, Goodenough, Low, Chenoweth, & Brodaty, 2014).

Noise levels within social spaces also have a significant effect on social interaction. High noise levels in the living room were associated with low levels of social interaction (Garre-Olmo et al., 2012). On the other hand, while high sound levels have been shown to reduce levels of social interaction, moderate levels of sound appear to be associated with more engaged behaviors (Cohen-Mansfield, Thein, Dakheel-Ali, & Marx, 2010), giving rise to the idea that a very quiet environment may also inhibit psychosocial activity.

Psychotherapeutic modalities

Systematic reviews of the evidence for the effectiveness of non-pharmacological approaches to assisting people with dementia, particularly those for the management of behavioral and psychological symptoms, support their use and show that they compare well against pharmacological interventions (Dyer, Harrison, Laver, Whitehead, & Crotty, 2018). An approach that consistently shows a significant positive effect is music therapy (Dyer et al., 2018; Kishita, Backhouse, & Mioshi, 2020; Oyebode & Parveen, 2019). Reminiscence therapy has also been the focus of many studies the highest quality of which have been the subject of a Cochrane review (O'Philbin, Woods, Farrell, Spector, & Orrell, 2018). Findings suggest that reminiscence therapy may improve psychosocial outcomes for people with dementia. Studies have shown that reminiscence therapy delivered on an individual basis may improve cognition and mood, whereas therapy delivered to a group may improve communication. The impact of reminiscence therapy on quality of life appeared to be most apparent when offered in care home settings.

While it might seem obvious, it is very rarely stated that these two approaches, unlike their pharmacological counterparts, require the support of the environment. They both require environments that enable the therapist to interact with the person, or people, with dementia in comfort and without distraction. The provision of these spaces should not be left to chance but be part of the design of the building being used in the care of people with dementia.

In the case of reminiscence therapy, it may be argued that a familiar environment provides constant opportunities for reminiscing. A familiar environment is one that is similar to that experienced by the person with dementia during the period that they remember best. This is usually early adulthood. The opportunity to increase the familiarity of the surroundings by the residents of aged care facilities, personalizing the environment, often by bringing in their own belongings, has been associated with the maintenance of activities of daily living and reductions in aggression, anxiety, and depression (Annerstedt, 1997; Charras et al., 2012; Garcia et al., 2012; Greene & Asp, 1985; Morgan & Stewart, 1999; Zeisel et al., 2003) and is also associated with higher levels of quality of life (Fleming et al., 2014). In contrast, a non-familiar atmosphere in a bathroom has been shown to cause problematic behaviors (Namazi & Johnson, 1996).

Sensory stimulation

If not well managed, the sensory environment can have detrimental effects on people with dementia who have difficulties in dealing with high levels of stimulation. Their ability to screen out unwanted visual and auditory stimuli appears to be reduced. They can become more confused, anxious, and agitated when overstimulated (Cleary, Clamon, Price, & Shullaw, 1988; Netten, 1993). Common causes of overstimulation are busy entry doors that are visible to residents, clutter, public address systems (Brawley, 1997; Cohen & Weisman, 1991), alarms, loud televisions (Evans, 1989; Hall, Kirschling, & Todd, 1986), corridors, and crowding (Nelson, 1995).

The building can contribute to the rehabilitation effort when it has been designed to reduce these unhelpful stimuli. There is, for example, strong evidence that residents of care homes are less verbally aggressive when the sensory environment is optimized (Zeisel et al., 2003, p. 708).

A well-designed building can provide a context in which rehabilitation is more likely to succeed. But, perhaps, it can be more active than that by including features specifically intended to improve the well-being of the residents. Two common examples are the inclusion of rooms specifically for sensory stimulation, such as Snoezelen rooms, and the provision of access to greenery and nature in the form of a garden. An Australian study was the first to demonstrate empirically an increase in pleasure associated with being in a landscaped garden (Cox, Burns, & Savage, 2004). Cox and colleagues examined how a Snoezelen room and a landscaped garden in a nursing home improved the well-being of care home residents who had dementia. These environments were compared to the experience of the normal living environment. The observed response of 24 residents with dementia was measured during time spent in the Snoezelen room, in the garden, and in the living room. Both the Snoezelen room and the garden decreased the signs of sadness shown by residents in comparison with the living room and significantly increased the signs of pleasure.

More recent studies, however, have cast doubt on the significance of the benefits of Snoezelen rooms. Smith and D'Amico reviewed the evidence and concluded that while positive, short-term effects can be detected, over-all the evidence is inconclusive (Smith & D'Amico, 2019). In contrast, a review of green space in care homes concluded that exposure to greenery and use of green space in care facilities showed promise in their ability to promote positive mental health (Carver, Lorenzon, Veitch, Macleod, & Sugiyama, 2020, p. 5). The reviewers drew attention to significant improve-ments in quality of life, reductions in depression, improved mood, increased interest in indoor pursuits, stress relief, and feelings of being mentally and physically refreshed. However, they were cautious about the strength of the evidence because of the low number of studies and the use of non-validated mental health measures. They described the field as being in its infancy. Unfortunately, we have not progressed much further in our understanding of the effects of Snoezelen rooms or gardens beyond the study completed by Cox and colleagues. They reported that regardless of setting, well-being was dependent on relationships, quality time, and closeness to other than mattered most (Cox et al., 2004, p. 43). Shortly after, Wood, Harris, Snider, and Patchel (2005) found that the presence of a pleasant, safe outside space had no affect that could be attributed to it that was not secondary to the impact of the relationships with the staff (Wood et al., 2005).

This draws attention to the limitations of the building as an active player in rehabilitation. A well-designed building can certainly provide a context for rehabilitation and avoid the negative impacts of a poorly designed build-ing, e.g., overstimulation, but when it comes to active rehabilitation care offered by staff and relationships are critical.

Interventions for improving functional abilities and abilities to undertake activities of daily living

It is a common practice to use features of the built environment as supports for a person with dementia's ability to perform activities of daily living (ADLs) by placing labels on drawers and cupboard doors, making objects visible through the doors, and removing distracting items (Chard, Liu, & Mulholland, 2008). More subtle environmental control such a reducing noise levels have been shown to improve ADLs (Garre-Olmo et al., 2012) and subtle environmental differences in exit control, safety, and homeliness between very similar facilities resulted in up to 50% difference in observed engagement in ADLs (Milke, Beck, Danes, & Leask, 2009). The effects of more obvious interventions were explored in an early study of residents in an 11 bed reduced stimulation unit. Within this unit, doors could be camouflaged, small tables were set up for eating and activities and the colors within the space were neutral. The use of televisions, radios, and telephones was limited and residents were free to ambulate, eat, and rest whenever they wished on the unit. A consistent daily routine scheduled rest and small-group activity periods (Cleary et al., 1988). Three months after admission to the facility, residents were significantly more involved in ADLs and required significantly less restraint than 3 months prior to admission. Agitation and wandering had decreased, while medication usage had not changed. Almost at the same time, while there was a very little information available to guide the design of environments for people with dementia, similar results were found when a group of patients with dementia were transferred from a psychiatric hospital to a purpose-designed unit (Fleming & Bowles, 1987). The evaluation of the unit suggested that the main impacts of this style of environment were to be found in improvements in self-help, socialization, and behavior although it is clear that these changes were brought about by the combination of both the environmental and psychosocial factors in operation in this specialized unit for people with dementia.

A more recent and thorough study of the functional and cognitive abilities of residents of small scale, homelike facilities produced very encouraging results (Milke, Leask, George, & Ziolkowski, 2015). The authors systematically and assessed the residents of three Alzheimer Care Centers (ACCs) over an 8-year period, which is a much longer time span than any other comparable study. The ACCs comprised groups of distinct self-contained houses linked by common areas that included a common room, activity spaces, and walking paths that led to exterior doors and a secure courtyard. They compared the changes that took place with estimates of the natural progression of Alzheimer's disease and found results that they describe as "frankly, startling." Residents experienced a slower and more consistent decline than was expected. The researchers reported that the homogenous and stimulating environment appeared to preserve the abilities of residents during their stay.

These findings are largely consistent with those reported in reviews of the literature, e.g., Chaudhury et al. (2017) collating information on much shorter studies but are even more compelling, greatly adding to the confidence that can be placed in the empirical support for considering the design of the building to be an integral part of the rehabilitation effort. A recent review specifically on investigations into the use of the environment to support everyday activities for people with dementia confirms this confidence in its conclusion that "this is an important area of research which appears to support a role for the environment in assisting people with dementia to perform a range of everyday tasks" (Woodbridge et al., 2018).

Considering rehabilitation as including efforts to limit or delay complications leads on to the recognition of the role of the building in preventing falls. People with dementia are eight times more likely to experience a fall than those of the same age without dementia (Allan, Ballard, Rowan, & Kenny, 2009). The provision of care in a specialized behavioral management area has been shown to reduce falls (Gonski & Moon, 2012). A significant reduction in injuries associated with falls has been achieved by providing furniture that puts the person with dementia closer to the ground through the use of bean bag chairs, futons, and mattresses placed on the floor (Scandura, 1995). The benefits of preventing falls by rearranging furniture, removing objects that may precipitate falls, repairing door steps, removing loose carpets, providing grab bars, improving lighting, repositioning beds and adjusting bed and chair heights, repairing roller walkers, and removing obstacles have been identified (Kallin, Jensen, Lundin Olsson, Nyberg, & Gustafson, 2004). Care must also be taken to avoid bold floor patterns and dark lines or surfaces that can disorient people with dementia (Passini, Pigot, Rainville, & Tetreault, 2000) and texture, joint presence, and color on pathways (Zamora, 2008).

Interventions to improve memory and cognition

One of the most basic activities that draws on the memory and cognitive abilities of the person with dementia is wayfinding. It is also an activity that can be easily facilitated, or made very difficult, by the design of the building. Research has shown that a simple building "where residents should be able to proceed from one decision point to the next as they walk along without having to plan for future decisions" is associated with good wayfinding (Passini, Rainville, Marchand, & Joanette, 1998). Being able to see where you want to go, often referred to as visual access, along with the integration of reference points and the implementation of several zones with a unique character have been identified as helpful for resident's wayfinding (Elmstahl, Annerstedt, & Ahlund, 1997; Marquardt & Schmieg, 2009; Netten, 1989; Passini et al., 2000).

Where direct visual access has not been provided in a building signage, furnishings, lighting, and color can assist with wayfinding. However, these cannot totally compensate for poor design (Marquardt, 2011). As signs are often used to assist wayfinding, it may be useful to describe the elements of a good sign. Signs should be clear and highlighted by a contrasting background, while those that are only relevant to staff should not contrast (Dinshaw, 2006). Signs on doors should not be above eye level, remembering that many old people have stooped posture. In fact, there is some evidence to support placing signs on the floor to compensate for the downcast gaze of many people with dementia (Namazi & Johnson, 1991). This study indicated that the best results, for getting residents to use a publicly available toilet on their unit, were obtained by using the word toilet on an arrow on the floor pointing to the toilet. The placing of a graphic depicting a toilet on the toilet door at eye level was also effective but not as effective as the arrow on the floor. Relevant, and only relevant, information needs to be presented in a variety of ways to maximize the chances of it being noticed and understood.

Signs and cues in the form of text and graphics are not the only way in which information about the location of spaces can be made available

The physical environment not only creates the wayfinding problems people have to solve but it can also provide information to solve these problems. ... Information should be presented by different means to allow for personal preferences and redundancy. ... Attention has to be paid to avoid distracting residents by nonrelevant information displays. The environment has to speak a language that the user .... can understand (Passini et al., 2000).

Some design guidelines suggest that the different means mentioned in this quotation include providing olfactory and auditory cues to identify and differentiate particular places, e.g., the corridor that your room is in, although the empirical evidence for this is very limited.

Design features such as these provide a passive context that supports the memory and cognition of the person with dementia but is there an environment that will actively improve memory and cognition? The fixed nature of buildings is an obstacle to this but if we are prepared to extend our definition of the environment to include virtual environments then the picture changes. A recent review of the use of virtual reality to improve cognitive functioning in people with neurocognitive disorders may improve congition and psychological functioning (such as reduction of anxiety and increased use of coping strategies) (Moreno et al., 2019).

It could be suggested, with tongue in cheek, that as the boundary between the real and virtual reality weakens through the use of assistive technologies, the environment may become an active agent in cognitive rehabilitation.

Self-management

Approaches to the self-management of some chronic diseases, e.g., diabetes, are well developed but this is not the case for dementia. Perhaps, this is tied up with epistemic invalidation of people living with dementia that results in them being regarded as incapable of making decisions about care or even of describing their own condition and needs (Carel & Kidd, 2014). Given that 70% of people with dementia live in the community (Australian Institute of Health and Welfare, 2012), it may be time to look more closely at this issue. There is some guidance available which helps people with dementia to prepare and maximize their opportunities to care for themselves. Specific recommendations for increasing the dementia friendliness of one's environment include:

- Ensure personal items and photos are on display to provide opportunities for reminiscence to reduce stress and anxiety.
- Place regularly used items in line of sight and group common items together to make them easier to find.
- Use labels to help locate and identify items.
- Make sure hot/cold indicators are clearly identified on taps, to avoid confusion.
- If you ever need to replace an appliance, make sure you do so with a familiar and recognizable model.
- Have distinctive colored doors with contrasting door frames to help with orientation.
  Source: (Alzheimer's Australia, n.d.).

A pilot investigation of a self-management program (Romero & Wenz, 2001) showed a reduction in depression and an improvement in social interaction. The parts of the program that point to the possibility of the environment being useful in this context were the focus on the maintenance of a sense of personal identity and maintaining engagement with everyday activities. The maintenance of personal identity has been discussed in relation to environmental support of reminiscence and engagement with everyday activities has been reviewed in the section on functional activities.

Technologies to compensate for failing mental and physical capacities

A recent review of assistive technologies for people with dementia living in supportive environments identified 61 relevant papers and concluded that there "was a significant lack of compelling evidence to indicate the technology intervention that is most effective" (Daly Lynn et al., 2019). Echoing the findings of a review published 5 years earlier that identified 41 papers and reported that the evidence for the effective use of assistive technology for people with dementia was very weak (Fleming & Sum, 2014). Common issues reported were difficulties using systems, lack of acceptance by the user, and the poor reliability of the technology.

The increasing number of papers and the obvious increase in the presence of technology in everyday life suggests that it is just a matter of time before assistive technology becomes useful to people living with dementia. Particularly, as those that have grown up with technology age with the ability to use it deeply ingrained in their long-term memory. Having said that, it is likely that the speed of progress would be increased by engaging more people with dementia in the design process (Daly Lynn et al., 2019).

The most recent review identified six streams of assistive technology most relevant to the life of a person with dementia in a supportive environment:
- Telecare
- Light therapy
- Robotic companions
- Well-being and leisure
- Simulated presence
- Orientation and activities of daily living (Daly Lynn et al., 2019).

Examples given in two of these, light therapy and orientation and activities of daily living, can be related to the consideration of the environment.

The primary purpose of light therapy is to reduce sleep disorders and disruptive behavior. It is based on the theory that these problems are caused, at least in part, by disturbances in the circadian rhythm and that exposure to bright light can stabilize that rhythm. As people living in nursing homes, or spending almost all of their time indoors in their own home, are less exposed to daylight, they need supplementary illumination. Unfortunately, the evidence for the effectiveness of light therapy is not strong enough to enable a recommendation for its use (Forbes, Blake, Thiessen, Peacock, & Hawranik, 2014).

A computerized device that could, potentially, be built into a bathroom, to help people with dementia wash their hands, while reducing caregiver burden was assessed in a single-subject study (Mihailidis, Boger, Craig, & Hoey, 2008). The device used artificial intelligence to autonomously guide six older adults with dementia through hand washing using audio and video prompts. Four of the six participants were able to achieve independence. However, this result required careful tailoring of the technology to meet the individual needs of the person with dementia.

At this stage of the development of assistive technologies, it may be sensible to be cautious about their adoption. While it is possible for people with dementia to learn to use new technologies, this is not easy and requires a great deal of support from skilled staff (Fleming & Sum, 2014; Lekeu, Wojtasik, der Linden Van, & Salmon, 2002). It is much easier, more practical and, possibly, more pleasant for the person with dementia to be provided with fittings, e.g., taps, that they can use because their use is recorded in their long-term memory. Even the ubiquitous position-change alarms that are installed in aged care homes to monitor movement and prevent falls have come under question because of a high rate of false alarms. A study on the effect of removing these devices and engaging staff in the development of alternative ways to prevent falls showed a statistically significant reduction in falls (Bressler, Redfern, & Brown, 2011).

Interventions to assist both formal (paid) carers and care partners

The previous sections have provided examples of some specific environmental characteristics that are of benefit to people living with dementia. In so far as these make life easier and better for them they must, surely, make life easier and better for their care partners. In broad terms, it seems obvious that an environment of the right size, layout, and atmosphere assists everyone who spends time in it. If empirical evidence is needed, we can look at studies of these characteristics. One such study compared behavior problems before and after transfer to a unit, where the dining area was both physically and numerically smaller (Schwarz, Chaudhury, & Tofle, 2004):

> The new dining spaces served eight to 10 residents compared with the 25 to 30 residents who had their meals in the large dining area before the renovation. Behavioral mapping data indicated that there were fewer incidents of disruptive and agitated behaviors in the new dining areas than in the larger dining space that served the residents prior to the renovation. Staff members seemed to be having more sustained conversations with the residents in the new dining spaces than they were having in the old dining space. The reduction of group size in the new dining areas reduced the possibility of the chain reaction of disruptive behaviors during mealtimes.

Other studies have looked at staff being able to see the residents from the places where they spend most of their time, i.e., having good visual access to residents. Staff working in facilities with good visual access spent less time locating and monitoring their patients (Morgan & Stewart, 1999). Good sight lines between the nurses' station and other key locations have been found to be influential in prompting or supporting informal social interactions (Campo & Chaudhury, 2012). In hospitals, the decentralization of the nurses' station to small bays located so as to improve monitoring by staff, and visibility of staff to patients, has been found to reduce the use of the nurse call system and improve contact between staff and patients (Burns, 2011).

With regard to the atmosphere of the environment, an Australian qualitative investigation of the views of staff and relatives on a new purpose designed (Cioffi, Fleming, Wilkes, Sinfield, & Le Miere, 2007) suggested that home-likeness is related to concepts such as a pleasant milieu, looking homely, a homelike eating environment, feeling homely, like a kitchen at home, tranquility, light and airy, serene, unrestricted, inviting for relatives, and comfortable for children. The authors concluded that an improved environment can enhance the QOL for residents, the "nursing home" experience for relatives and the working environment for staff. Relatives appreciated the airy homelike atmosphere with garden access, which increased their comfort with visiting and with having their family member in care. Staff reported that better access to equipment and greater ability to monitor residents helped them to provide better care. They were able to feel more comfortable about the safety of the residents.

Concluding remarks and clinical recommendations

The rehabilitative effect of a well-designed environment has not yet been proven to the standards used in trialing drugs and, in fact, may never be as the research designs used in drug trials, e.g., randomized control trials, do not work well when applied to evaluating environmental changes (Chenoweth et al., 2014). However, there is sufficient evidence that a range of environmental characteristics that include unobtrusive safety, small size, good visual access, appropriate levels of stimulation, familiarity, provision of a range of spaces, providing opportunities for engaged movement both indoors and outdoors, and being attractive and accessible to visitors, do provide a supportive context for rehabilitation.

However, mounting an argument for the importance of considering the role of the environment in rehabilitation should not cloud our judgment about the size of that importance. It has been estimated that the quality of the environment contributes 14.6% of the variance of quality of life (Fleming et al., 2014). This leaves a lot of room for other contributions, particularly that of the staff. It is very important to keep in mind that the care, and rehabilitation, of people living with dementia occurs within a complex system. Zeisel et al. have coined the term "ecopsychological" to encompass the full range of educational efforts, social support programs, community awareness raising, intergenerational programs as well as environmental design approaches required to be successful (Zeisel, Reisberg, Whitehouse, Woods, & Verheul, 2016).

For me the best indicator of success will be found in the behavior of 8 year olds. When I wake up on Sunday in Australia where there are a lot of 8 year olds saying to their mums and dads, "Let's go and see Granny in her home, it's so much fun being there," I'll know that we have got the whole, ecopsychological system right and that rehabilitation is just business as usual.

References

Allan, L. M., Ballard, C. G., Rowan, E. N., & Kenny, R. A. (2009). Incidence and prediction of falls in dementia: A prospective study in older people. *PLoS One, 4*(5), e5521. Retrieved from [Electronic Resource].

Alzheimer's Australia. The Dementia Guide: for people with dementia, their family and carers, n.d. Retrieved from https://www.dementia.org.au/files/VIC/documents/Alzheimers-Australia-Vic-Dementia-Guide-Web.pdf.

Annerstedt, L. (1997). Group-living care: An alternative for the demented elderly. *Dementia and Geriatric Cognitive Disorders, 8*(2), 136–142.

Australian Institute of Health and Welfare. (2012). *Dementia in Australia*. Retrieved from https://www.aihw.gov.au/reports/dementia/dementia-in-australia/contents/table-of-contents.

Barnes, S. (2006). Space, choice and control, and quality of life in care settings for older people. *Environment and Behavior, 38*(5), 589–604.

Brawley, E. C. (1997). *Designing for Alzheimer's disease. Strategies for creating better care environments*. New York: Wiley.

Bressler, K., Redfern, R. E., & Brown, M. (2011). Elimination of position-change alarms in an Alzheimer's and dementia long-term care facility. *American Journal of Alzheimer's Disease and Other Dementias, 26*(8), 599–605. https://doi.org/10.1177/1533317511432730.

Burns, A. (2011). Help patients see more clearly. *The Health Service Journal, 121*(6282), 26–27.

Byrnes, A. (2019). Human rights unbound: An unrepentant call for a more complete application of human rights in relation to older persons—And beyond. In *Paper presented at the Australian Association of Gerontology annual conference, Sydney*.

Campo, M., & Chaudhury, H. (2012). Informal social interaction among residents with dementia in special care units: Exploring the role of the physical and social environments. *Dementia, 11*(3), 401–423. https://doi.org/10.1177/1471301211421189.

Carel, H., & Kidd, I. J. (2014). Epistemic injustice in healthcare: A philosophical analysis. *Medicine, Health Care and Philosophy: A European Journal, 17*(4), 529–540.

Carver, A., Lorenzon, A., Veitch, J., Macleod, A., & Sugiyama, T. (2020). Is greenery associated with mental health among residents of aged care facilities? A systematic search and narrative review. *Aging & Mental Health, 24*(1), 1–7. https://doi.org/10.1080/13607863.2018.1516193.

Chard, G., Liu, L., & Mulholland, S. (2008). Verbal cueing and environmental modifications: Strategies to improve engagement in occupations in persons with alzheimer disease. *Physical and Occupational Therapy in Geriatrics, 27*(3), 197–211. https://doi.org/10.1080/02703180802206280.

Charras, K., Zeisel, J., Belmin, J., Drunat, O., Sebbagh, M., Gridel, G., & Bahon, F. (2012). Effect of personalization of private spaces in special care units on institutionalized elderly with dementia of the Alzheimer type. *Dementia: Non-Pharmacological Therapies*, 119–135.

Chaudhury, H., Cooke, H. A., Cowie, H., & Razaghi, L. (2017). The influence of the physical environment on residents with dementia in long-term care settings: A review of the empirical literature. *The Gerontologist, 58*, e325–e337.

Chenoweth, L., Forbes, I., Fleming, R., King, M. T., Stein-Parbury, J., Luscombe, G., … Brodaty, H. (2014). PerCEN: A cluster randomized controlled trial of person-centered residential care and environment for people with dementia. *International Psychogeriatrics, 26*(07), 1147–1160. https://doi.org/10.1017/S1041610214000398.

Cioffi, J. M., Fleming, A., Wilkes, L., Sinfield, M., & Le Miere, J. (2007). The effect of environmental change on residents with dementia: The perceptions of relatives and staff. *Dementia, 6*(2), 215–231.

Clare, L. (2017). Rehabilitation for people living with dementia: A practical framework of positive support. *PLoS Medicine, 14*(3). https://doi.org/10.1371/journal.pmed.1002245.

Cleary, T. A., Clamon, C., Price, M., & Shullaw, G. (1988). A reduced stimulation unit: Effects on patients with Alzheimer's disease and related disorders. *The Gerontologist, 28*, 511–514.

Cohen, U., & Weisman, G. D. (1991). *Holding on to home: Designing environments for people with dementia*. Baltimore: Johns Hopkins University Press.

Cohen-Mansfield, J., Thein, K., Dakheel-Ali, M., & Marx, M. S. (2010). Engaging nursing home residents with dementia in activities: The effects of modeling, presentation order, time of day, and setting characteristics. *Aging and Mental Health, 14*(4), 471–480. https://doi.org/10.1080/13607860903586102.

Cox, H., Burns, I., & Savage, S. (2004). Multisensory environments for leisure: Promoting well-being in nursing home residents with dementia. *Journal of Gerontological Nursing, 30*(2), 37–45.

Daly Lynn, J., Quinn, E., Rondón-Sulbarán, J., Ryan, A., Martin, S., & McCormack, B. (2019). A systematic review of electronic assistive technology within supporting living environments for people with dementia. *Dementia, 18*(7–8), 2371–2435. https://doi.org/10.1177/1471301217733649.

Dinshaw, C. (2006). Surveying nursing practice on wards for older people with mental health needs. *Nursing Older People, 18*(10), 25–31.

Dyer, S. M., Harrison, S. L., Laver, K., Whitehead, C., & Crotty, M. (2018). An overview of systematic reviews of pharmacological and non-pharmacological interventions for the treatment of behavioral and psychological symptoms of dementia. *International Psychogeriatrics, 30*(3), 295–309. https://doi.org/10.1017/S1041610217002344.

Elmstahl, S., Annerstedt, L., & Ahlund, O. (1997). How should a group living unit for demented elderly be designed to decrease psychiatric symptoms? *Alzheimer Disease & Associated Disorders, 11*(1), 47–52.

Evans, B. (1989). *Managing from day to day: Creating a safe and workable environment*. Minneapoolis, MN: Department of Veterans Affairs Medical Centre.

Fleming, R. (2011). An environmental audit tool suitable for use in homelike facilities for people with dementia. *Australasian Journal on Ageing, 30*(3), 108–112. https://doi.org/10.1111/j.1741-6612.2010.00444.x.

Fleming, R., & Bowles, J. (1987). Units for the confused and disturbed elderly: Development, design, programmimg and evaluation. *Australasian Journal on Ageing, 6*(4), 25–28.

Fleming, R., Goodenough, B., Low, L. F., Chenoweth, L., & Brodaty, H. (2014). The relationship between the quality of the built environment and the quality of life of people with dementia in residential care. *Dementia, 15*, 663–680.

Fleming, R., & Purandare, N. (2010). Long-term care for people with dementia: Environmental design guidelines. *International Psychogeriatrics, 22*(7), 1084–1096. https://doi.org/10.1017/s1041610210000438.

Fleming, R., & Sum, S. (2014). Empirical studies on the effectiveness of assistive technology in the care of people with dementia: A systematic review. *Journal of Assistive Technologies, 8*(1), 14–34.

Forbes, D., Blake, C. M., Thiessen, E. J., Peacock, S., & Hawranik, P. (2014). Light therapy for improving cognition, activities of daily living, sleep, challenging behaviour, and psychiatric disturbances in dementia. *Cochrane Database of Systematic Reviews*.

Garcia, L. J., Hébert, M., Kozak, J., Sénécal, I., Slaughter, S. E., Aminzadeh, F., ... Eliasziw, M. (2012). Perceptions of family and staff on the role of the environment in long-term care homes for people with dementia. *International Psychogeriatrics, 24*(5), 753–765. https://doi.org/10.1017/S1041610211002675.

Garre-Olmo, J., López-Pousa, S., Turon-Estrada, A., Juvinyà, D., Ballester, D., & Vilalta-Franch, J. (2012). Environmental determinants of quality of life in nursing home residents with severe dementia. *Journal of the American Geriatrics Society, 60*(7), 1230–1236. https://doi.org/10.1111/j.1532-5415.2012.04040.x.

Gonski, P. N., & Moon, I. (2012). Outcomes of a behavioral unit in an acute aged care service. *Archives of Gerontology and Geriatrics, 55*(1), 60–65. https://doi.org/10.1016/j.archger.2011.06.013.

Greene, J. A., & Asp, J. (1985). Specialized management of the Alzheimer's disease patient: Does it make a difference? A preliminary progress report. *Journal of the Tennessee Medical Association, 78*(9), 559–563.

Hall, G., Kirschling, M. V., & Todd, S. (1986). Sheltered freedom—An Alzheimer's unit in an ICF. *Geriatric Nursing, 7*, 132–137.

Hoglund, J. D., Dimotta, S., Ledewitz, S., & Saxton, J. (1994). Long-term care design: Woodside place—The role of environmental design in quality of life for residents with dementia. *Journal of Healthcare Design, 6*, 69–76.

Kallin, K., Jensen, J., Lundin Olsson, L., Nyberg, L., & Gustafson, Y. (2004). Why the elderly fall in residential care facilities, and suggested remedies. *Journal of Family Practice, 53*(1), 41–52.

Kishita, N., Backhouse, T., & Mioshi, E. (2020). Nonpharmacological interventions to improve depression, anxiety, and quality of life (QoL) in people with dementia: An overview of systematic reviews. *Journal of Geriatric Psychiatry and Neurology, 33*(1), 28–41. https://doi.org/10.1177/0891988719856690.

Lekeu, F., Wojtasik, V., der Linden Van, M., & Salmon, E. (2002). Training early Alzheimer patients to use a mobile phone. *Acta Neurologica Belgica, 102*(3), 114–121.

Low, L. F., Draper, B., & Brodaty, H. (2004). The relationship between self-destructive behaviour and nursing home environment. *Aging & Mental Health, 8*(1), 29–33.

Marquardt, G. (2011). Wayfinding for people with dementia: A review of the role of architectural design. *Health Environments Research and Design Journal, 4*(2), 75–90. https://doi.org/10.1177/193758671100400207.

Marquardt, G., Bueter, K., & Motzek, T. (2014). Impact of the design of the built environment on people with dementia: An evidence-based review. *Health Environments Research & Design Journal, 8*(1), 127–157. https://doi.org/10.1177/193758671400800111.

Marquardt, G., & Schmieg, P. (2009). Dementia-friendly architecture. Environments that facilitate wayfinding in nursing homes. *Zeitschrift für Gerontologie und Geriatrie, 42*(5), 402–407. https://doi.org/10.1007/s00391-008-0029-x.

Mihailidis, A., Boger, J., Craig, T., & Hoey, J. (2008). The COACH prompting system to assist older adults with dementia through handwashing: An efficacy study. *BMC Geriatrics, 8*(1), 28.

Milke, D. L., Beck, C. H. M., Danes, S., & Leask, J. (2009). Behavioral mapping of residents' activity in five residential style care centers for elderly persons diagnosed with dementia: Small differences in sites can affect behaviors. *Journal of Housing for the Elderly*, *23*(4), 335–367. https://doi.org/10.1080/02763890903327135.

Milke, D. L., Leask, J., George, C., & Ziolkowski, S. (2015). Eight years of data on residents in small dementia-care settings suggest functional performance is maintained. *Journal of Housing for the Elderly*, *29*(3), 298–328. https://doi.org/10.1080/02763893.2015.10 55026.

Moreno, A., Wall, K. J., Thangavelu, K., Craven, L., Ward, E., & Dissanayaka, N. N. (2019). A systematic review of the use of virtual reality and its effects on cognition in individuals with neurocognitive disorders. *Alzheimer's and Dementia: Translational Research and Clinical Interventions*, *5*, 834–850. https://doi.org/10.1016/j.trci.2019.09.016.

Morgan, D. G., & Stewart, N. J. (1999). The physical environment of special care units: Needs of residents with dementia from the perspective of staff and family caregivers. *Qualitative Health Research*, *9*(1), 105–118.

Mountain, G. (2005). Rehabilitation for people with dementia: Pointers for practice from the evidence base. In M. Marshall (Ed.), *Perspective on rehabilitation and dementia* (pp. 50–70). London: Jessica Kingsley.

Namazi, K. H., & Johnson, B. D. (1991). Physical environmental cues to reduce the problems of incontinence in Alzheimer's disease units. *American Journal of Alzheimer's Disease and Other Dementias*, *6*(6), 22–28. https://doi.org/10.1177/153331759100600605.

Namazi, K. H., & Johnson, B. D. (1996). Issues related to behavior and the physical environment: Bathing cognitively impaired patients. *Geriatric Nursing*, *17*(5), 234–238.

Nelson, J. (1995). The influence of environmental factors in incidents of disruptive behaviour. *Journal of Gerontological Nursing*, *21*(5), 19–24.

Netten, A. (1989). The effect of design of residential homes in creating dependency among confused elderly residents: A study of elderly demented residents and their ability to find their way around homes for the elderly. *International Journal of Geriatric Psychiatry*, *4*(3), 143–153.

Netten, A. (1993). *A positive environment? Physical and social influences on people with senile dementia in residential care.* Aldershot, England: Ashgate.

O'Philbin, L., Woods, B., Farrell, E. M., Spector, A. E., & Orrell, M. (2018). Reminiscence therapy for dementia: An abridged Cochrane systematic review of the evidence from randomized controlled trials. *Expert Review of Neurotherapeutics*, *18*(9), 715–727. https://doi.org/10.1080/14737175.2018.1509709.

Oyebode, J. R., & Parveen, S. (2019). Psychosocial interventions for people with dementia: An overview and commentary on recent developments. *Dementia*, *18*, 8–35.

Passini, R., Pigot, H., Rainville, C., & Tetreault, M. H. (2000). Wayfinding in a nursing home for advanced dementia of the Alzheimer's type. *Environment and Behavior*, *32*(5), 684–710. https://doi.org/10.1177/00139160021972748.

Passini, R., Rainville, C., Marchand, N., & Joanette, Y. (1998). Wayfinding with dementia: Some research findings and a new look at design. *Journal of Architectual and Planning Research*, *15*, 133–151.

Romero, B., & Wenz, M. (2001). Self-maintenance-therapy in Alzheimer's disease. *Neuropsychological Rehabilitation*, *11*, 333–355.

Scandura, D. A. (1995). Freedom and safety: A Colorado centre cares for Alzheimer's patients. *Health Progress*, *76*(3), 44–46.

Schwarz, B., Chaudhury, H., & Tofle, R. B. (2004). Effect of design interventions on a dementia care setting. *American Journal of Alzheimer's Disease and Other Dementias*, *19*(3), 172–176.

Smith, B. C., & D'Amico, M. (2019). Sensory-based interventions for adults with dementia and Alzheimer's disease: A scoping review. *Occupational Therapy in Health Care*, 1–31. https://doi.org/10.1080/07380577.2019.1608488.

Steele, L., Swaffer, K., Phillipson, L., & Fleming, R. (2019). Questioning segregation of people living with dementia in Australia: An international human rights approach to care homes. *Laws, 3*, 18. https://doi.org/10.3390/laws8030018.

Torrington, J. (2006). What has architecture got to do with dementia care? Explorations of the relationship between quality of life and building design in two EQUAL projects. *Quality in Ageing, 7*(1), 34.

United Nations. (2006). *Convention on the rights of persons with disabilities.*

Wood, W., Harris, S., Snider, M., & Patchel, S. A. (2005). Activity situations on an Alzheimer's disease special care unit and resident environmental interaction, time use, and affect. *American Journal of Alzheimer's Disease and Other Dementias, 20*(2), 105–118. https://doi.org/10.1177/153331750502000210.

Woodbridge, R., Sullivan, M. P., Gilhooly, K. J., Gilhooly, M. L. M., McIntyre, A., Wilson, L., … Crutch, S. (2018). Use of the physical environment to support everyday activities for people with dementia: A systematic review. *Dementia, 17*(5), 533–572. https://doi.org/10.1177/1471301216648670.

Zamora, T. (2008). Influence of pavement design parameters in safety perception in the elderly. *International Journal of Industrial Ergonomics, 38*(11 – 12), 992–998. https://doi.org/10.1016/j.ergon.2008.03.007.

Zeisel, J., Reisberg, B., Whitehouse, P., Woods, R., & Verheul, A. (2016). Ecopsychosocial interventions in cognitive decline and dementia: A new terminology and a new paradigm. *American Journal of Alzheimer's Disease and Other Dementias, 31*(6), 502–507. https://doi.org/10.1177/1533317516650806.

Zeisel, J., Silverstein, N. M., Hyde, J., Levkoff, S., Lawton, M. P., & Holmes, W. (2003). Environmental correlates to behavioral health outcomes in Alzheimer's special care units. *Gerontologist, 43*(5), 697–711.

CHAPTER 11

Supporting everyday functioning of people living with dementia: The role of care partners

Laura N. Gitlin[a] and Michael Bruneau Jr.[b]
[a]College of Nursing and Health Professions, Drexel University, Philadelphia, PA, United States
[b]Health Sciences Department, Drexel University, Philadelphia, PA, United States

Introduction

Mrs. Smith cares for her husband who is 80 years of age and has moderate symptoms of dementia and other chronic conditions that affect his mobility. Since his diagnosis 4 years prior, Mrs. Smith has been having difficulty managing her husband's increasing physical dependence as he is a fall risk, has difficulty getting in and out of the shower, chair, and bed. She is also managing a range of behavior changes. Mr. Smith for example paces, asks questions repeatedly, tries to leave home, follows Mrs. Smith throughout the home, misplaces items and becomes agitated, and rejects help. Medications are not effective, triggered side effects, and were discontinued. By chance, Mrs. Smith learned about the Alzheimer's Disease Association from a neighbor and has since received helpful information but she is not interested in attending their support groups. Their children live in another city and are unable to assist on a daily basis although they occasionally visit to provide Mrs. Smith some brief respite. As the Smiths do not receive in-home help, Mrs. Smith stopped working so she can provide full-time hands-on care at home. Because of this, finances are strained and Mrs. Smith feels isolated and depressed, has back pain from the physical strain of helping Mr. Smith in and out of bed and on and off chairs, and she is not sleeping well. She has missed several of her own doctor's appointments and sometimes forgets to take her own medications for her heart condition.

Mrs. Smith is one of 16 million family members in the United States with the full responsibility of providing long-term care, and one of over the 50 million families worldwide who are living with dementia (Alzheimer's Disease International, 2019; World Health Organization, 2017). Dementia is a complex neurodegenerative disease characterized by increasing functional dependence and disability along with other clinical symptoms such as

Dementia Rehabilitation
https://doi.org/10.1016/B978-0-12-818685-5.00011-8

189

behavioral changes that also impact the physical and emotional functioning of people living with dementia and their care partners. Functional dependence, a hallmark of the disease, is universally experienced, occurring across all disease etiologies and advancing with disease progression (Tschanz et al., 2011). Most people living with dementia live at home and with disease progression become increasingly dependent on a care partner, typically a family member, who, similar to Mrs. Smith, provide hands-on care, assisting with daily activities of living and assuring safety and quality of life. As the physical, emotional, financial, and social consequences of dementia and caregiving are profound, supporting families and people living with dementia is a worldwide public health priority.

Although to date there are no known pharmacological treatments that arrest, treat or delay functional decline or address other dementia-related symptoms, there are proven nonpharmacological approaches with demonstrated efficacy in symptom management (Bennett et al., 2019; Gitlin, Hodgson, Choi, & Marx, 2020). Promising approaches target either the person living with dementia directly, the physical environment or living space, the care partner, or a combination thereof. Exemplars include but are not limited to tailoring activities to abilities and interests, cognitive stimulation, exercise, environmental modification or education and support of care partners. Regardless of the target, approaches are typically dependent on the availability, capability, and readiness of care partners to enact strategies as part of daily care routines or to oversee, supervise or fully implement a given function-enhancing strategy (Gitlin & Rose, 2016b). By slowing the rate of functional decline, even for a brief period, and/or reducing excess disability (dependence over and above that caused by the disease process), studies have shown that we can improve quality of life for people living with dementia and their care partners (Gitlin et al., 2018; Gitlin, Cigliana, Cigliana, & Pappa, 2017). Given the reliance on and centrality of care partners in implementing nonpharmacological approaches and to supporting the daily function of people living with dementia, an essential consideration is how to involve and support care partners in this endeavor such that use of proven nonpharmacological strategies is not burdensome to family members.

This chapter tackles the critical consideration as to how to support care partners in the use of nonpharmacological strategies and minimize their burden in doing so. Using a multifactorial framework, the Good Life Model for dementia people living with dementia we discuss the financial, emotional, and physical impacts of functional dependency for the person and care partners. We also examine the role of care partners as implementers of evidence-based programs designed to address daily function. We present exemplar interventions tested in randomized clinical trials that have demonstrated efficacy for daily function from which to discuss possible roles of care partners in their implementation. Finally, we conclude by identifying best practices gleaned from clinical trials concerning how to involve care partners in the use of these approaches that support the daily function of people living with dementia.

Theoretical stance

To understand daily function in people living with dementia, we draw upon the "Good Life" model (Lawton, 1983) adapted for dementia (Gitlin & Hodgson, 2018). The Good Life Model for dementia postulates a multifactorial approach to understanding objective and subjective factors that inform a sense of "self" and personhood or which make up what a person perceives as the quality of life. As shown in Fig. 1, this model suggests that having a "good life" (quality of life) is more than managing medical issues and health. Rather it is multifactorial, composed of four highly interactive quadrants. Lawton identified quadrants as objective criteria involving

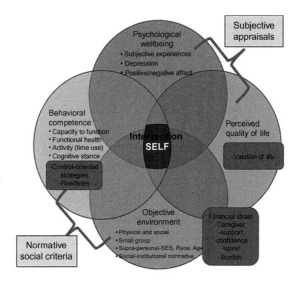

Fig. 1 Good Life Model for dementia. Note: *Dark blue* (*dark gray* in print version) boxes reflect newly emerging constructs of interest; *light blue* (*gray* in print version) boxes and intersection (intervention/self) reflect Lawton's implications. (*Adapted from Gitlin, L. N. & Hodgson, N. (2018). Better living with dementia: Implications for individuals, families, communities, and societies. Elsevier: Academic Press.*)

behavioral competence and the environment, and subjective criteria involving psychological well-being, and perceived quality of life. In turn, each quadrant is composed of specific domains with measurable properties.

The model provides a framework for identifying the specific objective and subjective factors that shape a "good life" for any one individual as well as possible targets for intervening to enhance everyday living. For example, supporting participation in a meaningful activity (behavioral competence) by modifying objective home environmental conditions (e.g., lighting, seating, access, noise, and so forth), and educating a care partner in verbal cueing techniques to initiate and sequence (e.g., objective environment) can enhance the behavioral competence and perceived quality of life of the person living with dementia. In turn, this alignment may not directly affect other quadrants and/or domains such as depressive symptoms (a domain within psychological well-being), which may require other interventions or targeted strategies to address. The model also affords an understanding of when a quadrant and within it a particular domain may serve as a target for intervention, a mediator or moderator of a particular outcome, or the outcome itself of an intervention designed to address daily function (Gitlin, 2018).

Three key themes can be deduced when applying this framework to an understanding of daily function and its impact on people living with dementia and their care partners. First, people living with dementia are more than their health or cognitive status. Second, a "good life" for an individual/care partner, reflects a combination of unique preferences, subjective states and objective conditions. Third, to support a good life and address daily function involves developing tailored approaches that take into account what matters most to individuals/care partners in each of the quadrants. Finally, the model provides guidance as to which domains may be modifiable or not and possibly impacts of nonpharmacological strategies for individuals and care partners.

With regard to the specific focus of this chapter, the Good Life Model for dementia suggests that consideration be given to all quadrants to fully understand ways to support daily function. That is, the model facilitates a nuanced understanding of the impact of functional decline (behavioral competence) on psychological well-being and perceived quality of life of people living with dementia and care partners and how objective environmental conditions inform daily functioning for any one individual or family unit. It also suggests that consideration be given to how supporting each of the quadrants of a good life for the person living with dementia impacts more specifically care partner(s) (who are a consideration in the quadrant referring to objective environmental conditions).

Impacts of functional challenges on well-being of people living with dementia and care partners

Attention to dementia-related functional challenges has been limited in dementia care and research. Only a few studies have documented its profound effects on everyday living for both people living with dementia and care partners. With the Good Life Model as the frame, the consequences of functional changes can be understood in terms of each of its quadrants such as the time needed to provide care (behavioral competence), perceived burden (psychological well-being), financial strain (objective environmental considerations), and perceived quality of life. There is no doubt that with disease progression, people living with dementia confront multiple difficulties including in care transitions (e.g., from hospital to home), difficulties with medication management and self-care, participation in meaningful activities, increased fall risk, pain, sleep problems, and home hazards (Black et al., 2013; Gitlin, Hodgson, Piersol, Hess, & Hauck, 2014; Provencher et al., 2020).

Foremost is that functional decline signals the need for more hands-on care. A recent study using a population-based data set, the Health and Retirement Study, found that at the incidence of dementia diagnosis ($n = 1530$), care partners were already providing 151 h per month and that 1.3 individuals were involved in providing care. However, by 8-years post-incidence, care partners provided close to double the number of hours of hands-on care (283 h) and 2.2 individuals were involved in providing care (Jutkowitz et al., 2017). Another study using the Aging, Demographics, and Memory Study and Health and Retirement Study datasets similarly showed that greater functional dependence was associated with more time providing care, heightened burden, and higher out-of-pocket costs for care partners (Jutkowitz et al., 2017).

Also, there is evidence suggesting that care partners of people living with dementia with high functional dependence have a greater need for supportive services, disease knowledge and skills to manage at home compared to care partners of people living with dementia with greater functional abilities (Gitlin et al., 2017). Furthermore, care partners of this highly functionally dependent group report greater impact, depressive symptoms, and more upset than their counterparts.

Care partners are also responsible for evaluating the functional capacity of the person living with dementia on a daily basis and making decisions as to the type and amount of support needed as well as ways to assure their safety. Nevertheless, care partners are rarely informed by health professionals as to the person living with dementia's functional abilities and thus typically are left on their own to guess the type and amount of support and vigilance needed along the disease trajectory. A study comparing 88 care partners' evaluation of the functional capacity of people living with dementia, to a "gold standard," that of an occupational therapist's determination using a standard tool, found that 83% ($n=73$) either over or underestimated the functional capacity of the person for whom they provided care (Piersol, Herge, Copolillo, Leiby, & Gitlin, 2016). Alternately, as shown in Fig. 2, only 17% ($n=15$) of care partner's appraisal of functional dependence of the person living with dementia was concordant with the objective determinations of the health professional. That is, most care partners either believed the person living with dementia could do more or less than that which they were capable of (e.g., bathing by self, staying home or in a room alone, using the oven) resulting in risks. Of the 83% with discordant appraisals, 61% ($n=52$) overestimated abilities, whereas 22% ($n=19$) underestimated the abilities of the person living with dementia. Whereas overestimation may result in the use of complex communications that may be confusing to the person living with dementia, and unsafe care practices (e.g., leaving the person alone, permitting oven use or smoking alone), underestimation of abilities may result in restricting activity participation and doing too much for the individual, resulting in excess disability. In either case of over or underestimations, the mismatch has significant consequences for the person

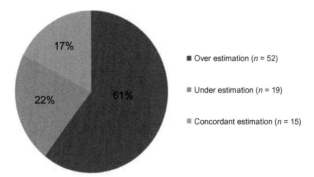

Fig. 2 Caregiver appraisal of Person's functional ability compared to health professionals ($N=88$).

living with dementia (either promoting excess disability or not meeting functional and safety needs). For care partners, this mismatch can result in heightening their risk for frustration, depression, and burden.

Another consequence of functional decline is its impact on the ability of the person living with dementia to participate in valued activities. Lack of engagement in activities that provide a sense of purpose and role continuity is a frequent complaint among care partners and people living with dementia (Parisi, Roberts, Szanton, Hodgson, & Gitlin, 2017). Disengagement, a common experience at dementia onset and thereafter, results in significant psychosocial consequences including isolation, boredom, behavioral changes; and among care partners, increased concern for the quality of life of people living with dementia and themselves.

Exemplar evidence-based programs to address functional decline

Understanding the multifaceted consequences of functional decline for people living with dementia and care partners as well as the impact on each quadrant of the Good Life Model for dementia can inform intervention development. Whereas nonpharmacological strategies have been identified as first-line treatment for behavioral changes and there are treatment guidelines (Gitlin, Kales, & Lyketsos, 2012; Kales, Gitlin, & Lyketsos, 2019a, 2019b), that is not the case for addressing functional decline and its associated challenges for both people living with dementia and care partners (Wesson et al., 2013). As stated earlier, there are no known pharmacologic agents for slowing functional decline, and those being tested, do not address the needs of care partners nor the consequences of disease progression for them. On the other hand, recent scoping, systematic and meta-analyses of studies of nonpharmacological approaches, suggest various strategies that can effectively address functional dependence (Bennett et al., 2019). Although there is much room for improvement in this area and effect sizes for outcomes are small and time-limited, these interventions are promising with results showing benefits for both people with dementia and care partners along meaningful dimensions.

Here we highlight interventions targeting functional dependence and which have been tested in randomized clinical trials or which demonstrate feasibility and for which the evidence is emerging. We discuss their level of evidence and examine the involvement of care partners in their delivery. Table 1 summarizes the primary and secondary targets of each program.

Table 1 Possible roles of care partners in implementing proven nonpharmacologic interventions that address daily function.

Program	Primary target of intervention (PLWD, care partner, both)	Secondary target (PLWD, care partner)	Role of care partner					Time commitment and demands of the intervention
			Training	Setup	Monitoring	Cueing		
Tailored activity program	PLWD	Care partner	X	X	X	X		(a) Participate in eight sessions with occupational therapist; (b) use activities (setup, initiate, cue, supervise)
COPE program	Care partner	PLWD	X	X	X	X		(a) Participate in up to 12 sessions with nurse and occupational therapists; (b) use strategies on a daily basis
Exercise	PLWD	Care partner	X	X	X	X		(a) Screen the PLWD's risk for cardiovascular, metabolic and renal disease or musculoskeletal injury; (b) obtain physician clearance or transport the PLWD for a preexercise evaluation; (c) become trained in the administration and interpretation of health/fitness assessments; (d) follow ACSM exercise guidelines for older adults and special considerations for PLWD; (e) encourage, engage guide and monitor the PLWD throughout each exercise session
Cognitive stimulation	PLWD	Care partner	X	X	X	X		(a) Identify songs to sing or other props to create a welcome and friendly environment; (b) learn how to facilitate opening recall exercises, (c) lead conversations and implement mental stimulating activities

Pet therapy	PLWD	Care partner	X	X	X	X	(a) Check that the care partner nor the PLWD suffer from any animal-related allergies; (b) determine if owning the animal is physically and financially feasible or if animal assisted therapy is a better option for the care partner and PLWD; (c) consider the size of the animal and whether the animal may be intimidating for the PLWD or themselves
Music/art therapy	PLWD	Care partner	X	X	X	X	(a) Consider the PLWD's physical health, and communication cognitive abilities; (b) decide if a creative or receptive process is appropriate

Note: PLWD, people living with dementia.

As studies do not directly assess the role of care partners in intervention delivery, we speculate as to the nature of their involvement including the potential amount of time required to learn and use a new approach, the level of difficulty of implementation, and whether setup, monitoring and oversight may be needed.

Tailored activity program (TAP)

One promising nonpharmacologic approach to address functional limitations is the use of activities that capitalizes on preserved capabilities and life-long social roles and interests. People living with dementia can effectively engage in activities when they are graded to their abilities (Trahan, Kuo, Carlson, & Gitlin, 2014). Results from multiple clinical trials suggest that using tailored activities reduces behavioral symptoms (Cohen-Mansfield et al., 2010; Gitlin et al., 2008, 2017; Kolanowski, Litaker, & Buettner, 2005), and result in less time needed in caregiving (Gitlin et al., 2008), and less burden and improved well-being in care partners (Novelli et al., 2018). TAP involves up to eight sessions at home conducted by an occupational therapist who assesses the person living with dementia for abilities and interests, the care partners level of stress and care routines and the physical environment. Based on the assessment, three activities are developed that are tailored to the unique characteristics and care partners are instructed in stress reduction techniques to reduce their distress and ways to setup and supervise the activities. The Tailored Activity Program has also been tested in outpatient, inpatient hospital, and residential settings. In these latter settings, care providers (nurse assistants, recreational therapists) deliver the prescribed activities. The target of this program is primarily the person living with dementia including behavioral symptoms. Secondarily, the program is designed to improve overall well-being and confidence of the care partner. One study showed that by using activities introduced in the intervention, care partners reported up to 5 h of time freed from daily care (Gitlin, Winter, Dennis, Hodgson, & Hauck, 2010). However, in the home, the benefits of activity are dependent on the availability and readiness of a care partner who has the time, energy, and motivation to provide prescribed activities which may entail setting up the environment (lighting, seating, activity materials), supervising the activity, cueing to assist the person living with dementia in sequencing and/or, organizing the activity, as well as structuring daily routines to include these activities. Thus, there is a need for considerable investment on the part of the care partner in terms of their time, availability, and willingness to use activities geared to a person's capabilities. The Tailored Activity Program is presently in use in various countries and settings, although it is not yet fully integrated into dementia care delivery throughout health systems worldwide. A new iteration of TAP involves training volunteers to visit homes and use prescribed activities to afford respite for care partners and minimize dependence on their availability and time to use activities therapeutically.

COPE program

COPE is another in-home program that involves up to 10 home visits conducted by an occupational therapist and two home visits by a nurse. COPE is presently being testing in different countries and in the state of Connecticut (Fortinsky et al., 2016), it has been tested in one efficacy trial thus far. The results of this trial are promising and show that at 4-months post-intervention, families receiving COPE reported less functional dependence in activities of daily living, and were more engaged in daily activities, compared to those in a minimal control group. Also, at the 4-month point, COPE care partners, compared to controls, reported improved well-being, and increased confidence in using environmental modifications and effective communication strategies. Care partners at 9-months were twice as likely as controls (40% vs 20%, $P = 0.02$) to report that COPE helped them a "great deal" to keep their relative at home. In this program, care partners are the primary target and they must be engaged in all visits and be active learners of new skills to communicate effectively, simplify activities and the environment, and manage comorbidities (Gitlin et al., 2010). Hence, considerable time and effort are required on the part of the care partner for COPE to be effectively implemented.

Exercise

Exercise is a subset of physical activity that integrates a planned, structured, and repetitive program designed to improve one or more components of health-related physical fitness. For PLWD who are often older in age, the benefits of physical activity and exercise are numerous. The major benefits for PLWD are similar to those for any older adult and include an increase in skeletal muscle strength, flexibility, mobility, cardiorespiratory fitness, and body composition, all of which have been shown to improve physical function, maintain functional independence and reduce risk of falls and fall-related injuries (Cress et al., 1999; Manty et al., 2009; Miller, Rejeski, Reboussin, Ten Have, & Ettinger, 2000; Pahor et al., 2014). Moreover, exercise can reduce depressive symptoms, and when performed within the context of a group setting, provide opportunities for social engagement; however, no exercise studies to date have specifically targeted PLWD within the context of group settings.

While the benefits of exercise are promising, some have expressed concern about the safety of exercise training for people living with dementia. As with older adults in general, individuals may be living with other medical conditions such as cardiovascular, metabolic and/or renal diseases, and therefore, may be at an increased risk for accidental falls that may make exercise training counterintuitive. However, much of the literature has found no evidence that the risks of physical activity and exercise outweigh its many benefits, and as such, age should not be a barrier to either initiation and engagement of exercise for older adults as positive improvements are attainable at any age and the relative adaptations to exercise for older adults are comparable to their younger counterparts. However, special considerations should be made when designing and implementing exercise programs for people living with dementia as they may have poor endurance and coordination, sore feet or muscles, and/or be living with other illness or depression. For that reason, care partners should be realistic about how much activity the person living with dementia can accomplish, ensure that the person living with dementia has an ID bracelet with the care partner's contact information and wears comfortable loose-fitting clothes and shoes that are appropriate for exercise, and make sure the person living with dementia drinks fluids before, during, and after exercise. Thus, use of exercise remains promising yet is dependent on care partner involvement for screening for medical readiness, setting up and/or monitoring exercise performance and providing motivation to adhere to a prescribed regimen.

Preparticipation screening

Care partners have an important role when using exercise as a therapeutic modality with people living with dementia. First, care partners may be involved in assuring that exercise is safe. With regard to safe exercising, care partners can administer valid self-screening tools such as the Exercise Assessment and Screening for You (EASY) tool. This is a six-item questionnaire to screen for health issues and concerns and from which to develop a tailored physical activity program that is appropriate for different health circumstances and situations (Resnick et al., 2008). Another role for care partners is monitoring performance during exercise. The EASY tool also provides recommendations and resources when a participant experiences musculoskeletal joint pain or swelling, experiences chest pressure during rest or mild activity, and/or identifies a heightened risk for falls (Chodzko-Zajko, Resnick, & Ory, 2012). However, validation of the EASY tool has not been established in people living with dementia despite its widespread acceptance and endorsement from reputable organizations such as the American Geriatrics Association, Gerontological Advanced Practice Association, and American College of Sports Medicine (ACSM, 2018).

Preexercise evaluation

In addition to administering self-or-partner-assisted screening tools to gauge whether beginning a physical activity and exercise training program is safe and appropriate for people living with dementia, care partners are in the position of having to recognize when a preexercise evaluation is warranted. According to the American College of Sports Medicine (Riebe et al., 2015), persons wishing to begin a physical activity or exercise program should first address whether or not they are currently physically active (Yes/No), then determine whether they are currently living with cardiovascular, metabolic or renal disease (Yes/No), and if so, whether they are symptomatic/asymptomatic (Yes/No). If asymptomatic, identification of signs/symptoms of disease are then ruled out before determining whether medical clearance for physical activity and exercise are recommended and what the starting exercise prescription should be. Reasons for asking about the current physical activity habits of people living with dementia is important because it reduces the burden for both the person living with dementia and her/his care partner, along with the additional medical costs associated with obtaining medical clearance when already engaging in physical activity, since the risk of sudden cardiac death and acute myocardial infarction is extremely low and occurring most frequently in those who are sedentary and who try to engage in vigorously intense physical activity to which they are unaccustomed (ACSM, 2018).

Health-fitness testing

Following the preparticipation health screening and pre-exercise evaluation, people living with dementia and their care partners can begin engaging in light to moderate-intensity physical activity and exercise programs. If uncertain about what the initial exercise workload should be, several valid and reliable physical performance tests are available.

Exercise prescription

Unfortunately, no universally accepted exercise prescription guidelines exist for people living with dementia. However, data from recent systematic reviews and meta-analyses highlight that adherence to the World Health Organization's physical activity recommendation of 150 min per week is recommended for people living with dementia (Panza et al., 2018). As there are few guidelines specific to people living with dementia, best practice is to follow the exercise prescription guidelines for older adults, which include the performance of moderately intense (5–6 on an OMNI 1–10 rating of perceived exertion scale) aerobic exercise for 30–60 min on 5 or more days per week (ACSM, 2018). Resistance exercise performed at light-to-moderate intensity, flexibility exercise performed to the point of slight discomfort, and neuromotor exercise, which combines balance, agility, and proprioceptive training, are also recommended 2 or more days per week. However, the extent to which people living with dementia and/or their care partners can meet these recommendations is uncertain, and additional studies need to further examine the feasibility of this prescription, determine whether refinement of the exercise prescription is needed, and identify its effect on biomarkers implicated with the pathophysiology of Alzheimer's disease and related dementias. Clearly, however, the role of care partners is essential to exercise engagement from determining risk and seeking medical approval, to setting up and monitoring performance.

Special considerations
Lastly, when people living with dementia engage in exercise training, a number of special precautions should be considered by the care partner and/or in consultation with a health professional. First, because people living with dementia are often older in age, the intensity and duration of the exercise training should be light for adults who are deconditioned, functionally limited or have limitations that impact their ability to perform daily tasks. Second, the progression of the exercise training program should be individualized to the person living with dementia's preference and abilities (ACSM, 2018). Third, if performing resistance exercise training, people living with dementia should be oriented to selectorized machines or free weights and supervised and monitored throughout the exercise training session. Fourth, if the person living with dementia has chronic comorbidities, perform and embrace physical activity as tolerated and consult with the person living with dementia's physician or allied health provider to learn more about how medication usage and/or comorbidities may affect their ability to engage in certain activities prescribed, recommended and enjoyed. Finally, the integration of behavioral strategies such as social support, self-efficacy, and perceived safety may enhance exercise participation,

so care partners or health/fitness professionals prescribing or supervising exercise for people living with dementia should provide positive reinforcement and regular feedback to enhance exercise adherence.

Cognitive stimulation: Cognitive stimulation is an intervention that aims to help people living with dementia maintain memory and achieve higher cognitive function by formulating strategies to compensate for declining function. Studies employing cognitive stimulation have shown promise but have been limited by a lack of standardization. In a 2012 systematic review, Woods, Aguirre, Spector, and Orrell (2012) found evidence that cognitive stimulation programs appeared to benefit cognition in people living with dementia but these studies tended to vary in methodological quality, including small sample sizes and provide a limited amount of detail surrounding the randomization of participants to study interventions. As such, the authors concluded that while cognitive stimulation therapy appears to provide benefit for people living with dementia, additional studies were needed.

However, in a more recent update of the literature, Kim et al. (2017) conducted a systematic review and meta-analysis of 14 randomized controlled trials including a total of 731 people living with dementia on the efficacy of cognitive stimulation and found people living with dementia to exhibit a moderate benefit with significant mean differences in cognition and quality of life between treatment and control groups. However, in subset analyses, cognitive stimulation therapies did not translate into improvements in behavioral and psychological symptoms, mood, nor activities of daily living, thus bringing into question its ecological validity. Cognitive stimulation may, therefore, be effective in improving cognition and quality of life for people living with dementia; however, the magnitude of these effects is moderate and do not translate into other behavioral and emotional manifestations that frequently occur in people living with dementia. Such findings should, therefore, be interpreted in context by care partners considering the use of cognitive stimulation for the person living with dementia; however, emphasis on the feasibility and apparent improvement in both cognitive function and quality of life should be highlighted.

When implementing cognitive stimulation for people living with dementia, care partners fulfill several important roles and responsibilities. First, care partners need to be trained in identifying songs to sing or selecting props that can be used to foster a welcoming and friendly environment during the initiation of the cognitive stimulation therapy session. Second, care partners need to become skilled in the structure and content of cognitive stimulation therapy sessions and with the facilitation of recall exercises needed to effectively implement mental stimulating activities. Lastly, barriers to implementing cognitive stimulation therapy in the home is a key issue for care partners of people living with dementia (Khan, Corbett, & Ballard, 2014). While manuals and cost-effective cognitive stimulation therapy training courses have become available, these courses are mostly targeted toward health-care professionals, rather than care partners themselves. Consequently, care partners may need to rely more heavily on the knowledge, skills, and abilities obtained by health-care professionals attending these trainings in order to provide effective cognitive stimulation therapy at home.

Music, art, and pet therapies: In addition to the use of exercise and cognitive stimulation therapy, which are two of the primary modes of therapeutic support with functional outcomes that care partners can provide for people living with dementia, a number of creative art therapies have begun to be recognized as having therapeutic value. Music therapy is a kind of active engagement program offered in older adult programs that have demonstrated physical, psychological, and emotional benefit; however, the effects for people living with dementia are less recognized and uncertain. To determine the potential benefit of music therapy for PLWD, Gomez Gallego and Gomez Garcia (2017) determined the effects of a 6-week music therapy program in 42 people living with dementia and found significant improvement in memory, orientation, depression and anxiety, delirium, hallucinations, agitation, irritability, and language disorders. Although these clinical improvements are impressive, the effect on cognition was seen in as little as four music therapy sessions, which is meaningful from an implementation perspective and may minimize excessive time and energy on the part of the care partner. The authors concluded that music therapy should be combined with other art therapies such as dance/movement therapy to improve motor and functional impairment. To further substantiate these findings, Zhang et al. (2017) systematically reviewed and meta-analyzed 34 studies integrating the use of music therapy as an enhancement strategy for behavioral and cognitive function in samples of people living with dementia. The authors found music therapy to be effective when people living with dementia received an interactive therapy compared to a standard of care control group and concluded that positive evidence and support exist for the use of music therapy as a treatment of cognitive function, depression, and quality of life.

Similar to music therapy, art therapy is believed to be a feasible modality for care partners to implement into their care for people living with dementia. Art therapy involves the use of art media as a primary mode of communication. Persons referred to art therapists themselves do not need to have experience or skill in the art. Rather the person engaging with art therapy focuses more on the person's ability to change and grow through the use of art in both a safe and facilitating environment. Consequently, the use of art therapy has largely been considered an intervention for managing the manifestations of dementia and to address the symptoms related to behaviors in people living with dementia and to improve the person's quality of life. However, quantitative evidence supporting this premise is lacking. In a recent systematic review examining the effects of art therapy as an adjuvant therapy for dementia compared to other nonpharmacologic care interventions, Deshmukh, Holmes, and Cardno (2018) determined that insufficient evidence exists regarding the efficacy of art therapy due to a small number of studies that were of low methodological quality neglecting to elicit clear changes in clinical outcomes between intervention and control groups in cognitive function, apathy, depression, and mental quality of life. Thus, while the use of art therapy may be theoretically sound as a mode of communication, more adequately powered clinical trials of higher quality are needed in people living with dementia.

Pet therapy involves the use of animals to promote improved mood and behaviors for people living with dementia. In recent decades, pet therapy has been used for both neurologic and psychiatric disorders. In people living with dementia, interactions with pets appear to have positive effects on behaviors such as aggressiveness and anxiety and quality of life and relationship measures. Peluso et al. (2018) reviewed the literature on animal-assisted therapy in older adults to highlight evidence and controversies in dementia care and offer insight into future perspectives in other neurological diseases. Among the studies reviewed, which were found to be of poor methodological quality due to weaknesses in small sample sizes, lack of randomization and inclusion of an active control group, matching and blinding, pet therapy did not improve measures of cognition; however, measures of anxiety, depression and sadness, and motor activity significantly improved. Therefore, the inclusion and use of pet therapy may be promising in the future, but additional studies are needed with higher methodological rigor to substantiate their effects for people living with dementia.

Care partners have a number of important roles and factors to consider when deciding to implement pet therapy in the home. First and foremost, the care partner needs to determine if either she/he or the person living with dementia has any animal-related allergies that may be counterintuitive to pet therapy. Second, an understanding of both the physical and financial responsibilities need to be considered and evaluated before deciding to integrate pet therapy into the home. Should either the physical or financial implications of pet ownership be infeasible, care partners may instead opt for animal-assisted therapy, which can provide many of the benefits of pet ownership under the guidance of an animal-assisted therapist. However, should animal-assisted therapy be pursued, care partners may require a written prescription or letter certifying the need for an emotional-support animal for the person living with dementia.

For each of the programs described, different levels of involvement of care partners are required as shown in Table 1. Future research on each of these modalities should examine more specifically the role of the care partner, time commitment to learning technique, for setup, supervising and monitoring as well as for any potential benefits.

Best practices in engaging care partners

As shown in Table 1, for each of the potential programs or interventions that address daily function in people living with dementia, care partners serve similar roles including having to be involved in setting up and monitoring the activity, exercise or particular strategy and/or assuring safety when engaging in a program or activity. The burdens associated with these roles have not been directly measured or previously considered. Alternately, there may be hidden benefits for care partners when providing nonpharmacological programs that extend beyond the outcomes examined in efficacy trials. For example, it may be that participating in pleasant events or meaningful activities with people living with dementia such as in the tailored activity, art therapy, or cognitive stimulation approaches, has positive unmeasured benefits. Furthermore, the knowledge that one is providing the best possible evidence-informed care may boost a care partner's morale and sense of efficacy. Nevertheless, nonpharmacological programs as shown in Table 1, may over-rely on care partners in order to have their beneficial effects for people living with dementia.

Additionally, it is unclear what it takes for care partners to effectively engage in nonpharmacological approaches. For example, there appears to be a certain level of readiness that is necessary on the part of care partners to initially volunteer for a trial testing a nonpharmacologic approach and then to engage in its implementation (Gitlin & Rose, 2016b).

Table 2 lists five common areas for which care partners need education in order to effectively participate in, administer and oversee any one of these nonpharmacological treatments.

Table 2 Common challenges encountered when instructing care partners in implementing nonpharmacologic strategies to support PLWD daily function.

Area that needs to be addressed	What caregiver needs to learns
Care partner wants PLWD to learn new things, initiate on own, and/or to get better	• Gear activity to present abilities of PLWD • Structure daily routines to provide PLWD with a sense of control and security • Use effective communications that match PLWD abilities and to cue PLWD to initiate or carry out an activity.
Care partner wants PLWD to do things properly or the right way and believes benefits derived only if PLWD follows rules or engages in an activity in a certain way	• There is no right or wrong. • Have to be flexible • Goal is for engagement • Goal is for PLWD to derive a sense of purpose
Care partner feels upset and stressed such that doing one more thing (e.g., setting up an activity, engaging in exercise) is too burdensome	• Use simple stress reduction techniques (deep breathing, walking for exercise, meditation, mindfulness) • Take time for self • Attend medical visits for self • Pace self-throughout the day, week • Using the nonpharmacological strategies may make caregiving less burdensome over time
Care partner communications geared toward correcting PLWD, overly explaining, using open-ended questions (e.g., what do you want to do today), and offering too many choices	• Open-ended communications can be confusing at moderate-to-severe disease stage • Depending on abilities, give 2 choices at most • Provide simple directions at time when needed

Conclusion

How families care for and provide daily assistance is key to the functionality, safety, and well-being of people living with dementia and if a "good life" with dementia is achieved. Although families still receive the message from health-care systems that "nothing can be done," that is simply not the case. We do have evidence-based approaches that are of low to no risk that can support daily function and other domains of a "good life" in persons living with dementia. These approaches, however, are dependent on care partners to implement; yet little attention has been given to the potential burden on care partners when being instructed in and using these nonpharmacological strategies. As we advance evidence-based approaches to support daily function, consideration must be given to the role and consequences of these programs on care partners. Furthermore, as more people living with dementia live alone and with the shrinking number of care partners available to provide hands-on support, identifying alternative modalities for delivery (e.g., use of volunteers) of these approaches will be imperative.

References

Alzheimer's Disease International. (2019). *World Alzheimer's report 2019: Attitudes to dementia*. Retrieved from https://www.alz.co.uk/research/WorldAlzheimerReport2019.pdf.

American College of Sports Medicine. (2018). *ACSM's guidelines for exercise testing and prescription*. Philadelphia: Wolters Kluwer.

Bennett, S., Laver, K., Voigt-Radloff, S., Letts, L., Clemson, L., Graff, M., et al. (2019). Occupational therapy for people with dementia and their family carers provided at home: A systematic review and meta-analysis. *BMJ Open, 9*(11), e026308. Retrieved from https://pubmed.ncbi.nlm.nih.gov/31719067.

Black, B. S., Johnston, D., Rabins, P. V., Morrison, A., Lyketsos, C., & Samus, Q. M. (2013). Unmet needs of community-residing persons with dementia and their informal caregivers: Findings from the maximizing independence at home study. *Journal of the American Geriatrics Society, 61*(12), 2087–2095.

Chodzko-Zajko, W. J., Resnick, B., & Ory, M. G. (2012). Beyond screening: Tailoring physical activity options with the EASY tool. *Translational Behavioral Medicine, 2*(2), 244–248.

Cohen-Mansfield, J., Marx, M. S., Dakheel-Ali, M., Regier, N. G., Thein, K., & Freedman, L. (2010). Can agitated behavior of nursing home residents with dementia be prevented with the use of standardized stimuli? *Journal of the American Geriatrics Society, 58*(8), 1459–1464.

Cress, M. E., Buchner, D. M., Questad, K. A., Esselman, P. C., deLateur, B. J., & Schwartz, R. S. (1999). Exercise: effects on physical functional performance in independent older adults. *The Journals of Gerontology. Series A, Biological Sciences and Medical Sciences, 54*(5), M242–M248. Retrieved February 29, 2020 from http://www.ncbi.nlm.nih.gov/pubmed/10362007.

Deshmukh, S. R., Holmes, J., & Cardno, A. (2018). Art therapy for people with dementia. *The Cochrane Database of Systematic Reviews, 9*, CD011073.

Fortinsky, R. H., Gitlin, L. N., Pizzi, L. T., Piersol, C. V., Grady, J., Robison, J. T., et al. (2016). Translation of the Care of Persons with Dementia in their Environments (COPE) intervention in a publicly-funded home care context: Rationale and research design. *Contemporary Clinical Trials, 49*, 155–165.

Gitlin, L. N. (2018). Reflections on a professional journey to making home life better for older adults and families. *Annual Review of Gerontology and Geriatrics, 38*(1), 89–108.

Gitlin, L. N., Arthur, P., Piersol, C., Hessels, V., Wu, S. S., Dai, Y., et al. (2018). Targeting behavioral symptoms and functional decline in dementia: A randomized clinical trial. *Journal of the American Geriatrics Society, 66*(2), 339–345.

Gitlin, L. N., Cigliana, J., Cigliana, K., & Pappa, K. (2017). Supporting family caregivers of persons with dementia in the community: Description of the "memory care home solutions" program and its impacts. *Innovation in Aging, 1*(1), 1.

Gitlin, L. N., & Hodgson, N. (2018). *Better living with dementia: Implications for individuals, families*. Communities and Societies: Academic Press Inc.

Gitlin, L. N., Hodgson, N., Choi, S., & Marx, K. (2020). Interventions to address functional decline in persons with dementia: Closing the gap between what a person "does do" and what they "can do:". In R. Park (Ed.), *Neuropsychology of Alzheimer's disease and other dementias* (2nd). USA: Oxford University Press.

Gitlin, L. N., Hodgson, N., Piersol, C.V., Hess, E., & Hauck, W.W. (2014). Correlates of quality of life for individuals with dementia living at home: the role of home environment, caregiver, and patient-related characteristics. *The American Journal of Geriatric Psychiatry*, *22*(6), 587–597.

Gitlin, L. N., Kales, H. C., & Lyketsos, C. G. (2012). Nonpharmacologic management of behavioral symptoms in dementia. *JAMA*, *308*(19), 2020–2029.

Gitlin, L. N., & Rose, K. (2016b). Impact of caregiver readiness on outcomes of a nonpharmacological intervention to address behavioral symptoms in persons with dementia. *International Journal of Geriatric Psychiatry*, *31*(9), 1056–1063. https://doi.org/10.1002/gps.4422. PMCID: PMC4970967.

Gitlin, L. N., Winter, L., Burke, J., Chernett, N., Dennis, M. P., & Hauck, W. W. (2008). Tailored activities to manage neuropsychiatric behaviors in persons with dementia and reduce caregiver burden: A randomized pilot study. *American Journal of Geriatric Psychiatry*, *16*(3), 229–239.

Gitlin, L. N., Winter, L., Dennis, M. P., Hodgson, N., & Hauck, W.W. (2010). A biobehavioral home-based intervention and the well-being of patients with dementia and their caregivers: The COPE randomized trial. *JAMA*, *304*(9), 983–991.

Gomez Gallego, M., & Gomez Garcia, J. (2017). Music therapy and Alzheimer's disease: Cognitive, psychological, and behavioural effects. *Neurologia (Barcelona, Spain)*, *32*(5), 300–308.

Jutkowitz, E., Kane, R. L., Gaugler, J. E., MacLehose, R. F., Dowd, B., & Kuntz, K. M. (2017). Societal and family lifetime cost of dementia: Implications for policy. *Journal of the American Geriatrics Society*, *65*(10), 2169–2175.

Kales, H. C., Gitlin, L. N., & Lyketsos, C. G. (2019a). *The DICE approach: Guiding the caregiver in managing the behavioral symptoms of dementia*. University of Michigan.

Kales, H. C., Gitlin, L. N., & Lyketsos, C. G. (2019b). When less is more, but still not enough: Why focusing on limiting antipsychotics in people with dementia is the wrong policy imperative. *Journal of the American Medical Directors Association*, *20*(9), 1074–1079.

Khan, Z., Corbett, A., & Ballard, C. (2014). Cognitive stimulation therapy: Training, maintenance and implementation in clinical trials. *Pragmatic and Observational Research*, *5*, 15–19.

Kim, K., Han, J. W., So, Y., Seo, J., Kim, Y. J., Park, J. H., et al. (2017). Cognitive stimulation as a therapeutic modality for dementia: A meta-analysis. *Psychiatry Investigation*, *14*(5), 626–639.

Kolanowski, A. M., Litaker, M., & Buettner, L. (2005). Efficacy of theory-based activities for behavioral symptoms of dementia. *Nursing Research*, *54*(4), 219–228.

Lawton, M. P. (1983). Environment and other determinants of well-being in older people. *The Gerontologist*, *23*(4), 349–357.

Manty, M., Heinonen, A., Leinonen, R., Tormakangas, T., Hirvensalo, M., Kallinen, M., et al. (2009). Long-term effect of physical activity counseling on mobility limitation among older people: A randomized controlled study. *The Journals of Gerontology. Series A, Biological Sciences and Medical Sciences*, *64*(1), 83–89.

Miller, M. E., Rejeski, W. J., Reboussin, B. A., Ten Have, T. R., & Ettinger, W. H. (2000). Physical activity, functional limitations, and disability in older adults. *Journal of the American Geriatrics Society*, *48*(10), 1264–1272.

Novelli, M. M. P. C., Machado, S. C. B., Lima, G. B., Cantatore, L., Sena, B. P., Rodrigues, R. S., et al. (2018). Effects of the tailored activity program in Brazil (TAP-BR) for persons with dementia: A randomized pilot trial. *Alzheimer Disease and Associated Disorders*, *32*(4), 339–345.

Pahor, M., Guralnik, J. M., Ambrosius, W. T., Blair, S., Bonds, D. E., Church, T. S., et al. (2014). Effect of structured physical activity on prevention of major mobility disability in older adults: The LIFE study randomized clinical trial. *JAMA, 311*(23), 2387–2396.

Panza, G. A., Taylor, B. A., MacDonald, H. V., Johnson, B. T., Zaleski, A. L., Livingston, J., et al. (2018). Can exercise improve cognitive symptoms of Alzheimer's disease? *Journal of the American Geriatrics Society, 66*(3), 487–495.

Parisi, J. M., Roberts, L., Szanton, S. L., Hodgson, N. A., & Gitlin, L. N. (2017). Valued activities among individuals with and without cognitive impairments: Findings from the National Health and aging trends study. *The Gerontologist, 57*(2), 309–318.

Peluso, S., De Rosa, A., De Lucia, N., et al. (2018). Animal-assisted therapy in elderly patients: evidence and controversies in dementia and psychiatric disorders and future perspectives in other neurological diseases. *Journal of Geriatric Psychiatry and Neurology, 31*(3), 149–157. https://doi.org/10.1177/0891988718774634.

Piersol, C. V., Herge, E. A., Copolillo, A. E., Leiby, B. E., & Gitlin, L. N. (2016). Psychometric properties of the functional capacity card Sort for caregivers of people with dementia. *OTJR : Occupation, Participation and Health, 36*(3), 126–133.

Provencher, V., Clemson, L., Wales, K., Cameron, I. D., GItlin, L. N., Greiner, A., et al. (2020). Supporting at-risk older adults transitioning from hospital to home: Who benefits from an evidence-based patient-centered discharge planning intervention? Post-hoc analysis from a randomized trial. *BMC Geriatrics, 20*(84), 1–10.

Resnick, B., Ory, M. G., Hora, K., Rogers, M. E., Page, P., Bolin, J. N., et al. (2008). A proposal for a new screening paradigm and tool called exercise assessment and screening for you (EASY). *Journal of Aging and Physical Activity, 16*(2), 215–233.

Riebe, D., Franklin, B. A., Thompson, P. D., Ewing Garber, C., Whitfield, G. P., Magal, M., et al. (2015). Updating ACSM's recommendations for exercise Preparticipation health screening. *Medicine & Science in Sports & Exercise, 47*(11), 2473–2479. Retrieved from http://ezproxy2.library.drexel.edu/login?url=http://search.ebscohost.com/login. aspx?direct=true&db=c8h&AN=110468702&site=ehost-live.

Trahan, M. A., Kuo, J., Carlson, M. C., & Gitlin, L. N. (2014). A systematic review of strategies to foster activity engagement in persons with dementia. *Health Education & Behavior, 41*(1 Suppl), 70S–83S.

Tschanz, J. T., Corcoran, C. D., Schwartz, S., Treiber, K., Green, R. C., Norton, M. C., et al. (2011). Progression of cognitive, functional, and neuropsychiatric symptom domains in a population cohort with Alzheimer dementia: The Cache County dementia progression study. *The American Journal of Geriatric Psychiatry, 19*(6), 532–542.

Wesson, J., Clemson, L., Brodaty, H., Lord, S., Taylor, M., Gitlin, L., et al. (2013). A feasibility study and pilot randomised trial of a tailored prevention program to reduce falls in older people with mild dementia. *BMC Geriatrics, 13*, 89.

Woods, B., Aguirre, E., Spector, A. E., & Orrell, M. (2012). Cognitive stimulation to improve cognitive functioning in people with dementia. *Cochrane Database of Systematic Reviews*, (2), CD005562. https://doi.org/10.1002/14651858.CD005562.pub2.

World Health Organization. (2017). *Global action plan on the public health response to dementia 2017–2025.* Geneva: World Health Organization. Retrieved from https://apps.who.int/iris/bitstream/handle/10665/259615/9789241513487-eng. pdf;jsessionid=EFA821F9B7606753F89C04A1CB6AA197?sequence=1.

Zhang, Y., Cai, J., An, L., Hui, F., Ren, T., Ma, H., et al. (2017). Does music therapy enhance behavioral and cognitive function in elderly dementia patients? A systematic review and meta-analysis. *Ageing Research Reviews, 35*, 1–11.

Further reading

Forbes, D., Forbes, S. C., Blake, C. M., Thiessen, E. J., & Forbes, S. (2015). Exercise programs for people with dementia. *The Cochrane Database of Systematic Reviews*, (4), CD006489. https://doi.org/10.1002/14651858.CD006489.pub4.

Gitlin, L. N., & Rose, K. (2016a). Impact of caregiver readiness on outcomes of a nonpharmacological intervention to address behavioral symptoms in persons with dementia. *International Journal of Geriatric Psychiatry*, *31*(9), 1056–1063.

Young, J., Angevaren, M., Rusted, J., & Tabet, N. (2015). Aerobic exercise to improve cognitive function in older people without known cognitive impairment. *Cochrane Database of Systematic Reviews*. Retrieved from http://onlinelibrary.wiley.com/doi/10.1002/14651858.CD005381.pub4/abstract.

CHAPTER 12

Physical comorbidities of dementia: Recognition and rehabilitation

Susan Kurrle
Faculty of Medicine & Health, University of Sydney, Sydney, NSW, Australia

Introduction

Multiple comorbid medical conditions are common in the older population both with and without dementia. A number of these medical conditions may occur more commonly in people with dementia than in people without dementia. A review of the scientific literature has previously been conducted to understand more about these physical comorbidities which are associated with dementia (Kurrle, Brodaty, & Hogarth, 2012). This chapter describes these comorbidities and provides recommendations to address them using a rehabilitation lens.

For this chapter, comorbidity is defined as a disease or condition that coexists with dementia (of any cause) and is likely to be related pathophysiologically to dementia. The comorbidities of dementia included in this chapter are

- falls
- delirium
- weight loss and malnutrition
- epilepsy
- frailty
- sleep disorders
- oral disease
- visual dysfunction

Falls

Falls are a major health issue in older people. A fall can precipitate a downward spiral of immobility, reduced confidence, and incapacity which may result in early institutionalization and death. Studies have consistently shown

Dementia Rehabilitation
https://doi.org/10.1016/B978-0-12-818685-5.00012-X

that dementia is associated with an increased risk of falls which is twice that of cognitively intact older people (Shaw, 2002). The annual incidence of falls in older people with dementia is 70%–80% and this high rate of falling is also seen in younger people with dementia. Dementia is also associated with a three to fourfold increase in the risk of hip fracture and a threefold increase in 6-month postfracture mortality rate compared to older people without dementia.

There are many possible reasons why dementia increases the risk of falls. Gait abnormalities are seen commonly in people with dementia, particularly in those with vascular dementia, dementia with Lewy bodies, and Parkinson's disease with dementia (Morley, 2016). Postural hypotension is commonly seen in people with dementia with Lewy bodies and Parkinson's disease with dementia, and decreased postural instability is common to all dementias. Centrally active medications such as antipsychotics and antidepressants are well known to increase the risk of falls and these are commonly prescribed in people with dementia.

Impaired motor planning skills, reduced attention span, and inaccurate judgment of reaching ability in people with dementia has been shown to increase the risk (Taylor et al., 2018). Agitation, restlessness, and wandering also increase the risk of falls. People with dementia, particularly Alzheimer's disease and dementia with Lewy bodies, have impaired visual and visuospatial skills which increase the risk of falling. People with dementia may also have an unrealistic perception of their own motor abilities resulting in impulsivity and risk-taking behavior which also contributes to the risk of falling.

There is strong evidence for interventions to prevent falls in the general older population (Sherrington et al., 2019), but no studies have been successfully shown that falls can be prevented specifically in people with dementia living in the community. Studies in nursing homes have indicated that multifactorial interventions may be effective in preventing or reducing falls in a population of frail older people, some of whom have dementia. Medication management, strength and balance training, treatment of postural hypotension, treatment of osteoporosis, treatment of cataracts, occupational therapy home hazard assessment, use of hip protectors and helmets, and falls alarms, are some of the interventions that have been shown to reduce falls or fall-related injuries in the older population. See Chapter 5 for further discussion on maintaining and improving physical function in people with dementia.

Rehabilitation recommendations

1. Exercise-based interventions for people with dementia both in the community and in nursing homes have the potential to improve falls risk factors associated with reduced physical and cognitive function. These interventions should be simple and tailored to the abilities of the person with dementia and include the involvement of the care partner where possible. They should include strength and balance components and where possible be supervised by a physiotherapist or exercise physiologist (Lewis, Peiris, & Shields, 2017).
2. Consider use of calcium and Vitamin D, and bisphosphonates or denosumab if low BMD or previous fracture are present to to reduce the risk of fractures in people with dementia.

Delirium

Delirium is a mental disorder characterized by rapid onset, an altered level of consciousness, disturbances in attention, orientation, memory, thinking, perception and behavior, and a fluctuating course. It occurs in up to 60% of older people admitted to the hospital, and approximately three-quarters of patients who develop delirium have a diagnosis of dementia (Inouye, Westendorp, & Saczynski, 2014).

Delirium may manifest itself as hyperactive, hypoactive, or as a mixed form of delirium. Signs include being easily distracted, having periods of altered perception, exhibiting disorganized speech, having periods of restlessness and agitation alternating with lethargy, and having a clear variation in cognitive function for a day.

Dementia is the strongest risk factor for the occurrence of delirium. The presence of dementia increases the risk of delirium occurring fivefold, with up to three-quarters of all episodes of delirium occurring in people with dementia. The presence of delirium is associated with increased hospital length of stay, increased health service costs, increased mortality, increased rates of admission to nursing homes, and increased functional disability. Many cases go unrecognized as dementia is blamed for the occurrence of the acute confusional state. Symptoms of delirium may persist for up to 6 months after discharge from hospital, and in some cases, the delirium may never resolve completely.

It is suggested that people with dementia are more likely to develop delirium because there is an underlying vulnerability of the brain due to the changes related to the dementia disease process. Although the pathophysiology of delirium is poorly understood, it shares with dementia the features of decreased cerebral metabolism, cholinergic deficits, and chronic inflammation, and there are disruptions in higher cortical function. Lower cognitive reserve (e.g., lower education level) predicts a higher risk of delirium, and people with more severe dementia tend to have more severe delirium with longer recovery time than those with milder dementia.

A number of multifactorial interventions have been shown to improve outcomes for hospitalized patients with delirium. These include education of nursing and medical staff on the detection and management of delirium and use of appropriate ward accommodation (Kurrle et al., 2019) and regular reorientation and early mobilization where appropriate to prevent prolongation of delirium and further functional decline (Hshieh et al., 2015).

Rehabilitation recommendations

1. Nurse in an appropriate specialized ward environment and ensure that spectacles, hearing aids, and walking aids are available. The person with dementia should be kept as mobile as possible, with regular walking and simple exercises as appropriate for their underlying medical condition.

Weight loss and malnutrition

Weight loss accompanied by malnutrition is one of the major manifestations of Alzheimer's disease (AD) and is also seen in other dementias. Alois Alzheimer mentioned this particular manifestation in his case report of Johann F saying "his body weight falls slowly and steadily" (Alzheimer, 1911). People with dementia are likely to lose up to 10% of their body weight during the disease.

Many studies have identified low body weight, thinness, and weight loss as clinical characteristics of people with dementia, particularly Alzheimer's disease, and especially in the later stages of the disease process, and weight loss is considered by many to be one of the principal manifestations of Alzheimer's disease (Gillette Guyonnet et al., 2007). Even at an early stage of the disease process, changes may be apparent and weight loss may precede the diagnosis of dementia by up to 20 years (Stewart et al., 2005). People with vascular dementia and frontotemporal dementia are also reported to experience weight loss and malnutrition as are people with Down syndrome and Alzheimer's disease.

Many factors have been suggested to explain the occurrence of weight loss and malnutrition, sometimes in the presence of adequate food intake.

These include alterations in eating patterns, decreased ability to feed oneself due to dyspraxia, poor dentition or dry mouth, loss of olfactory function, changed sense of satiety, dysphagia, and the presence of behavioral symptoms such as agitation, anxiety, or apathy. Medications can also affect appetite, and although the cholinesterase inhibitors may cause anorexia and vomiting, their use has also been shown to be a protective factor in preventing weight loss in some studies.

Intervening to prevent or address malnutrition is important in order to decrease the consequences of malnutrition which include reduced muscle strength, increased risk of falls, loss of independence, increased risk of pressure ulceration, impaired immunity, and the increased chance of infection, and increased risk of death.

Targeted nutritional interventions using oral nutritional supplements are effective in addressing poor nutrition and weight loss, but it is important to ensure that the person with dementia does not compensate for the increase in energy intake by decreasing normal food intake. Education of both family care partners and professional carers in the importance of adequate nutrition has been shown to maintain or increase body weight. Environmental factors are also important and include maintaining a home-like environment, using tablecloths, simple utensils and appropriate seating, and having background music and attractive, easy-to-eat food (such as finger foods).

The use of enteral feeding in late-stage dementia remains controversial and nasogastric and gastrostomy tube placement has not been shown to improve nutrition or survival. Careful feeding by the hand of people with severe dementia is likely to be more effective than enteral feeding (Callahan et al., 2000).

Rehabilitation recommendations

1. The nutritional intervention comprises: search for reversible medical or socio-environmental causes increased calorie/protein intake (oral supplementation by food and/or by dietary supplements) and regular daily physical activity including both aerobic exercises such as walking and simple strength exercises to improve uptake of protein and improved muscle function.

Epilepsy

Epileptic seizures are defined as brief, unprovoked disturbances of consciousness, behavior, motor function, or sensation and are known to have a higher frequency of occurrence in older people. However, in people with dementia there is an approximately sixfold increase in the likelihood of seizures compared to an age-matched population (Amatniek et al., 2006).

Studies indicate that approximately 10% of people with dementia suffer a seizure during their disease. The risk is greater for people with younger onset dementia where an 87-fold increase in the risk of seizures is reported in the 50- to 59-year-old age group. This drops to a threefold increase in the population aged 85 years and over with dementia. In people with Down syndrome and dementia more than half of the population studied had suffered seizures in comparison with seizures occurring in approximately 10% of people with Down syndrome and no dementia. The seizure rate is slightly higher in people with vascular dementia than in those with Alzheimer's disease (Beagle et al., 2017).

Both generalized and partial seizures are seen in people with dementia. As a rule of thumb, partial seizures are more common early in dementia, and generalized seizures are more common later in dementia. There are many case studies and reports of seizures associated with dementia and these include descriptions of unexplained falls, amnestic wandering, transient epileptic amnesia, and dementia contributing to complex partial status epilepticus.

The presentation of a person with dementia with a syncopal episode or fainting episode, or "funny turn" in the absence of other possible causes, should alert the clinician to a possibility of a seizure. An EEG that confirms the presence of seizures will assist in making the diagnosis, but often this cannot easily be performed. Diagnosis may rely on the history of the incident, including observations by the care partner. A trial of an anticonvulsant may assist in making the diagnosis; valproate, carbamazepine, gabapentin, and lamotrigine have been recommended as medications for seizures (Mendez & Lim, 2003).

Rehabilitation recommendations

1. Be aware that seizures occur more commonly in people with dementia and consider the possibility of seizures where people with dementia or their care partners report the occurrence of a faint or funny turn or unusual fall.
2. Consider treatment with anticonvulsants if more than one possible seizure has occurred.

Frailty

Frailty is a state of reduced physiological reserves (in the domains of physical ability, cognition, and health) which leads to increased vulnerability. It has been operationalized as a combination of weight loss, low grip strength, self-reported exhaustion, slow walking speed, and low physical activity (Hoogendijk et al.,

2019). Many studies have reported an association between frailty and cognitive impairment, with a higher degree of physical frailty associated with more severe cognitive impairment, and it has been suggested that frailty and cognitive impairment may share a common underlying pathogenesis.

Several underlying links in etiology have suggested that cardiovascular and cerebrovascular disease are risk factors for both frailty and Alzheimer's disease and diabetes, and raised levels of pro-inflammatory cytokines such as interleukin-1 and interleukin-6, CRP, and TNF-α are common to both and indicate a state of a low-grade chronic inflammation. Other possible common underlying mechanisms include decreased energy production at the cellular level, metabolic changes, and oxidative stress (Atkinson et al., 2005).

There is evidence from many cohort studies indicating that decreases in strength and walking speed ("frailty") antedate the onset of dementia by many years. In a cohort study of more than 800 older people, significantly more cases of Alzheimer's disease developed in those participants considered frail than in those who were not considered as frail, over several years of follow-up. Slow gait speed and low grip strength have been associated with impaired cognitive function in several cohort studies, with low-handgrip strength predicting cognitive decline in one study of 600 people over age 85 years. A decline in motor function has been suggested as an indicator of the progression of subclinical dementia (Wang, Larson, Bowen, & van Belle, 2006).

Frailty can be treated with multifactorial interventions including physical exercise, nutritional supplementation, and addressing polypharmacy where present (Dent et al., 2017). It has also been suggested that the association between pre-frailty status and cognitive impairment presents an opportunity for preventative interventions with the combined aim of preventing the onset of frailty and slowing cognitive decline. Improved diet and regular aerobic and resistance exercise are likely to improve the physical status and may also slow cognitive decline.

Rehabilitation recommendations

1. Regular exercise including both aerobic exercise such as walking and resistance/strength training are known to lower inflammatory markers and have been shown to improve both physical function and memory.

Sleep disorders

Age-related changes in sleep patterns are well documented in the general older population. Changes occur in several areas including increases in sleep latency, sleep arousals, sleep stage shifts and awakenings, and a reduction in total sleep time. Sleep apnoea is also seen more commonly in the older population, and cognitive changes associated with sleep apnoea syndrome may mimic symptoms and signs of dementia. There is also some evidence that sleep apnoea may occur more often in people with dementia, usually in the later stages of the disease (Andrade, Bubu, Varga, & Osorio, 2018).

In dementia, particularly in Alzheimer's disease, when compared to age-matched controls, there is reduced sleep efficiency, increased amounts of non-rapid eye movement sleep (NREM sleep), and an increase in the number of awakenings. There is also a decrease in the amount of rapid eye movement sleep (REM sleep), a reduction in total sleep time, and significantly more sleep-wake rhythm disturbances, including inversion of the sleep-wake cycle and subsequent day-night sleep reversal (Ancoli-Israel & Vitiello, 2006).

In observational studies, up to 50% of people with dementia (or their care partners) report sleep disturbances. The severity of these changes in sleep appears to increase as the severity of the dementia increases. Daytime sleepiness was associated with lower MMSE scores and greater impairments in functional status. Disrupted sleep patterns have a significant impact on quality of life for both the person with dementia and care partner with chronic sleep deprivation playing a key role in the decision to institutionalize the person with dementia.

A number of interventions may reduce sleep disturbance in people with dementia (Ooms & Ju, 2016). Exposure of the eyes to adequate light during the day can have a profound effect on sleep quality and timing probably through the effect of light as the primary synchronizer for the brain's "body clock." Bright light therapy on its own has been used with variable results in people with dementia, but as part of a multifactorial sleep improvement program, increased light exposure along with daily walking and sleep hygiene measures improved sleep quality in people with dementia. Sedating medication should be used with care due to adverse effects. Melatonin has been used to reset circadian rhythms in travelers experiencing jetlag, but its use as a treatment in dementia is not confirmed.

Rehabilitation recommendations

1. Encourage good sleep hygiene measures, discourage daytime napping, and engage the person with dementia in regular activities. Maintain regular sleep-wake routines and meal schedules.
2. Ensure that factors which may disturb sleep have been assessed and managed, for example pain, heat, cold, infection, before considering the use of sedative medication to manage sleep disturbance.
3. Consider a routine of daily physical exercise with adequate exposure to daylight.

Oral disease

Poor oral health is more common in people with dementia than with age-matched controls. Xerostomia (dry mouth), plaque accumulation, and caries are more common, and people with dementia have fewer natural teeth and use dentures less often. This has been shown even before a diagnosis of dementia has been made, and chronic inflammation has been suggested as a link between poor cognition and poor dentition (Ellefsen, Holm-Pederson, Morse, et al., 2008). Whether the link is casual, or correlational is unclear.

The effect of cognitive impairment on oral health is multifactorial. Factors include a deterioration in the ability to self-care and inability to follow instructions, decreased motivation and reduced executive function, and increasing dyspraxia and agnosia.

There is also a decreased ability to adapt to changes such as dental plates or new dentures and reduced expressive and receptive communication skills result in difficulties reporting dental symptoms. Combative behavior during personal care and increasing care partner burden may decrease motivation to maintaining oral health. The emergence of sucking reflexes and involuntary tongue movements in the later stage of dementia makes mouth care very difficult to deliver (Delwel, Binnekade, Perez, et al., 2018).

Medications used by people with dementia can cause xerostomia, particularly the antipsychotic and anticonvulsant medications, but a decrease in salivary function has been found in people with dementia on no medication indicating that there is likely to be compromising of salivary function related to dementia.

Common symptoms and signs of dental problems in the later stages of dementia include refusal, or inability, to eat or drink or open the mouth, halitosis, drooling, holding or pulling at the face, restlessness, agitation, or aggressive behavior.

Management of oral disease should begin in the early stages of the disease once a diagnosis has been made. Referral should be made for a dental consultation with the aim of maintenance of good oral health. A regimen of twice-daily teeth and gum brushing should be instituted so that it becomes a normal part of daily care. Education for family and professional carers should include what is appropriate oral care for a person with dementia.

Rehabilitation recommendations

1. Ensure twice daily brushing of teeth becomes part of the normal activities of daily living for a person with dementia. Encourage them to do this independently.

2. Avoid complications of a dry mouth by encouraging regular sips or drinks of water and the use of saliva stimulators such as lemon-flavored sweets or mouth gel.

Visual dysfunction

A substantial body of research identifies visual dysfunction in Alzheimer's disease, vascular dementia, and other dementias. People with dementia may present with complaints of visual problems quite early in the disease process. A visual variant of Alzheimer's disease (posterior cortical atrophy) has been suggested with visual symptoms occurring before problems with memory are identified (Kaese, Ghika, & Borruat, 2015).

Many visual symptoms have been identified (Armstrong & Kergoat, 2015).Visual field defects may be present with normal neuroimaging. Other symptoms include blurred vision, difficulty reading or judging distances, and problems in identifying and locating familiar objects or people. Changes in contrast sensitivity and visual acuity, particularly in conditions of low light, as well as changes in color vision, may be experienced. Impaired visual acuity may be linked to increased occurrence of visual hallucinations. Deficits in color discrimination and stereoacuity are not invariably correlated with the severity of dementia, and they may emerge early in the disease process for some people with dementia, while changes in visual fields may occur early or later in the disease. Additional abnormalities may be seen in ocular motility, visual motion evoked potentials, saccadic movements and tracking, and pattern electroretinograms.

Visual dysfunction in dementia may form the basis of difficulties experienced by people with dementia in activities of daily living. Some of the common visual problems identified by people with dementia and care partners, where the opinion of an ophthalmologist or optometrist was sought, include difficulty with reading, writing, depth perception, identifying or locating familiar objects or people, driving, walking, manipulating objects, dressing, and judging distances. A particular note of visual dysfunction is required if the person with dementia drives or operates machinery.

Many population-based studies have shown significant associations between cognitive impairment/dementia and visual dysfunction (Gussekloo, de Craen, Oduber, et al., 2005). Impaired visual acuity was associated with lower MMSE scores and slower cognitive speed after adjustment for vision-related items in two studies. Retinal nerve fiber layer thickness is reduced in people with Alzheimer's disease compared to age-matched controls. Age-related macular degeneration with the loss of retinal ganglionic cells in the macula is significantly associated with cognitive impairment compared to age-matched controls. An increased incidence of open-angle glaucoma has also been found in people with Alzheimer's disease.

Rehabilitation recommendations

1. Be aware that during dementia, visual problems may arise which can have a significant impact on the performance of assessment tasks, and function in activities of daily living including mobility.
2. Review by optometrist or ophthalmologist should be undertaken early in the disease process, to address refractive errors, check intraocular pressures, and assess the presence of cataracts.
3. Visual acuity and contrast sensitivity may be improved by the correction of conditions such as cataracts and making environmental changes such as improved lighting and the use of high contrast markers.

Conclusion

While much attention is paid to the cognitive symptoms and the behavioral and psychological changes that occur in people with dementia, there is a lack of knowledge about the health conditions that occur commonly in people with dementia. Many of these conditions are treatable and should be looked for as part of the complete management of a person with dementia.

Raising awareness of the significant increase in the likelihood of seizures in people with dementia may lead to the recognition of epilepsy as the cause for syncope or falls rather than the inappropriate diagnosis and treatment of cardiac or cerebrovascular disease. Recognition of the need for early dental care after a diagnosis of dementia is made, and the importance of regular ongoing management can make a big difference to the ability of a person with dementia to eat normal food and reduce discomfort and pain from oral disease. Understanding the role of nutrition is important in preventing malnutrition and subsequent infections and pressure injuries.

There are some areas where there remain questions about management. For instance, the prevention and management of falls remain an area where further research is needed to better understand how to reduce the doubling in fall rates and subsequent falls-related injuries that occur in people with dementia. It is important to know how to take into account the visual changes that occur in dementia when carrying out cognitive testing, as these visual changes can affect performance. More needs to be understood about the unexplained weight loss that occurs in people with dementia despite good dietary intake.

These physical conditions which accompany dementia can complicate management and reduce the quality of life of people with dementia and their care partners. Recognizing and responding to them can lead to marked improvements in care and quality of life for this population.

References

Alzheimer, A. (1911). Über eigenartige Krankheitsfälle des späteren Alters. *Zeitschrift für die gesamte Neurologie und Psychiatrie, 4*(1), 356. https://doi.org/10.1007/BF02866241.

Amatniek, J. C., Hauser, W. A., Del Castillo-Castaneda, C., Jacobs, D. M., Marder, K., Bell, K., … Stern, Y. (2006). Incidence and predictors of seizures in patients with Alzheimer's disease. *Epilepsia, 47*(5), 867–872. https://doi.org/10.1111/j.1528-1167.2006.00554.x.

Ancoli-Israel, S., & Vitiello, M. V. (2006). Sleep in dementia. *The American Journal of Geriatric Psychiatry, 14*(2), 91–94. https://doi.org/10.1097/01.JGP.0000200973.93494.aa.

Andrade, A. G., Bubu, O. M., Varga, A. W., & Osorio, R. S. (2018). The relationship between obstructive sleep apnea and Alzheimer's disease. *Journal of Alzheimer's Disease, 64*(s1), S255–s270. https://doi.org/10.3233/jad-179936.

Armstrong, R., & Kergoat, H. (2015). Oculo-visual changes and clinical considerations affecting older patients with dementia. *Ophthalmic & Physiological Optics, 35*, 352–376.

Atkinson, H. H., Cesari, M., Kritchevsky, S. B., Penninx, B. W., Fried, L. P., Guralnik, J. M., & Williamson, J. D. (2005). Predictors of combined cognitive and physical decline. *Journal of the American Geriatrics Society, 53*(7), 1197–1202. https://doi.org/10.1111/j.1532-5415.2005.53362.x.

Beagle, A. J., Darwish, S. M., Ranasinghe, K. G., La, A. L., Karageorgiou, E., & Vossel, K. A. (2017). Relative incidence of seizures and myoclonus in Alzheimer's disease, dementia with Lewy bodies, and frontotemporal dementia. *Journal of Alzheimer's Disease, 60*(1), 211–223. https://doi.org/10.3233/jad-170031.

Callahan, C. M., Haag, K. M., Weinberger, M., Tierney, W. M., Buchanan, N. N., Stump, T. E., & Nisi, R. (2000). Outcomes of percutaneous endoscopic gastrostomy among older adults in a community setting. *Journal of the American Geriatrics Society, 48*(9), 1048–1054. https://doi.org/10.1111/j.1532-5415.2000.tb04779.x.

Delwel, S., Binnekade, T., Perez, R., et al. (2018). Oral hygiene and oral health in older people with dementia: A comprehensive review with focus on oral soft tissues. *Clinical Oral Investigations, 22*, 93–108.

Dent, E., Lien, C., Lim, W. S., Wong, W. C., Wong, C. H., Ng, T. P., … Flicker, L. (2017). The Asia-Pacific clinical practice guidelines for the Management of Frailty. *Journal of the American Medical Directors Association, 18*(7), 564–575. https://doi.org/10.1016/j.jamda.2017.04.018.

Ellefsen, B., Holm-Pedersen, P., Morse, D., et al. (2008). Caries prevalence in older persons with and without dementia. *Journal of the American Geriatrics Society, 56*(1), 59–67.

Gillette Guyonnet, S., Abellan Van Kan, G., Alix, E., Andrieu, S., Belmin, J., Berrut, G., … International Academy on Nutrition and Aging Expert Group. (2007). IANA (International Academy on Nutrition and Aging) Expert Group: Weight loss and Alzheimer's disease. *The Journal of Nutrition, Health & Aging, 11*(1), 38–48.

Gussekloo, J., de Craen, A., Oduber, C., et al. (2005). Sensory impairment and cognitive functioning in oldest-old subjects: The Leiden 85+ study. *American Journal of Geriatric Psychiatry, 13*(9), 781–786.

Hoogendijk, E. O., Afilalo, J., Ensrud, K. E., Kowal, P., Onder, G., & Fried, L. P. (2019). Frailty: Implications for clinical practice and public health. *The Lancet, 394*(10206), 1365–1375. https://doi.org/10.1016/S0140-6736(19)31786-6.

Hshieh, T. T., Yue, J., Oh, E., Puelle, M., Dowal, S., Travison, T., & Inouye, S. K. (2015). Effectiveness of multicomponent nonpharmacological delirium interventions: A meta-analysis. *JAMA Internal Medicine, 175*(4), 512–520. https://doi.org/10.1001/jamainternmed.2014.7779.

Inouye, S. K., Westendorp, R. G. J., & Saczynski, J. S. (2014). Delirium in elderly people. *The Lancet, 383*(9920), 911–922. https://doi.org/10.1016/S0140-6736(13)60688-1.

Kaese, P., Ghika, J., & Borruat, F. (2015). Visual signs and symptoms in patients with the visual variant of Alzheimer disease. *BMC Ophthalmology, 15*, 65.

Kurrle, S., Bateman, C., Cumming, A., Pang, G., Patterson, S., & Temple, A. (2019). Implementation of a model of care for hospitalised older persons with cognitive impairment (the Confused Hospitalised Older Persons program) in six New South Wales hospitals. *Australasian Journal on Ageing, 38*(Suppl. 2), 98–106. https://doi.org/10.1111/ajag.12690.

Kurrle, S., Brodaty, H., & Hogarth, R. (2012). *Physical comorbidities of dementia.* Cambridge: Cambridge University Press.

Lewis, M., Peiris, C. L., & Shields, N. (2017). Long-term home and community-based exercise programs improve function in community-dwelling older people with cognitive impairment: A systematic review. *Journal of Physiotherapy, 63*(1), 23–29. https://doi.org/10.1016/j.jphys.2016.11.005.

Mendez, M., & Lim, G. (2003). Seizures in elderly patients with dementia: Epidemiology and management. *Drugs and Aging, 20*(11), 791–803. https://doi.org/10.2165/00002512-200320110-00001.

Morley, J. E. (2016). Gait, falls, and dementia. *Journal of the American Medical Directors Association, 17*(6), 467–470. https://doi.org/10.1016/j.jamda.2016.03.024.

Ooms, S., & Ju, Y. E. (2016). Treatment of sleep disorders in dementia. *Current Treatment Options in Neurology, 18*(9), 40. https://doi.org/10.1007/s11940-016-0424-3.

Shaw, F. E. (2002). Falls in cognitive impairment and dementia. *Clinics in Geriatric Medicine, 18*(2), 159–173. https://doi.org/10.1016/s0749-0690(02)00003-4.

Sherrington, C., Fairhall, N. J., Wallbank, G. K., Tiedemann, A., Michaleff, Z. A., Howard, K., … Lamb, S. E. (2019). Exercise for preventing falls in older people living in the community. *Cochrane Database of Systematic Reviews, 1.* https://doi.org/10.1002/14651858.CD012424.pub2.

Stewart, R., Masaki, K., Xue, Q. L., Peila, R., Petrovitch, H., White, L. R., & Launer, L. J. (2005). A 32-year prospective study of change in body weight and incident dementia: The Honolulu-Asia Aging Study. *Archives of Neurology, 62*(1), 55–60. https://doi.org/10.1001/archneur.62.1.55.

Taylor, M. E., Butler, A. A., Lord, S. R., Delbaere, K., Kurrle, S. E., Mikolaizak, A. S., & Close, J. C. T. (2018). Inaccurate judgement of reach is associated with slow reaction time, poor balance, impaired executive function and predicts prospective falls in older people with cognitive impairment. *Experimental Gerontology, 114*, 50–56. https://doi.org/10.1016/j.exger.2018.10.020.

Wang, L., Larson, E. B., Bowen, J. D., & van Belle, G. (2006). Performance-based physical function and future dementia in older people. *Archives of Internal Medicine, 166*(10), 1115–1120. https://doi.org/10.1001/archinte.166.10.1115.

CHAPTER 13

Improving functional independence: Dementia rehabilitation programs

Yun-Hee Jeon[a], Nicole Milne[a], Cassandra Kaizik[a], and Barbara Resnick[b]
[a]Sydney Nursing School, The University of Sydney, Sydney, NSW, Australia
[b]School of Nursing, The University of Maryland, Baltimore, MD, United States

Introduction

"The right to live independently and to be included in the community stems from some of the most fundamental human rights standards" (Council of Europe Commissioner for Human Rights, 2012). Maintaining functional independence—the ability to perform essential everyday activities safely and autonomously—even in the face of physical, cognitive, social, and emotional challenges, is a marker of well-being of people of all ages, including those living with dementia. People living with dementia retain the capacity to enjoy a meaningful life with the most appropriate care and support (Vernooij-Dassen & Jeon, 2016). This strongly aligns with the concept of social health, emphasizing the person's ability to fulfill their potential and obligations, to adapt and self-care despite their frailties, limitations, and disabilities, and to participate in social activities (Huber et al., 2011, 2016).

According to the World Health Organisation (World Health Organisation, 2019), rehabilitation is broadly defined as "a set of interventions needed when a person is experiencing or is likely to experience limitations in everyday functioning due to aging or a health condition, including chronic diseases or disorders, injuries or traumas." Rehabilitation emphasizes person-centeredness and the person's functional independence, not the disease, through the measures of preventing and slowing down their loss of function, or its further decline, improving, restoring, and maintaining the function, and compensating for lost function (World Health Organisation, 2011, 2019).

In the past two decades, a steadily increasing number of dementia-specific rehabilitation programs that adopt the principles of rehabilitation have

Dementia Rehabilitation
https://doi.org/10.1016/B978-0-12-818685-5.00013-1
227

been tested. These include multidisciplinary or specialist-led community programs, multimodal rehabilitation programs, function-focused care, and cognitive rehabilitation (altogether "rehabilitation programs" hereafter). We distinguish these from rehabilitative interventions which address a single therapy such as exercise, cognitive stimulation, reminiscence, speech therapy, or a specific aspect of functions (e.g., physical, cognitive or social function, or communication) which have been reviewed in the preceding chapters.

Current approaches and evidence

A total of 28 rehabilitation programs included in this chapter have been organized in three settings: home based, institution based, and clinic/center based. As shown in Tables 1–3, there was considerable variability in the nature of the programs. With the exception of function-focused care (Boltz, Chippendale, Resnick, & Galvin, 2015; Galik, Resnick, Hammersla, & Brightwater, 2014; Galik, Resnick, Lerner, Hammersla, & Gruber-Baldini, 2015; Henskens, Nauta, Scherder, Oosterveld, & Vrijkotte, 2017) and inpatient hospital-based programs (Raggi et al., 2007; Tanaka et al., 2017; Toba et al., 2014), most programs involved community–dwelling participants with mild to moderate dementia ($n = 21$) and were most commonly undertaken individually in participants' homes with care partner input ($n = 12$). Three programs were delivered in groups and two used both group and individual sessions. The total duration of the programs ranged from 4 to 234 hours, conducted over 3 weeks to 2 years, and generally occurring in 1 hour or 90-minute sessions.

The majority of programs were delivered by occupational therapists or psychologists, either alone or with other health care professionals such as registered nurses, speech therapists, geriatricians, and occasionally neurologists. Multimodal interventions tended to include multidisciplinary teams.

Home-based rehabilitation

Twelve of the 28 programs reviewed were for community–dwelling people with dementia and delivered in their homes. The programs were specialist-led, in forms of cognitive rehabilitation and occupational therapy, or multidisciplinary team based. Notably, all but one (Callahan et al., 2017) program in this category improved individuals' everyday functioning. Most home-based programs included environmental assessment and modifications except for cognitive rehabilitation.

Specialist-led home-based rehabilitation

As with the goal of occupational therapy (OT), OT-led programs focus on enabling people to perform activities of everyday living. This is achieved through a person-centered approach, and by modifying tasks or the environments in which they are performed. Gitlin et al.'s (Gitlin, Corcoran, Winter, Boyce, & Hauck, 2001) home environmental intervention in the United States was led by experienced OTs and involved care partner education on the role and impact of physical and social environments on individuals' functional ability and behavior. The goal was to address the person with dementia's behavioral concerns and improve functional independence. The program consisted of five 90-min sessions delivered over 3 months. At 3 months post-intervention, compared with the control group, the intervention group had significantly less decline in the person with dementia's instrumental activities of daily living, self-care, and behavior concerns (Gitlin et al., 2001).

A Dutch community-based occupational therapy program, by an experienced occupational therapist over 5 weeks (two 1-h visits per week), also focused on improving the person with dementia's function and promoting independence (Graff et al., 2006). Following a comprehensive assessment of the person with dementia, a client-centered, dementia specific, occupational guideline was used, involving both the person with dementia and their care partner. Post-intervention, the intervention group functioned significantly better than the wait-list control group. These group differences were maintained at 12 weeks (Graff et al., 2006).

However, one American OT-led program was not shown to be effective in improving function or reducing/delaying functional decline. Despite its lengthy intervention period and intensive approach of up to 24×90-minute individual sessions over 2 years, the addition of in-home occupational therapy to collaborative care did not improve outcomes in comparison to collaborative care alone after 24 months (Callahan et al., 2017).

Cognitive rehabilitation is an individualized, goal-oriented program with an emphasis on improving everyday functioning rather than improving cognition per se. Personalized rehabilitation methods may include the use of compensatory strategies, external aids, environmental adaptations, and procedural learning (Clare et al., 2019). There are many similarities between cognitive rehabilitation and OT-led rehabilitation. The main difference is that cognitive rehabilitation includes memory rehabilitative strategies such as the use of verbal and visual mnemonics, forward cueing, errorless learning, spaced retrieval, semantic association, dual coding and repetition, action-based encoding, chaining, prompting, and fading (e.g., Germain et al., 2019; Kelly, Lawlor, Coen, Robertson, & Brennan, 2019).

Table 1 Home-based rehabilitation programs targeting functional independence (*n* = 12).

Author, year, country	Program description	Delivered by (#multidisciplinary team)
Specialist-led home-based rehabilitation (*n* = 9)		
Callahan et al., 2017 USA	Collaborative care and home-based occupational therapy involved: (i) initial in-home evaluation to develop care plan; (ii) 3 cycles of home visits and telephone contact; (iii) evaluation repeated at beginning of each cycle; (iv) home visits more spread in each progressive cycle	OT
Clare et al., 2010 UK	Cognitive rehabilitation included personally meaningful goals, supported by addressing practical aids and strategies, techniques for learning new information, practice in maintaining attention and concentration, and techniques for stress management. Care partners, if available, joined for the end of each session to support implementation and practice	OT
Clare et al., 2019 UK	Cognitive rehabilitation involving a problem-solving approach to work on client chosen rehabilitation goals; emotion regulation and behavioral activation strategies; optimizing participants' existing use of strategies to manage cognitive disability; providing practice in maintaining attention and concentration; directing to relevant support services; care partner support	OT or RN
Fernández–Calvo et al., 2015 Spain	Cognitive stimulation and cognitive rehabilitation (e.g., errorless learning, spaced retrieval, semantic association, generation, dual coding, repetition and external memory aids) incorporating: (i) new recreational and cognitive tasks; (ii) a module of functional activities based on real-life situations; (iii) cognitive training exercises to carry out at home with the care partner; and (iv) psychoeducational activities	OT
Germain et al., 2019 Belgium	Cognitive rehabilitation included: (i) identifying ADL difficulties; (ii) selecting realistic and potentially rewarding areas to focus on; (iii) defining specific program to adapt each ADL selected (requires detailed analysis of performance); (iv) relevant strategies for each ADL (errorless progressive adaptation and spaced retrieval technique, written instructions with step-by-step procedure, repeated exercises, adaptation of environment), explained to relatives to ensure practice at home	Psychologist and/ or OT

Sample size (¥dyads)	Dementia severity	Program dose: number of sessions × time (duration in wks)	Tools used to measure function	Study design (*significant improvement in function)
¥n = 180	AD Mild–moderate	8 × 90 min (16 wks) + 8 × 90 min (32 wks) + 8 visits (1 year) *Tot 36 h*	ADCS-ADL	RCT
¥n = 69	Mild (MMSE > 18)	8 × 60 min (8 wks) *Tot 8 h*	COPM	★RCT
¥n = 427	Mild (MMSE > 18)	10 × 60–90 min (13 wks) + 4 × 60–90 min (26 wks) *Tot 14–21 h*	BGSI	★RCT
n = 61	Mild	48 × 90 min (16 wks) *Tot 72 h*	RDRS-2	★RCT
¥n = 52	Mild–moderate	13 × 60 min (13 wks) + 9 × 60 min (39 wks) *Tot 22 h*	Profinteg scale	★Pre-post

Continued

Table 1 Home-based rehabilitation programs targeting functional independence ($n = 12$)—cont'd

Author, year, country	Program description	Delivered by ([#]multidisciplinary team)
Graff et al., 2006 Netherlands	Cognitive and behavioral occupational therapy based on client-centered occupational therapy guidelines for people with dementia, to train people with dementia in the use of aids to compensate for cognitive decline and care partners in coping with behaviors and supervision	OT
Gitlin et al., 2001 USA	Home environmental intervention involved in educating care partners about the environmental impact on dementia related behaviors: helping them to: (i) simplify objects in the home; (ii) break-down tasks and (iii) involve other family network or formal supports in daily caregiving tasks. It targeted a specific aspect of daily care as problematic, with strategies redefined, and/or new recommendations introduced throughout. Cognitive restructuring and validation used to instill care partners' greater perceived control and confidence to manage the problem	OT
Kelly et al., 2019 Ireland	Cognitive rehabilitation addressed person with dementia goals, and incorporated techniques for learning new information, encouraged relaxation and the use of learning strategies and memory aids every day: Memory rehabilitative strategies (verbal and visual mnemonics, forward cueing, spaced retrieval, direct instruction; Procedural memory strategies (action-based encoding, chaining, prompting, and fading). Where possible, care partners attended the end of each session and were provided with a summary and encouraged to support practice	Psychologist
Regan et al., 2017 Australia	Brief cognitive rehabilitation addressed individually relevant goals, supported by the provision of the MAXCOG information resource. Strategies focused on positive resources, intact functions, retained skills, and activities clients could still take part in	Counsellor, neuro-psychologist

Sample size ($^{¥}$dyads)	Dementia severity	Program dose: number of sessions × time (duration in wks)	Tools used to measure function	Study design (*significant improvement in function)
$^{¥}n = 135$	Mild–moderate	10 × 60 min (5 wks) $Tot\ 10h$	AMPS, IDDD	*RCT
$^{¥}n = 171$	Moderate-moderately severe	5 × 90 min (13 wks) $Tot\ 7.5h$	Modified FIM-ADL; Lawton IADL	*RCT (IADL only)
$^{¥}n = 3$	Mild (MMSE 18–24)	8 × 60–90 min (8 wks) $Tot\ 8–12h$	BGSI, Lawton IADL	*Pre-post, single-case MBD (BGSI only)
$^{¥}n = 40$	MCI & early stage AD	4 × 60 min (4 wks) $Tot\ 4h$	Bayer-ADL COPM	*RCT (COPM only)

Continued

Table 1 Home-based rehabilitation programs targeting functional independence (*n* = 12)—cont'd

Author, year, country	Program description	Delivered by (#multidisciplinary team)
Multidisciplinary home-based rehabilitation (*n* = 3)		
Carbone et al., 2013 Italy	Home assistance model of rehabilitation consisted of: (i) memory training, reality orientation therapy, occupational therapy, reminiscence therapy, validation therapy, motor rehabilitation, milieu therapy, music therapy, supportive psychotherapy; (ii) family counseling and psychoeducational counseling; (iii) aids and adaptations to compensate for disability and reduce possible environmental triggers for behaviors	#OT, RN, Psychologist, Social assistant
Gitlin et al., 2010 USA	Biobehavioral home-based intervention also known as COPE, is an extended version of Gitlin et al. (2001) with the additional of RN input. COPE involved: (i) assessments; (ii) care partner education; and (iii) care partner training; training in problem-solving, communication, activity engagement, task simplification	#OT, RN
Jeon, Krein, et al., 2019 Australia	Interdisciplinary home-based reablement program (I-HARP) involved: (i) comprehensive assessment; (ii) interdisciplinary, tailored care planning using person-centered goal setting; (iii) implementation of the plan through a series of home visits; (iv) care partner support; and (v) minor home alterations and assistive devices	#OT, RN, case coordinator, (other allied health service)

Notes: MCI: Mild Cognitive Impairment; AD: Alzheimer's disease; OT: Occupational Therapist; RN: Registered Nurse. Mth/mths: month/months; Wk/wks: week/weeks; Grp: Group; Ind: Individual; Tot: Total.
Pre-Post; Pre- and post-intervention study; Single case MBD: Single subject multiple baseline design; RCT: Randomized controlled trial; CRT: Cluster-randomized trial; pRCT: Controlled partial-randomized study; Non-RCT: not randomly allocated controlled trial.
MMSE: Mini Mental State Examination; BI: Barthel Index; BGSI: Bangor Goal-Setting Interview; COPM: Canadian Occupational Performance Measure; FIM: Functional Independence Measure; RDRS-2: Rapid Disability Rating Scale; AADL: Advanced Activities of Daily Living; SAS: Social Activity Scale; Bayer-ADL: Bayer Activities of Daily Living Scale; DAD: Disablement Assessment for Dementia; Katz ADL: Activities of Daily Living; Lawton IADL: Instrumental Activities of Daily Living; ADCS ADL: Alzheimer's Disease Cooperative Study Group Activities of Daily Living Scale; AMPS: Assessment of Motor and Process Skills; IDDD: Interview of Deterioration of Daily Activities in Dementia.
COPE: Care of Persons with Dementia in their Environments; MAXCOG: Maximizing Cognition.

Sample size ($^¥$dyads)	Dementia severity	Program dose: number of sessions × time (duration in wks)	Tools used to measure function	Study design (*significant improvement in function)
$^¥n = 22$	Mild–moderate	36 × 360 min (13 wks) Tot 243 h	BI, Katz ADL, Lawton IADL	★Pre–post (BI only)
$^¥n = 209$	Mild–severe (MMSE 1–23)	12 × 90 min (18 wks) Tot 18 h	FIM	★RCT
$^¥n = 18$	Mild–moderate	11 × 90 min home visit + 1.5 × 60-min care partner support (18 wks) Tot 18 h	DAD	★RCT

Table 2 Institution-based multimodal rehabilitation programs targeting functional independence (*n*=7).

Author, year, country	Setting (§informal care partner involved)	Program description (†Grp; ‡Grp & Ind-combined/compared)	Delivered by (#multidisciplinary team)
Inpatient hospital-based rehabilitation (*n*=4)			
Boltz et al., 2015 USA	§Hospital medical unit (acute care)	Family-centered, Function-focused care involved: (i) environmental and facility policy review; (ii) staff education and training; (iii) family/person with dementia education linked to joint care partner/nurse assessment; jointly developed individualized goals and treatment plans; coaching of primary nurse to communicate and provide a copy of plan to post-acute providers; post-acute follow-up to provide ongoing education and modification of the care plan; coaching of family care partner to communicate program goals and expectations to the post-acute care providers	RN, Care staff
Raggi et al., 2007 Italy	§Hospital specialized unit	Comprehensive rehabilitation: Reality Orientation Therapy integrated with once daily sessions of computerized cognitive training consisting of a series of 30 computer tasks tapping into different functional areas at varying levels of difficulty	#Neurologist, Psychologist, Education specialist, RN
Tanaka et al., 2017 Japan	Geriatric health service facility	‡Brain-activating rehabilitation (BAR), post-intensive rehabilitation involved reality orientation, reminiscence, physical activity	Not stated
Toba et al., 2014 Japan	Geriatric health service facility	Intensive rehabilitation involved reminiscence, reality orientation, memory rehabilitation, music therapy, physical exercise, occupational therapy, speech communication therapy and learning sessions. Individual functional profiles were assessed with regard to both abilities and disabilities and training activities were selected jointly by therapists and participants	#Physio, Occupational, or Speech therapist

Sample size (¥dyads)	Dementia severity	Program dose: number of sessions × time (duration in wks)	Tools used to measure function	Study design (*significant improvement in function)
¥n = 86	Not stated	Variable–until discharge (on average 4 days)	BI	*Comparative repeated measures
n = 50	Mild–severe	Variable–until discharge (on average 26 days)	Katz ADL, Lawton IADL	*Pre-post
n = 60	Mild–severe (MMSE 5–25)	24 × 60 min (Grp); OR 24 × 20 min (Ind) (12 wks) *Tot 8–24 h*	NOSGER total	RCT
n = 212	Not stated	39 × personal session (13 wks) *Tot 39 h*	BI, SAS	Non-RCT

Continued

Table 2 Institution-based multimodal rehabilitation programs targeting functional independence (n = 7)—cont'd

Author, year, country	Setting (§informal care partner involved)	Program description (†Grp; ‡Grp & Ind-combined/compared)	Delivered by (#multidisciplinary team)
Long-term care facility-based rehabilitation (n = 3)			
Galik et al., 2014 USA	§Nursing home	Function focused care for the cognitively impaired (FFC-CI) involved: (i) environmental and facility policy review; (ii) staff education and training to incorporate appropriate skills and strategies for actively engaging cognitively impaired residents in functional and physical activities that are person-centered. Coordinated by a trained RN who worked with intervention sites to implement program through staff in-services, education sessions, handouts and supported a staff champion of the program	RN, care staff
Galik et al., 2015 USA	Dementia Assisted Living	Function focused care for the cognitively impaired Same as above	RN, Care staff
Henskens et al., 2017 Netherlands	§Nursing home	Movement-oriented restorative care focused on stimulating physical activity and independent functioning in daily care and activities; incorporates important aspects of function-focused care and restorative care, such as establishing goals with each resident, educating nursing staff and families	#Nursing/care staff, Allied health staff, Geriatricians, Activity supervisors, Volunteers

Notes: Mth/mths: month/months; Wk/wks: week/weeks; Grp: Group; Ind: Individual; Tot: Total.
OT: Occupational Therapist; RN: Registered Nurse.
Pre-Post; Pre- and post-intervention study; RCT: Randomized controlled trial; CRT: Cluster-randomized trial; Non-RCT: not randomly allocated controlled trial.
MMSE: Mini Mental State Examination; BI: Barthel Index; SAS: Social Activity Scale; Katz ADL: Activities of Daily Living; Lawton IADL: Instrumental Activities of Daily Living; NOSGER: Nurses' Observation Scale for Geriatric Patients.

Sample size ([¥]dyads)	Dementia severity	Program dose: number of sessions × time (duration in wks)	Tools used to measure function	Study design (*significant improvement in function)
$n = 103$	Moderate–severe (MMSE ≤ 15)	26 wks	BI	★CRT
$n = 96$	Moderate–severe (MMSE ≤ 15)	(26 wks)	BI	CRT
$n = 61$	Moderate–severe	(52 wks)	BI	Non-RCT

Table 3 Clinic/Center-based rehabilitation targeting functional independence (*n* = 9).

Author, year, country	Setting (§informal care partner involved)	Program description (†Grp; ‡Grp & Ind-combined/compared)
Amieva et al., 2016 France	§Outpatient clinic	3 Groups compared: (i) structured group program of standard tasks designed to involve various cognitive functions such as memory, attention, language, or executive function; (ii) group reminiscence therapy (e.g., schooldays, birthday, wedding, working life, holidays); and (iii) individualized cognitive rehabilitation therapy consisted of activities according to personally relevant goals for participants
Ávila, Carvalho, Bottino, & Miotto, 2007 Brazil	§Outpatient clinic (+ home visits)	‡Neuropsychological rehabilitation involved different memory techniques aimed at facilitating learning and recall of material: motor movements; verbal association; categorization; and ADL training with simulation of ordinary daily situations and use of external aids like diaries, calendars, and notebooks
Brueggen et al., 2017 Germany	§Outpatient clinic	†Modified CORDIAL: (i) identification of problems and treatment goals; (ii) use of external memory aids; (iii) introduction and implementation of daily routine and structured framework for the day; (iv) organization and implementation of pleasurable and meaningful activities; (v) reminiscence; (vi) evaluation of achieved goals and future planning; (vii) advanced training in tasks for transferring strategies to daily life
Chew et al., 2015 Singapore	§Outpatient clinic	†Multimodal cognitive and physical rehabilitation included: (i) multicomponent physical exercise program of light aerobic exercises, range of motion and resistance exercises, as well as balance training; (ii) cognitive stimulation and rehabilitation with social and mental activities such as reminiscence therapy; and (iii) tailored activities and person-centered care
Cornelis et al., 2018 Belgium	§Memory clinic (+ home visits)	Multicomponent rehabilitation involved: (i) assessment and goal setting; (ii) rehabilitation (teaching compensatory and environmental strategies to people with dementia and up-skilling care partners to support person with dementia autonomy using cognitive and behavioral interventions); (iii) counseling; (iv) adaptations to the living environment or assistive devices

Delivered by (#multidisciplinary team)	Sample size (¥dyads)	Dementia severity	Program dose: number of sessions × time (duration in wks)	Tools used to measure function	Study design (*significant improvement in function)
Psychologist	¥$n = 311$	Mild–moderate	13 × 90 min (13 wks) + 15 × 90 min (91 wks) *Tot 42 h*	DAD	⋆RCT
#Psychologist and Speech Therapist	$n = 16$	Mild–moderate	22 × 60 min Grp (22 wks); OR 22 × 40 min Ind (22 wks) *Tot 14–22 h*	Bayer-ADL	Pre-post
Psychologist, OT	$n = 16$	Mild	12 × 120 min (12 wks) *Tot 24 h*	Bayer-ADL, NSL	pRCT
#RN coordinator, Physio-therapist, OT, Psychologist	¥$n = 55$	Mild	8 × 180 min (8 wks) *Tot 24 h*	BI, Lawton IADL	Pre-Post
#Geriatrician, Neurologist, OT, Social worker/RN, Psychologist	¥$n = 30$	Not stated	25 × 60 min (52 wks) including 2 home visits *Tot 25 h*	Katz ADL, Lawton IADL, AADL	Pre-Post

Continued

Table 3 Clinic/Center-based rehabilitation targeting functional independence (*n* = 9)—cont'd

Author, year, country	Setting (§informal care partner involved)	Program description (†Grp; ‡Grp & Ind-combined/compared)
Kim, 2015 South Korea	Day care center	‡Cognitive rehabilitation focused on a personally meaningful goal with sessions consisting of practical strategies and aids, compensation strategies, and the techniques for stress management to improve performance and functioning in relation to goals. Group sessions focused on: (i) practicing time-and-place orientation through paper-and-pencil tasks and use of a calendar and personal memory notebook or cellular phone at the start of each session; (ii) matching faces and names and learning memory and sustaining attention through paper-and-pencil tasks
Lam et al., 2010 Hong Kong	Social center, Nursing home	†Functional enhancement comprised skills training and problem solving in individually selected (relevant) daily activities using cognitive behavioral approach
Loewenstein, Acevedo, Czaja, & Duara, 2004 USA	Clinic (not specified)	Cognitive rehabilitation: (i) learning face–name associations; (ii) practicing time-and-place orientation through rehearsal, use of the calendar and memory notebook; (iii) activating procedural and motor memory by manipulating the objects as though they were using them; (iv) sustaining attention and activating visuomotor processing within a computer task; (v) training to make change for a purchase using different amounts; and (vi) balancing a cheque book by hand and with a calculator after paying three actual utility bills. Encouraged to practice tasks at home with other's assistance
Zanetti et al., 2001 Italy	Day hospital	Procedural memory stimulation involved 13 basic and instrumental activities of daily living (ADLs) were trained, prompting and informing people with dementia about each task to be performed. People with dementia were assisted by cues, reinforcement, and verbal and nonverbal prompts, or modeling of the task

Notes: Mth/mths: month/months; Wk/wks: week/weeks; Grp: Group; Ind: Individual; Tot: Total.
Pre-Post: Pre- and post-intervention study; RCT: Randomized controlled trial; pRCT: Controlled partial-randomized study.
MMSE: Mini Mental State Examination; BI: Barthel Index; AADL: Advanced Activities of Daily Living; Bayer-ADL: Bayer Activities of Daily Living Scale; NSL: Nuremberg Aging Observation Scale; COPM: Canadian Occupational Performance Measure; DAD: Disablement Assessment for Dementia; Katz ADL: Activities of Daily Living; Lawton IADL: Instrumental Activities of Daily Living; AMPS: Assessment of Motor and Process Skills; PPT: Physical Performance Test; DAFS: Direct Assessment of Functional Status.
CORDIAL: Cognitive Rehabilitation and cognitive-behavioral treatment for early dementia in Alzheimer disease.

Delivered by (#multidisciplinary team)	Sample size (¥dyads)	Dementia severity	Program dose: number of sessions × time (duration in wks)	Tools used to measure function	Study design (*significant improvement in function)
RN	n = 43	Mild (MMSE ≥ 18)	8 × 60 min (30 min Grp & 30 min Ind) (8 wks) Tot 8 h	Modified BI COPM	*RCT (COPM)
OT	n = 74	Mild–moderate	16 × 45 min (8 wks) Tot 12 h	Chinese DAD, AMPS	RCT
Neuro-psychologist	n = 44	Mild	24 × 45 min (12–16 wks) Tot 18 h	Bayer-ADL	RCT
OT	n = 18	Mild–Moderate	15 × 60 min (3 wks) Tot 15 h	PPT, DAFS	★Two-group pre-post

Goal-oriented cognitive rehabilitation evaluated by Clare et al. (2019) is characterized by establishing client-directed rehabilitation goals, and action planning to achieve those goals in the client's own environment and real-life context. Depending on the client's need, the intervention involved "applying emotion regulation and behavioural activation strategies, reviewing and optimising participants' existing use of strategies to manage cognitive disability, providing practice in maintaining attention and concentration, signposting to relevant services, and offering support for study partners" (Clare et al., 2019, p. 711). This intervention was implemented through 10 weekly 1-hour dyadic individual sessions over a 3-month period followed by four 1-hour maintenance sessions over the subsequent 6 months (total 14–21 h). A parallel-group multicenter single-blind RCT showed statistically significant, large positive effects in the intervention group at three and 6 months on goal attainment for the person with dementia and care partner. However, no significant effect was found in the person with dementia's quality of life, mood, self-efficacy, and cognition, nor the partner's stress level and quality of life, both short and long term (Clare et al., 2019). Notably, an earlier intervention of Clare et al. (2010) conducted in a clinic setting with a smaller dose and duration of cognitive rehabilitation (1-h/week over 8 weeks, total 8 h) showed a significant functional improvement.

A brief cognitive rehabilitation program in Australia (Regan et al., 2017) showed no significant group by time interaction on activities of daily living (ADL). However, the intervention group displayed significantly higher performance and satisfaction with primary goals post-intervention than the control group (Regan et al., 2017). The negative result in ADL may be due to the fact the participants had mild cognitive impairment or early-stage Alzheimer's disease, whose ADL decline might not have been severe enough to show change over the short program duration (4 weeks). Similarly, cognitive rehabilitation tested in Ireland showed no significant improvement in instrumental activities of daily living (IADL), while goal attainment showed improvement post-intervention and follow-up (Kelly et al., 2019).

Cognitive rehabilitation is the most frequently studied program in this review, however, its effectiveness in improving functional independence is mixed. This may be due to inconsistency in dose and duration, the outcome measure for function, and delivery setting (clinic, day care, hospital, or home). Some patterns of effectiveness emerged. All home-based cognitive rehabilitation demonstrated improvement in individuals' functional independence, either based on the measure of activities of daily living or the measure of goal performance. Clinic or center-based cognitive rehabilitation showed fewer positive outcomes.

Multidisciplinary home-based rehabilitation

The COPE (Care of Person with Dementia in their Environments) program, developed by Gitlin and her team in the United States, aims "to re-engage the person with dementia in daily activities and increase functionality, thereby alleviating caregiver burden" (Gitlin, Winter, Dennis, Hodgson, & Hauck, 2010, p.984), involving both the person with dementia and their informal care partners. The COPE program took into account the person with dementia's capabilities, underlying medical conditions, and physical and social environments. The principles were an individually tailored approach, addressing concerns and issues identified by the care partners, and using goals and action planning strategies. COPE consisted of comprehensive assessments (person with dementia's dis/abilities, medical conditions, physical environment, communication, and care partner-identified concerns); care partner education (person with dementia capabilities, potential effects of medications, pain, constipation, dehydration); and care partner training (problem solving, communication, engaging people with dementia in activities, and simplifying tasks). The COPE program involved 10 OT home visits over 4 months and two nursing sessions. The nurse provided health-related information to the care partner, collected blood and urine samples, assessed for signs of dehydration, and reviewed medications. At 4 months, compared with controls, COPE participants with dementia had less functional dependence and less dependence in IADLs, but no group differences were observed at 9 months. COPE care partners perceived greater benefits (well-being, knowledge, and skills in caregiving) than their control counterparts at both 4- and 9 months (Gitlin et al., 2010).

An Australian multimodal reablement program, interdisciplinary home-based reablement program (I-HARP) (Jeon, Krein, et al., 2019), shares a number of commonalities with COPE: a 4-month home visit program delivered by an OT and registered nurse (RN), individually tailored to address the person's total environment, comorbid health conditions, and multimorbidity based on comprehensive assessments. I-HARP included a strong emphasis on interdisciplinary teamwork with greater involvement of the RN and other allied health professionals, and person–centeredness/client direction, incorporating cognitive rehabilitation techniques (e.g., compensatory and restorative techniques) and minor home modifications and assistive devices. I-HARP consisted of (1) 12 home visits of 90 minutes (5–6×OT, 3–4×RN, plus 2–4 additional options of a physiotherapist, speech pathologist, or psychologist); (2) minor home modification and/or assistive devices; and (3) 1.5 hours of care partner support sessions. A face-to-face case interdisciplinary conference was undertaken after initial assessments and ongoing communication occurred between all clinicians throughout the intervention. At 4 months post-intervention, the I-HARP pilot showed strong results in terms of goal attainment, improved mobility and independence, functional independence, no entry to higher care, and both self-perceived and observed client's well-being and confidence. The control group declined more than the intervention group on functional independence after 12 months (effect size of 0.33) (Jeon, Krein, et al., 2019).

The most time and resource-intensive multimodal intervention was an Italian home care assistance program or "personalized functional reactivation treatment" (Carbone et al., 2013). This consisted of physical and cognitive rehabilitation for people with mild to moderate dementia, home environment modification, and psychological support for care partners delivered by a multidisciplinary team of occupational therapists, nurses, psychologists, and social assistants. In all, 6-hour sessions were conducted in the home 3 times per week for 3 months, a total of 243 hours. At the end of treatment, there was a significant improvement in scores on an ADL measure, the Barthel Index (rising from 75.5 to 87.3), with all items improving except for transfers and mobility. However, there was no corresponding improvement in another set of ADL measures, Katz ADL and Lawton IADL. At 3-month follow-up, basic ADLs had returned to baseline levels (Carbone et al., 2013).

Institution-based multimodal rehabilitation

Institution-based rehabilitation programs target patients and residents in their respective care environment and are categorized into inpatient hospital based ($n = 4$) and long-term care facility based ($n = 3$) (see Table 2).

Inpatient hospital-based rehabilitation

A 13-week intensive rehabilitation program in Japan (Toba et al., 2014) offered in an intermediate health facility, which is a subacute geriatric health service, was tailor made to meet the individual needs of people with dementia and delivered by a multidisciplinary team (OT, physiotherapist, speech therapist). This entailed assessment of individual functional profiles of capabilities and deficits, and selection of training activities drawn from reminiscence, reality orientation, memory rehabilitation, music therapy, physical exercise, occupational therapy, and speech communication therapy. The control group engaged in usual activities such as exercise, singing, and playing games. While there was a significant improvement in activities of daily living within the intervention group following the program, this did not differ from the control group.

Tanaka et al. (2017) evaluated an extended version of this intensive rehabilitation program, by offering a 12-week brain-activating rehabilitation program, a combination of cognitive rehabilitation, reminiscence therapy, reality orientation, and physical activity, to those who had recently completed the intensive rehabilitation program. Compared to usual care, no significant improvement in functional independence was found in the group-based or individual-based intervention participants.

A comprehensive multidisciplinary hospital-based rehabilitation program provided to people with dementia with mild to severe dementia at a specialized unit in Italy (Raggi et al., 2007) showed significant improvement on function at discharge, with an average length of stay of 26 days.

Boltz et al. (2015) implemented function-focused care for the cognitively impaired (FFC-CI, see below for details) with people with dementia in a hospital setting in the United States. This program introduced organizational change including staff education, collaborations between staff, family, and the community team. Despite an initial reduction in function, intervention participants improved significantly on function 14-days post-discharge, this was still evident at 60 days.

Long-term care facility-based rehabilitation

Function-focused care, interchangeably termed restorative care, is generally undertaken in institutional facilities (i.e., nursing homes). It involves fostering greater use of physical activity and independent functioning by residents enacted through interactions between care staff and residents and supported by organizational processes. For example, staff walking a resident to the bathroom instead of using incontinence pads (Galik et al., 2014). Developed by Galik and Resnick in the United States, function-focused care for the cognitively impaired (FFC-CI) intervention involves environmental and policy assessment, staff, and family education, developing individualized resident goals, and ongoing mentoring/motivating nursing staff and people with dementia. A 6-month cluster randomized study of the FFC-CI program (Galik et al., 2014) took place in four nursing homes involving residents with moderate to severe dementia. The intervention sought to change the attitudes and behaviors of staff to focus more on improving residents' functional independence, by teaching and mentoring staff to implement appropriate strategies and skills, and to actively engage residents in person–centered, physical, and functional activities. There was a significant improvement in function after 3 months in the intervention compared to control sites which were not maintained at 6 months.

However, a trial of FFC-CI involving residents with dementia in assisted living facilities in the United States found no significant difference in function between the intervention group and an educational control group over 6 months. Function declined in both groups (Galik et al., 2015). A Dutch version of FFC for nursing home residents with moderate to severe dementia, called "movement-oriented restorative care", did not demonstrate significant improvements in function over 12 months (Henskens et al., 2017).

Clinic/center-based rehabilitation

Nine rehabilitation programs, mostly cognitive rehabilitation ($n = 7$), were offered to community-dwelling older people with dementia in outpatient clinics, memory clinics, day centers, or day hospital. Notably, only 3 of the 7 cognitive rehabilitation programs in this setting showed improvement in function (Amieva et al., 2016; Kim, 2015; Zanetti et al., 2001).

The multicenter, ETNA3 randomized trial (Amieva et al., 2016), conducted in France, investigated the effects of group cognitive training, group reminiscence therapy, and individualized cognitive rehabilitation, in comparison to usual medical treatment. Participants had mild to moderate Alzheimer's disease. The program consisted of weekly, 90-minute sessions for 3 months, followed by 6-weekly maintenance sessions for the next 21 months. The program also involved a weekly telephone call to the care partner for feedback or questions during the first 3 months, followed by a 6-weekly telephone call. The cognitive rehabilitation component involved a tailor-made program of meaningful activities undertaken with the person with dementia and their care partner and setting personally relevant goals. For those who completed individualized cognitive rehabilitation, there was a significant improvement in function and a 6-month delay in institutionalization at 2 years compared to usual medical treatment, but this effect was not observed for participants in the group cognitive training or group reminiscence. A combined group and individualized cognitive rehabilitation program offered over 8-weeks in a day center in South Korea (Kim, 2015) showed no change in ADLs post-intervention and no significant difference between the intervention group and controls. Similar to earlier studies on home-based cognitive rehabilitation, significant improvements were observed in ratings of occupation performance and satisfaction.

A multicomponent rehabilitation program in Belgium (Cornelis et al., 2018), focused on everyday functioning and a person-centered, goal-oriented approach. The program involved up to 25 individual sessions for people with dementia and their care partners over a year, conducted in a memory clinic, with 2 home visits. There was no control group. There was a significant decline in basic, instrumental, and advanced activities of daily living over 12-months, with most participants worsening in their function (range 45.5%–77.3%).

In a multimodal cognitive and physical rehabilitation program in Singapore (Chew, Chong, Fong, & Tay, 2015), participants with mild dementia and their care partners attended weekly 3-hour group sessions for 8 consecutive weeks. Each session included 30 minutes of tailored, individualized activities, based on individual treatment goals. The program had no significant impact on function, which might be because of a ceiling effect. Another group based functional enhancement program in Hong Kong, delivered by an OT in two, 45-minute sessions per week for 8 weeks at a social center and a nursing home showed no difference between the control and intervention groups (Lam et al., 2010).

Theoretical underpinnings

Only eight of the 28 programs specified theories that informed the development and evaluation of the intervention. Refer to Box 1 for further explanations for the theories below.

BOX 1 Theories that have informed rehabilitation programs in dementia.

Biopsychosocial and Biopsychosocial-environmental theory: Proposed by Engel (1977), the biopsychosocial approach recognized the many and varied factors influencing a person's health and experience of illness, which were absent from the purely biomedical model of the time. Building on Engel's foundation, the biopsychosocial-environmental theory extends this to highlight consideration of the person's environmental, or "ecological" factors.

Ecology of aging theory: Within the field of "environmental gerontology" or the "ecology of aging," Lawton and Nahemow (1973) have further explored the interaction of the aging individual with his or her environment which is expressed in the competence-environmental press framework and the person-environment-fit. A competence-environmental press framework (Lawton & Nahemow, 1973) explains processes and outcomes of changing individual's competency requiring their environment demands to be adjusted to prevent or enhance their capability to function optimally. The notion of person-environment-fit further explains that to understand person-environment relations, as people age, it is crucial not to

(Continued)

BOX 1 Theories that have informed rehabilitation programs in dementia—cont'd

consider personal and environmental factors as separate constructs, but to instead examine the "fit" between personal competencies/functional needs and the conditions of the person's environment. Here, the person encompasses biological health, sensory, and motor skills, and cognitive function while the environment includes both intimate and broad personal environments, social environment, as well as the physical environment. The fit, or the match, between the person and the environment denotes adaptation that is often manifested in individuals' everyday activities (Lawton & Nahemow, 1973).

The Disablement Process Model (DPM): Verbrugge and Jette (1994) describe the "risk factors" for the transition to a disability, referring to extra-individual (e.g., home modifications) and intra-individual (e.g., coping styles) factors. The DPM suggests that disability-related outcomes may be minimized by environmental interventions or enhancing environmental supports; the physical environment influences well-being, either an increasing risk or providing protection (Verbrugge & Jette, 1994).

Ecological systems theory: Often referred to as the "bioecological model," Bronfenbrenner's theory conceptualizes development as a process that occurs through the life course and recognizes equally the role of biopsychological characteristics of the individual and their environment (Bronfenbrenner, 1979). Ecological systems theory informs the Social Ecological Model (SEM), a framework for understanding relationships between individual and environmental factors in health, incorporating intrapersonal, interpersonal, and environmental and policy factors that can affect behavior (Sallis et al., 2008).

Social cognitive theory: Developed by Albert Bandura, initially as the Social Learning Theory in the 1960s, the social cognitive theory postulates that people acquire knowledge and understanding in the social context through observations and interactions with others and environments, which is often considered as reciprocal interactions between the person, behavior, and environment. It recognizes the importance of internal and external reinforcements influenced by past experiences in forming and shaping individuals' learning and behaviors (Bandura, 1986).

The Canadian Model of Occupational Performance (CMOP): Canadian Association of Occupational Therapists (1991, 1997), the CMOP is a social model that illustrates the relationship between persons, their social/environment context, and occupation. Occupation may be self-care, leisure, and/or productivity. Occupational performance is the result of interaction and interdependence between person, environment, and occupation. The person is connected to the environment, and occupation occurs in the interaction between persons and their environment. Both models of practice also convey person-centered practice and can be linked back to overarching theories of ecological and bioecological systems, biopsychosocial/environmental theory.

> **BOX 1 Theories that have informed rehabilitation programs in dementia—cont'd**
>
> *The Model of Human Occupational (MOHO) Performance*: Kielhofner and Posatery (1980) view humans as interacting with and within the environment to participate in occupations. The environment includes physical, social, cultural, economic, and political aspects. Human doing, or the occupation aspect of the model, includes participation, performance, skill, and the many factors that influence this in an individual.

Development of the home-based rehabilitation programs that consider environmental modifications or enhancements to reduce disability and enhance function, was informed and shaped by biobehavioral and biopsychosocial-environmental theories and the models of person-environmental fit from the ecology of aging theory (Lawton & Nahemow, 1973) and disablement process (Verbrugge & Jette, 1994). These home-based programs (Gitlin et al., 2001, 2010; Jeon, Krein, et al., 2019) focused on the interaction of environment and whole person and aimed to remove environmental barriers known to reduce a person's competency and instead adjust the environment to maximize the person's ability, considering all aspects of their functioning health, sensory and motor skills, and cognition. Notably, both the COPE program (Gitlin et al., 2010) and the I-HARP (Jeon, Krein, et al., 2019) addressed comorbidity and multimorbidity issues as well as modifiable environmental stressors surrounding the person with dementia to reduce any sensorial, physical, and cognitive demands that did not fit with their competence in daily activities.

The "function-focused care" programs, set within a hospital or aged-care facility, considered organizational and policy factors while addressing environmental and personal (direct care staff and residents) factors. As such, they were underpinned by ecological systems theory, which informs the social–ecological model. A social–ecological framework reflects the multifaceted levels interacting within a system (Sallis, Owen, & Fisher, 2008), for example, within a hospital or residential care facility, and how individuals and the environment interact within that system. Function-focused care was also guided by Bandura's social cognitive theory (Bandura, 1986) taking into account the influences that may impact achieving behavior/institutional change and maintenance.

The community occupational therapy intervention used in Graff's study (2006) is underpinned by the Canadian Model of Occupational

Performance (CMOP) (Canadian Association of Occupational Therapists, 1991, 1997), a social model that illustrates the relationship between persons, their social/environment context and occupation. Graff et al. (2006) used both the CMOP and another occupational therapy practice model, the Model of Human Occupational (MOHO) (Kielhofner & Posatery, 1980) convey person-centered practice, incorporating client-directed goal setting within this practice.

Gaps in clinical and research knowledge

This review demonstrates that people with dementia can improve in their functioning, following an appropriate, targeted rehabilitation program. As shown in Tables 1–3, 17 of the 28 studies reported a significant post-intervention improvement in individuals' functional independence. Successful programs are more likely to be individually administered and conducted with people with mild to moderate dementia in a person's home environment.

Over two-thirds of the programs in this review engaged care partners, and this involvement may also be an important part of an effective program. As (Jeon, Krein, et al., 2019) found in their I-HARP pilot trial, the care partner's understanding of the principles of reablement, their trust toward interventionists, motivation, and willingness to be involved in the program might be critical to success.

The question of what an adequate program dose and duration entails is complex, and the examination of dose and duration details shown in Tables 1–3, does not show clear patterns. Studies reporting a significant improvement tended to involve greater dose (range 10–234 h) compared to those with nonsignificant results (range 4–39 h), although a higher dose did not guarantee improvement. There was little difference in program duration between studies with and without significant improvement (3–104 weeks, and 4 to 104 weeks, respectively). Programs of about 3–4 months in duration (with or without further maintenance) and about 15–22 hours of dose appear to be adequate to improve function. Individualized care might suggest that people would require different doses and durations. However, most studies did not allow for individualized dose and duration. The need for a predefined dose and duration is understandable given that rehabilitation requires many elements to be addressed for the program to be effective, and this is usual practice in clinical trials. At the same time, flexibility in dose and duration to make room for varying degrees of individual needs and preferences is a necessary consideration.

None of the papers reviewed provided cost evaluation, so it is not clear whether individualized programs are cost-effective. Program costs must be weighed up against savings in health, aged care, and social services (e.g., emergency presentations, hospital admissions, nursing home admission), each of which may be avoided or delayed following rehabilitation. An extended follow-up is required to provide this evidence (Gitlin et al., 2001).

While more than 50% of the studies reviewed here used randomized controlled designs, they were mostly pilot or feasibility studies. All but one specialist-led ($n = 8$) and all of the multidisciplinary ($n = 3$) home-based programs showed a significant improvement in function. The institution-based rehabilitation program (inpatient hospital-based and function-focus care) showed mixed results. Focusing on the randomized controlled trials with adequate statistical power (Callahan et al., 2017; Clare et al., 2019; Gitlin et al., 2010; Graff et al., 2006; Toba et al., 2014), a similar conclusion of mixed results can be made.

Recently, there has been considerable debate over the varying terminology of rehabilitation and the difference between rehabilitation, restorative care, and reablement. Reablement has been defined as usually a time-limited, goal-oriented, person-centered, and often multidisciplinary program that focuses on supporting the person's functional independence, by maintaining the existing function, regaining lost function (where possible), and adapting to functions that have been lost. Supports may include skills training, home modifications, or access to assistive devices (Aspinal, Glasby, & Rostgaard, 2016; Poulos & Poulos, 2019). With the exception of the multidisciplinary element, most of the rehabilitation programs reviewed in this chapter would share the same characteristics as this definition of reablement. However, only one program, I-HARP (Jeon, Krein, et al., 2019), described their program as reablement. Overall, Tables 1–3 provide somewhat contradicting features to some definitions of rehabilitation (Poulos & Poulos, 2019) distinguished as a specialized service in a hospital-based or community outreach context provided only after a certain point of ill-health, injury, or trauma. Consensus on the terminology in this field is yet to be established, however, the rehabilitation programs reviewed here are consistent with the WHO guidelines on health-related rehabilitation (World Health Organisation, 2011), which emphasize the cross-sectoral nature of rehabilitation services without restriction on setting or provider.

Clinical and research implications

Many key principles are found to have played a major role in the success of the programs.

- *Person-centered, individually tailored, and home-based approach:* In each of the studies that reported improved function, the program involved person-centered practice and conducted on an individual basis in the person's home. The practice of skills in the familiar home environment may contribute to program success. Nevertheless, the setting alone or the mode of delivery alone does not necessarily determine the outcome, as demonstrated in successful programs offered in an outpatient clinic (Amieva et al., 2016), day center (Kim, 2015), and hospitals (Raggi et al., 2007; Zanetti et al., 2001).
- *Comprehensive assessment of the person and their environment:* A comprehensive assessment of individual capacities, capabilities, and deficits that informs person-centered goal setting and action planning was a feature of some successful programs. Programs also had a strong emphasis on addressing deficits or enhancing the participant's social, functional, and physical environments.
- *Dementia severity and co/multi-morbidity:* The level of dementia severity and other co/multi-morbidity issues may affect outcomes. Dementia severity may also impact on detecting changes in the person's everyday functioning using commonly used ADL measures that do not necessarily detect small changes in functional independence due to ceiling effects. Importantly, the functional decline may not be solely caused by the neurodegenerative nature of dementia, but also age-related and/ or associated with other chronic illnesses (Kurrle, Brodaty, & Hogarth, 2012), and further impaired by the person's physical/social environment. When people with dementia have greater impairments in function, and greater co/multi-morbidity, a multidisciplinary team might be required to address these greater needs. With the exception of programs such as I-HARP (Jeon, Krein, et al., 2019) and COPE (Gitlin et al., 2010), most rehabilitation programs had limited or no attention to the issue of co/ multi-morbidity.
- *Assessment of functional ability:* The variety of tools used to assess function may also contributed, in part, to different outcomes between studies. Carbone et al. (2013), for example, reported a significant improvement in scores on the Barthel Index (Shah, Vanclay, & Cooper, 1989). However, in the same study, there was no change in basal and instrumental

activities of daily living, as assessed by the Lawton and Brody (1969) and Katz, Downs, Cash, and Grotz (1970) scales, respectively. The authors suggested the Barthel Index may be more sensitive to change than the latter scales. However, as indicated in Tables 1–3, the Barthel Index and Lawton and Katz scales all showed mixed results across studies. It also indicates that studies using different tools to measure function may not be directly comparable. Measures of goal attainment and satisfaction—the Bangor Goal Setting Interview (BGSI) (Clare, Nelis, & Kudlicka, 2016) and the Canadian Occupational Performance Measure (COPM) (Law et al., 2005)—have been successfully used in many cognitive rehabilitation evaluation. However, as discussed earlier, the studies that measured both ADL and goal attainment (Kelly et al., 2019; Kim, 2015; Regan et al., 2017) have shown conflicting results between the outcomes from the ADL measures and goal attainment scales. There is insufficient evidence to determine whether the goal attainment alone can determine the effectiveness of a rehabilitation program.

- *Experience and training of interventionists:* Many papers did not describe the interventionists' experience and/or training. However, those studies reporting significant results tend to emphasize the importance of interventionists' training and experience. For example, in the Dutch OT-led program, OTs were trained for 80 hours and experienced for a minimum of 240 hours of care relevant to the study (Graff et al., 2006). Gitlin et al. (2001) program required a licensed OT with a minimum of 1-year experience in-home care or working with older adults and 20 h of training.

- *Implementation research:* All studies reviewed tested for the efficacy or effectiveness of the rehabilitation program. There is a need for rigorous implementation research on scalability and sustainability of the appropriateness of these programs including how to embed them in everyday practice, service delivery, and policy development. In their evaluation for the implementation of function-focused care in assisted living, Resnick, Galik, Vigne, and Carew (2016) emphasized the importance of selecting the most suitable champions for change management: those in leadership positions or nurses in an administrative role who have access to resources and can facilitate necessary policy changes to assure implementation of the innovation (Resnick et al., 2016). Two Australian studies are currently being conducted: an implementation study of the COPE in the Australian context (Clemson et al., 2018) and a pragmatic RCT of the I-HARP in hospital and aged care settings (Jeon, Simpson, et al., 2019).

Models of care and implementation of rehabilitation programs

As demonstrated in this book, a substantial amount of evidence has been generated in the field of rehabilitation in dementia. This chapter has provided a synthesis of research evidence on rehabilitation programs designed to improve everyday functioning of people living with dementia. The "model of care" is an important concept in considering future directions for the implementation of dementia rehabilitation programs. A model of care is multidimensional and refers to overarching health service design within a broader health system context, that is informed by theories, evidence-based practice, and defined standards as well as values and principles. It consists of roles and structures, care management, and referral processes (Davidson, Halcomb, Hickman, Phillips, & Graham, 2006; NSW Health, 2015). One of the key principles that must be considered in developing and introducing a model of care is to establish an appropriate care setting, which is determined by the person's needs, functional capacity, health conditions as well as service accessibility. A Rehabilitation Model of Care report (NSW Health, 2015) provides useful guidance in this regard, describing that:

> … a rehabilitation patient journey is not a linear process and pathways are individually determined based on functional impairment, medical acuity and prognosis and access to rehabilitation services. Rehabilitation clients require different levels of care at different points in their rehabilitation journey. Patient flow considerations include those from the acute care setting to the sub-acute care setting and patient flow from the sub-acute care setting into an ambulatory care setting and ultimately the patient's return to the community and home (where possible) (NSW Health, 2015, p. 9).

Fig. 1 illustrates dynamic processes that need consideration in implementing rehabilitation programs in the real-world setting. The figure also provides important signposts in developing a rehabilitation model of care in the context of the broader health system. What is missing in this diagram is the role of the sectors that provide rehabilitation beyond health services, for example, aged care or social services.

Translating well-established evidence into everyday practice is key to improving care quality and requires multipronged approaches, engaging various stakeholders. As shown in Fig. 1, implementing an evidence-based rehabilitation program into a new setting requires consideration of a range of factors: workforce capacity (OTs, RNs, and other allied health professionals) and training; resources and time; client motivation and other relevant health conditions; care partner engagement and motivation; and

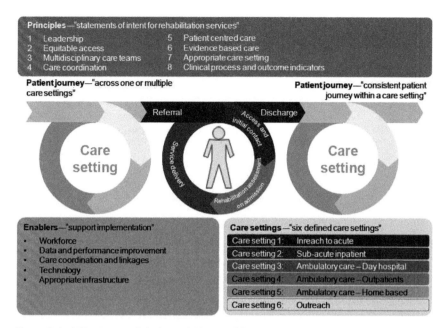

Fig. 1 Rehabilitation model of care (NSW Health, 2015, p. 11).

organizational leadership and culture. It also requires guidance around how the new intervention or program can be delivered in the real-world setting through a model of care.

Without appropriate care and support, dementia has detrimental impacts on the person's physical, social and psychological health, and quality of life. Developing and evaluating rehabilitation models of care that address unique needs and concerns of people with dementia and their family and take into account the current and continually evolving health and aged care system, is crucial in ensuring that rehabilitation is well embedded in everyday practice and service delivery.

References

Amieva, H., Robert, P. H., Grandoulier, A.-S., Meillon, C., De Rotrou, J., Andrieu, S., ... Meillon, C. (2016). Group and individual cognitive therapies in Alzheimer's disease: The ETNA3 randomized trial. *International Psychogeriatrics*, *28*(5), 707–717. https://doi.org/10.1017/S1041610215001830.

Aspinal, F., Glasby, J., & Rostgaard, T. (2016). Reablement: Supporting older people towards independence. *Age and Ageing*, *45*(5), 574–578.

Ávila, R., Carvalho, I. A. M., Bottino, C. M. C., & Miotto, E. C. (2007). Neuropsychological rehabilitation in mild and moderate Alzheimer's disease patients. *Behavioural Neurology*, *18*(4), 225–233. https://doi.org/10.1155/2007/915816.

Bandura, A. (1986). *Social foundations of thought and action: A social cognitive theory*. Englewood Cliffs, NJ: Prentice-Hall.

Boltz, M., Chippendale, T., Resnick, B., & Galvin, J. E. (2015). Testing family-centered, function-focused care in hospitalized persons with dementia. *Neurodegenerative Disease Management, 5*(3), 203–215. https://doi.org/10.2217/nmt.15.10.

Bronfenbrenner, U. (1979). *The ecology of human development: Experiments by nature and design*. Cambridge, MA: Harvard University Press.

Brueggen, K., Kasper, E., Ochmann, S., Pfaff, H., Webel, S., Wolfgang, S., ... Schneider, W. (2017). Cognitive rehabilitation in Alzheimer's disease: A controlled intervention trial. *Journal of Alzheimer's Disease, 57*(4), 1315–1324. https://doi.org/10.3233/JAD-160771.

Callahan, C. M., Boustani, M. A., Schmid, A. A., LaMantia, M. A., Austrom, M. G., Miller, D. K., ... Hendrie, H. C. (2017). Targeting functional decline in Alzheimer disease: A randomized trial. *Annals of Internal Medicine, 166*(3), 164–171. https://doi.org/10.7326/M16-0830.

Canadian Association of Occupational Therapists. (1991). *Occupational therapy guidelines for client-centred practice*. Toronto, ON: CAOT Publications ACE.

Canadian Association of Occupational Therapists. (1997). *Enabling occupation: An occupational therapy perspective*. Ottawa, ON: CAOT Publications ACE.

Carbone, G., Barreca, F., Mancini, G., Pauletti, G., Salvi, V., Vanacore, N., ... Sinibaldi, L. (2013). A home assistance model for dementia: Outcome in patients with mild-to-moderate Alzheimer's disease after three months. *Annali dell'Istituto Superiore di Sanità, 49*(1), 34–41. https://doi.org/10.4415/ann_13_01_07.

Chew, J., Chong, M. S., Fong, Y. L., & Tay, L. (2015). Outcomes of a multimodal cognitive and physical rehabilitation program for persons with mild dementia and their caregivers: A goal-oriented approach. *Clinical Interventions in Aging, 10*, 1687–1694. https://doi.org/10.2147/cia.S93914.

Clare, L., Kudlicka, A., Oyebode, J. R., Jones, R. W., Bayer, A., Leroi, I., ... Woods, B. (2019). Individual goal-oriented cognitive rehabilitation to improve everyday functioning for people with early-stage dementia: A multicentre randomised controlled trial (the GREAT trial). *International Journal of Geriatric Psychiatry, 34*(5), 709–721. https://doi.org/10.1002/gps.5076.

Clare, L. P., Linden, D. E. J. D., Woods, R. T. M., Whitaker, R. M., Evans, S. J. M., Parkinson, C. H. B. A., ... Rugg, M. D. P. (2010). Goal-oriented cognitive rehabilitation for people with early-stage Alzheimer disease: A single-blind randomized controlled trial of clinical efficacy. *The American Journal of Geriatric Psychiatry, 18*(10), 928–939.

Clare, L., Nelis, S., & Kudlicka, A. (2016). *Bangor goal-setting interview manual*. Retrieved from https://medicine.exeter.ac.uk/media/universityofexeter/schoolofpsychology/reach/documents/The_Bangor_Goal-Setting_Interview_Version_2_Manual_(BGSI_v.2)_Dec_2016.pdf. (Accessed 31 March 2020).

Clemson, L., Laver, K., Jeon, Y.-H., Comans, T. A., Scanlan, J., Rahja, M., ... Gitlin, L. N. (2018). Implementation of an evidence-based intervention to improve the wellbeing of people with dementia and their careers: Study protocol for 'Care of People with dementia in their Environments (COPE)' in the Australian context. *BMC Geriatrics, 18*(108). https://doi.org/10.1186/s12877-018-0790-7.

Cornelis, E., Gorus, E., Beyer, I., Van Puyvelde, K., Lieten, S., Versijpt, J., ... De Vriendt, P. (2018). A retrospective study of a multicomponent rehabilitation programme for community-dwelling persons with dementia and their caregivers. *British Journal of Occupational Therapy, 81*(1), 5–14. https://doi.org/10.1177/0308022617728680.

Council of Europe Commissioner for Human Rights. (2012). *The right of people with disabilities to live independently and be included in the community*. Council of Europe Commissioner for Human Rights.

Davidson, P., Halcomb, E., Hickman, L., Phillips, J., & Graham, B. (2006). Beyond the rhetoric: What do we mean by a 'model of care'? *Australian Journal of Advanced Nursing, 23*(3), 47–55.

Engel, G. (1977). The need for a new medical model: A challenge for biomedicine. *Science, 196*(4286), 129–136.

Fernández-Calvo, B., Contador, I., Ramos, F., Olazarán, J., Mograbi, D. C., & Morris, R. G. (2015). Effect of unawareness on rehabilitation outcome in a randomised controlled trial of multicomponent intervention for patients with mild Alzheimer's disease. *Neuropsychological Rehabilitation, 25*(3), 448–477. https://doi.org/10.1080/09602011.2014.948461.

Galik, E., Resnick, B., Hammersla, M., & Brightwater, J. (2014). Optimizing function and physical activity among nursing home residents with dementia: Testing the impact of function-focused care. *The Gerontologist, 54*(6), 930. https://doi.org/10.1093/geront/gnt108.

Galik, E. P. C., Resnick, B. P. C. F. F., Lerner, N. D. N. P. R. N., Hammersla, M. M. S. C., & Gruber-Baldini, A. L. P. (2015). Function focused care for assisted living residents with dementia. *The Gerontologist, 55*. https://doi.org/10.1093/geront/gnu173.

Germain, S., Wojtasik, V., Lekeu, F., Quittre, A., Olivier, C., Godichard, V., & Salmon, E. (2019). Efficacy of cognitive rehabilitation in Alzheimer disease: A 1-year follow-up study. *Journal of Geriatric Psychiatry and Neurology, 32*(1), 16–23. https://doi.org/10.1177/0891988718813724.

Gitlin, L. N., Corcoran, M., Winter, L., Boyce, A., & Hauck, W. W. (2001). A randomized, controlled trial of a home environmental intervention: Effect on efficacy and upset in caregivers and on daily function of persons with dementia. *Gerontologist, 41*(1), 4–14.

Gitlin, L. N., Winter, L., Dennis, M. P., Hodgson, N., & Hauck, W. W. (2010). A biobehavioral home-based intervention and the well-being of patients with dementia and their caregivers: The COPE Randomized Trial. *JAMA, 304*(9), 983–991. https://doi.org/10.1001/jama.2010.1253.

Graff, M. J. L., Vernooij-Dassen, M. J. M., Thijssen, M., Dekker, J., Hoefnagels, W. H. L., & Rikkert, M. G. M. (2006). Community based occupational therapy for patients with dementia and their care givers: Randomised controlled trial. *BMJ: British Medical Journal (International Edition), 333*(7580), 1196–1199. https://doi.org/10.1136/bmj.39001.688843.BE.

Henskens, M., Nauta, I. M., Scherder, E. J. A., Oosterveld, F. G. J., & Vrijkotte, S. (2017). Implementation and effects of Movement-oriented Restorative Care in a nursing home—A quasi-experimental study. *BMC Geriatrics, 17*. https://doi.org/10.1186/s12877-017-0642-x.

Huber, M., Knottnerus, J. A., Green, L., Horst, H. V. D., Jadad, A. R., Kromhout, D., … Smid, H. (2011). How should we define health? *BMJ, 343*. https://doi.org/10.1136/bmj.d4163.

Huber, M., van Vliet, M., Giezenberg, M., Winkens, B., Heerkens, Y., Dagnelie, P. C., & Knottnerus, J. A. (2016). Towards a 'patient-centred' operationalisation of the new dynamic concept of health: A mixed methods study. *BMJ Open, 6*(1). https://doi.org/10.1136/bmjopen-2015-010091.

Jeon, Y. H., Krein, L., Simpson, J. M., Szanton, S. L., Clemson, L., Naismith, S. L., … Brodaty, H. (2019). Feasibility and potential effects of interdisciplinary home-based reablement program (I-HARP) for people with cognitive and functional decline: A pilot trial. *Aging & Mental Health*, 1–10. https://doi.org/10.1080/13607863.2019.1642298.

Jeon, Y.-H., Simpson, J. M., Low, L.-F., Woods, R., Norman, R., Mowszowski, L., … Szanton, S. (2019). A pragmatic randomised controlled trial (RCT) and realist evaluation of the interdisciplinary home-bAsed Reablement program (I-HARP) for improving functional independence of community dwelling older people with dementia: An effectiveness-implementation hybrid design. *BMC Geriatrics, 19*(1), 199. https://doi.org/10.1186/s12877-019-1216-x.

Katz, S., Downs, T., Cash, H., & Grotz, R. (1970). Progress in the development of the index of ADL. *Gerontologist, 10*, 20–30. https://doi.org/10.1093/geront/10.1_Part_1.20.

Kelly, M. E., Lawlor, B. A., Coen, R. F., Robertson, I. H., & Brennan, S. (2019). Cognitive rehabilitation for early stage Alzheimer's disease: A pilot study with an Irish population. *Irish Journal of Psychological Medicine, 36*(2), 105–119. https://doi.org/10.1017/ipm.2017.23.

Kielhofner, G., & Posatery, B. J. (1980). A Model of Human Occupation, Part 1. Conceptual Framework and Content. *American Journal of Occupational Therapy, 34*, 572–581.

Kim, S. (2015). Cognitive rehabilitation for elderly people with early-stage Alzheimer's disease. *Journal of Physical Therapy Science, 27*(2), 543–546. https://doi.org/10.1589/jpts.27.543.

Kurrle, S., Brodaty, H., & Hogarth, R. (2012). *Physical comorbidities of dementia*. Cambridge: Cambridge University Press.

Lam, L. C. W., Lui, V. W. C., Luk, D. N. Y., Chau, R., So, C., Poon, V., … Ko, F. S. (2010). Effectiveness of an individualized functional training program on affective disturbances and functional skills in mild and moderate dementia—A randomized control trial. *International Journal of Geriatric Psychiatry, 25*(2), 133–141. https://doi.org/10.1002/gps.2309.

Law, M., Baptiste, S., Carswell, A., McColl, M., Polatajko, H., & Pollock, N. (2005). *Canadian occupational performance measure* (4th ed.). Ottowa: CAOT Publications ACE.

Lawton, M., & Brody, E. (1969). Assessment of older people: Self maintaining and instrumental activities of daily living. *Gerontologist, 9*, 179–186.

Lawton, M. P., & Nahemow, L. (1973). Ecology and the aging process. In *The psychology of adult development and aging* (pp. 619–674). Washington, DC: American Psychological Association.

Loewenstein, D. A., Acevedo, A., Czaja, S. J., & Duara, R. (2004). Cognitive rehabilitation of mildly impaired Alzheimer disease patients on cholinesterase inhibitors. *The American Journal of Geriatric Psychiatry, 12*(4), 395–402.

NSW Health. (2015). *NSW rehabilitation model of care: NSW health rehabilitation redesign project final report—model of care*. Retrieved from https://www.aci.health.nsw.gov.au/resources/rehabilitation/rehabilitation-model-of-care/rehabilitation-moc. (Accessed 31 March 2020).

Poulos, C. J., & Poulos, R. G. (2019). A function-focused approach in primary care for older people with functional decline. *Australian Journal of General Practice, 48*(7), 434–439.

Raggi, A., Iannaccone, S., Marcone, A., Ginex, V., Ortelli, P., Nonis, A., … Cappa, S. F. (2007). The effects of a comprehensive rehabilitation program of Alzheimer's disease in a hospital setting. *Behavioural Neurology, 18*(1), 1–6.

Regan, B., Wells, Y., Farrow, M., O'Halloran, P., Workman, B., & O'Halloran, P. (2017). MAXCOG-maximizing cognition: A randomized controlled trial of the efficacy of goal-oriented cognitive rehabilitation for people with mild cognitive impairment and early Alzheimer disease. *American Journal of Geriatric Psychiatry, 25*(3), 258–269. https://doi.org/10.1016/j.jagp.2016.11.008.

Resnick, B., Galik, E., Vigne, E., & Carew, A. P. (2016). Dissemination and implementation of function focused care for assisted living. *Health Education & Behavior, 43*(3), 296–304.

Sallis, J., Owen, N., & Fisher, E. (2008). Ecological models of health behavior. In K. Glanz, B. Rimer, & K. Viswanath (Eds.), *Health behavior and health education* (4th ed., pp. 465–485). San Francisco: John Wiley & Sons.

Shah, S., Vanclay, F., & Cooper, B. (1989). Improving sensitivity of the Barthel Index for stroke rehabilitation. *Journal of Clinical Epidemiology, 8*, 703. https://doi.org/10.1016/0895-4356(89)90065-6.

Tanaka, S., Honda, S., Nakano, H., Sato, Y., Araya, K., & Yamaguchi, H. (2017). Comparison between group and personal rehabilitation for dementia in a geriatric health service facility: Single-blinded randomized controlled study. *Psychogeriatrics*, *17*(3), 177–185. https://doi.org/10.1111/psyg.12212.

Toba, K., Nakamura, Y., Endo, H., Okochi, J., Tanaka, Y., Inaniwa, C., … Yamaguchi, H. (2014). Intensive rehabilitation for dementia improved cognitive function and reduced behavioral disturbance in geriatric health service facilities in Japan. *Geriatrics and Gerontology International*, *14*(1), 206–211. https://doi.org/10.1111/ggi.12080.

Verbrugge, L., & Jette, A. (1994). The disablement process. *Social Science and Medicine*, *38*(1), 1–14.

Vernooij-Dassen, M., & Jeon, Y.-H. (2016). Social Health and Dementia: The power of human capabilities (Guest editorial). *International Psychogeriatrics*, *28*(5), 701–703.

World Health Organisation. (2011). *WHO Guidelines on Health-Related Rehabilitation (Rehabilitation Guidelines)*. Retrieved from https://www.who.int/disabilities/care/rehabilitation_guidelines_concept.pdf.

World Health Organisation. (2019). *Rehabilitation: Key facts*. Retrieved from https://www.who.int/news-room/fact-sheets/detail/rehabilitation.

Zanetti, O., Zanieri, G., Di Giovanni, G., DeVreese, L. P., Pezzini, A., Metitieri, T., & Trabucchi, M. (2001). Effectiveness of procedural memory stimulation in mild Alzheimer's disease patients: A controlled study. *Neuropsychological Rehabilitation*, *11*(3–4), 263–272. https://doi.org/10.1080/09602010042000088.

Index

Note: Page numbers followed by *f* indicate figures, *t* indicate tables, and *b* indicate boxes.